CW00553192

KEPT BY THE POWER OF GOD

Other titles in the Biblical and Theological Classics Library:

Biblical Exegesis in the Apostolic Period — *Richard Longenecker*
Biblical Inspiration — *I. Howard Marshall*
The Cross in the New Testament — *Leon Morris*
New Testament Exposition – *Walter Liefeld*
The Progress of Redemption – *Willem VanGemeren*
Showing the Spirit – *D. A. Carson*
Theological Diversity and the Authority of the Old Testament – *John Goldingay*

Other titles by the same author:

The Gospel of Luke — A Commentary on the Greek Text
Last Supper and Lord's Supper
Luke — Historian and Theologian
New Testament Interpretation (Editor)
The Work of Christ

Kept by the POWER of GOD

A Study of Perseverance and Falling Away

I. HOWARD MARSHALL

First edition published 1969
by Epworth Press, London

Second edition published 1974
by Bethany House Publishers, Minneapolis, U.S.A.

This third edition published 1995
by The Paternoster Press, P.O. Box 300, Carlisle CA3 0QS, U.K.

01 00 99 98 97 96 95 7 6 5 4 3 2 1

British Library Cataloguing in Publication Data

Marshall, I. Howard
Kept by the Power of God. – 2Rev.ed. –
(Biblical & Theological Classics
Library)
I. Title II. Series
234

ISBN 0–85364–642–2

Typeset by Photoprint, Torquay, Devon
and Printed in the U.K. by Cox & Wyman Ltd., Reading

To my parents

Contents

Foreword

Dr. Marshall is an eminent New Testament scholar of evangelical convictions whose name is associated with scholarly work of the highest quality. It is a pleasure to be able to introduce this carefully written volume on the subject of perseverance and apostasy to an American audience. My enthusiasm for it is especially great owing to the decisive influence of Dr. Marshall's arguments on my own thinking along these lines. The book had a brief and limited exposure to a British public a few years back, but it never effectively penetrated the American evangelical community, something which I hope it will now be able to do. As a piece of meticulous exegesis, the fruits of which have wide theological implications, it is urgent this book receive a broad and careful reading.

The form of the book is simple and straightforward. The author does exactly what is needed to be done. He conducts a historical-grammatical investigation of all the Scriptural materials which treat the subject of apostasy and falling away, and produces ample evidence to support his thesis that the security of the believer is conditioned upon his faithfulness to Jesus Christ. It is simply not possible to maintain that the warnings in the Bible against turning away from the truth describe an imaginary or hypothetical danger. They are addressed to us all, and we all must heed them. Dr. Marshall's case rests on solid exegetical foundations, and is not to be set aside on dogmatic or *a priori* grounds. It is very common in this area of doctrine to hear people arguing from election or predestination, or irresistible grace so as to reach the opposite conclusion. But this will not do. To the word and to the testimony. Unless Dr. Marshall can be refuted exegetically, he cannot be refuted at all. The evidence of Scripture cannot be cancelled by the systems of men.

Biblical truths when they are carefully examined are often controversial and challenging. It is so with the biblical doctrine of apostasy. Belief in the unconditional perseverance of the saints, or eternal security, is very widely entertained by multitudes of evangelical Christians, even though it belongs generically to the Augustinian-Calvinistic tradition in theology, a doctrinal system which they do not generally hold in its other dimensions. Nevertheless, it is a fact that Dr. Marshall's argument is controversial and will not be immediately accepted. One reason for this is the understandable fear that the doctrine of conditional security may unsettle a proper and vital Christian assurance. After all, the Word of God continually reminds us of our spiritual rights and possessions, and breathes an atmosphere of settled confidence. There is nothing in Dr. Marshall's book that undercuts this assurance. We are kept by the power of God, as his title boldly states. However, he would not have us disregard the threats to perseverance which the Bible presents or the commands to abide steadfastly in the truth with which its pages abound. What this book will unsettle, and for this we applaud it, is a spurious assurance, indeed a presumption, of those who cling to eternal security while deliberately following lives of second or third rate discipleship. Such people do not want to see the doctrine of eternal security challenged and with good reason! Although it is not part of the original intention of the author, this book may have a wider theological impact on those who take it seriously than simply at one point. If it is true that the concept of eternal security is essentially a deduction, as I believe it is, from a set of Augustinian-Calvinistic premises, it is inevitable that a refutation of that concept will lead to an undermining of those premises. For what we have on the margins of this book is nothing less than a theology of salvation in which there is no dark shadow cast over the gospel by a fearful doctrine of double predestination. Dr. Marshall does not believe that God intentionally bypasses a group of sinners, denying his saving grace to them. On the contrary, God wills the salvation of all mankind, and has done everything to secure it. The good news is sincerely meant for all sinners. It remains only for each person to respond to God's offer and to receive his gift of love. Dr. Marshall embraces a fresh, liberating and biblical concept of how God saves sinners, and I believe it will prove appealing to large numbers who will hear him.

Clark H. Pinnock

Preface to the First Edition

In its endeavor to maintain a lively existence in the contemporary world the Christian Church has concentrated its attention on two matters. One is the need to unite Christians for the work of mission; the other is to find the right methods of communicating the Gospel in a secular environment. Another equally fundamental task has not yet received the attention it deserves. Year by year the number of members of the Christian Church who fall away from active discipleship remains large and shows no signs of diminishing. The witness of the Church is sadly impoverished by their lapse, and, more important, the Church is failing in its pastoral duty of strengthening the weak and retrieving the backslider.

The present book attempts to make a contribution to the study of the theological problem raised by backsliding. It is devoted to a presentation and exposition of the biblical and, in particular, the New Testament material which must form the basis for a theological understanding of perseverance and backsliding. Originally the study was made for the purpose of writing an academic thesis, but it is hoped that the revised and abbreviated presentation offered here will be of more than specialist interest, and will also help to show something of the resources which are available in the teaching of the New Testament for the pastor who is concerned to build up the people of God in their faith and to help them to know more fully the grace of the God who is able to keep them from falling.

The thesis on which the book is based was presented to the University of Aberdeen in 1963; the book itself was completed at the beginning of 1965, but an attempt has been made to bring the discussion up to date in the light of recent publications.

It is my pleasant duty to express thanks to all who have helped in the writing of this book. Professor A. M. Hunter, the supervisor of my research, offered ready help at all times. Professor J. Jeremias showed a kindly interest in the beginning of my studies in the University of Göttingen, and Principal F. Greeves, Professor K. Grayston, and my other colleagues made it easy for me to pursue my research while I was Assistant Tutor at Didsbury College, Bristol. A special debt of gratitude is due to my congregations in Darlington, especially at Bondgate, Methodist Church, who willingly put up with the hours which their pastor spent in the study. Mrs. Muriel Trenholm performed a valiant feat in typing out an untidy manuscript, and Mr. Arthur Trenholm was zealous in the work of correction. My wife has been a constant support throughout the task.

I wish to express my especial thanks to the trustees of the William Honyman Gillespie Trust for a research scholarship and for their patience in waiting to see some result from their award, and also to the Rev. G. S. Wakefield and the Epworth Press for accepting the book for publications.

An earlier form of the discussion of Luke 12:10 appeared in *Theology*, Vol. LXVII, No. 524 (February, 1964), and I am grateful to the Editor and the S.P.C.K. for permission to use the material here.

I.H.M.

Aberdeen,
September, 1968

Preface to the Second Edition

After a period of some five years during which this book has been out of print I am glad that it is now appearing in a second edition, and I should like to express my very sincere thanks to Bethany Fellowship for being willing to undertake its republication. It is perhaps not surprising that my attempt to re-examine the foundations of the doctrine of the perseverance of the saints has led to some criticisms of the argument and, on occasion, to some misunderstandings of the position expressed. I am grateful to those whose criticisms have enabled me to see weaknesses in the earlier edition of this book, and I have attempted to remove them in preparation of the new edition.

It may perhaps be worth commenting at the outset that I write as a conservative evangelical, one who accepts the Scriptures as his supreme authority in faith and life and who believes that they are the infallible Word of God. The aim of this book is accordingly to examine the teaching of the Bible on one particular doctrine and to attempt to reformulate that doctrine on the basis of biblical teaching.

Within conservative evangelicalism the dominant school of thought is Calvinism. It follows one line of scriptural teaching on the doctrine of perseverance by emphasising the eternal security of the regenerate believer. But there is another line of scriptural teaching which warns the believer against the danger of apostasy from the faith, and this has been emphasised by theologians of the Arminian school. Each school of thought has in my opinion tended to play down the significance of the scriptural teaching on which the other school has built its case; my concern is that justice be done to both aspects of the matter. If I appear to over-emphasise the 'apostasy' texts, it is simply because the dominant tendency in evangelicalism is to under-emphasise them.

It follows that this book is not a defense of Arminianism as such. The full Arminian position is as much open to error as is extreme Calvinism. My aim is to reach beyond the Calvinist-Arminian controversy to a position which is biblical, and which therefore accepts whatever is true in both Calvinism and Arminianism. I owe something in my upbringing to the influence of John Wesley. I do not follow him on every matter, for he too needs on occasion to be corrected by Scripture, but I agree with his own estimate of where the truth of the Gospel is to be found — 'within a hair's breadth' of Calvinism.

It should also be emphasised at the outset that I do not want to over-stress the danger of apostasy. My point is that the warnings in Scripture against falling away are not to be lightly explained away as hypothetical or unreal, but are meant to be taken with full seriousness as warnings against a real danger. But I did not entitle this book *Kept by the Power of God* without due consideration. That is where the heart of the matter is to be found. Our perseverance depends upon the grace of God, who has promised that He will keep us from falling, and perhaps we have a deeper appreciation of the greatness of His grace if at the same time we have a more realistic understanding of the dangers from which He continually guards us.

To reconcile these two strands in biblical teaching, the promises of eternal security and the warnings against falling away, is not easy. Our tendency is to push beyond the evidence to some kind of logical system which over-emphasises the sovereignty of God or human freedom. We have to learn not to go beyond the things that are written, and to be content with the full teaching of the Scriptures.

The republication of this book has some connection with a recent visit to Trinity Evangelical Divinity School, Deerfield, and I owe a special debt of gratitude to Dr. C. H. Pinnock, who was teaching there at the time; he very kindly commended this book to Bethany Fellowship.

During my visit to the USA it was my privilege to serve as guest lecturer in a number of seminaries, some of which were avowedly Calvinist in their basis, while others were Wesleyan. The warmth of the welcome and the depth of the Christian fellowship which I experienced in all of these institutions demonstrated to me that the things on which we may differ in detail pale into insignificance in the light of the things that unite us, our common salvation in Jesus Christ and our common adherence to the faith once for all delivered to the saints. May this book in some small way serve to strengthen this fellowship in Christian love and to lead us to an ever-deepening experience of the truth as it is in Christ Jesus.

I. Howard Marshall

Aberdeen,
April, 1974

Preface to the Third Edition

Twenty years after the publication of the second edition of this book by Bethany House Publishers I am grateful that it is being given a further lease of life by this reprint in the Biblical Classics Library of the Paternoster Press. Were I to be writing this book afresh at the present time, there would be some changes both in the manner of presentation (e.g. the use of inclusive language) and in the details of the content, although the general line of the argument and the conclusions would not be significantly different. There would also have to be some engagement with scholars who have subsequently contributed to the debate on the subject. However, the character of the series and the constraints of the method of publication require that this edition is essentially a reprint of the second edition. Nevertheless, I am grateful to the publishers for the opportunity to make some minor corrections, to update the bibliography, and also to include as an epilogue a subsequent article which may show how my thinking on the matter has developed. The epilogue originally appeared in R. L. Perkins (ed.), *Perspectives on Scripture and Tradition: Essays in Honor of Dale Moody* (Macon: Mercer Press, 1987) and was reprinted in my collection of essays, *Jesus the Saviour: Studies in New Testament Theology* (London: SPCK, 1990); I am grateful to the original publishers for permission to reprint.

I. Howard Marshall

Aberdeen, February, 1995

Abbreviations

AG	Arndt, W. F. and Gingrich, F.W., *A Greek-English Lexicon of the New Testament and Other Early Christian Literature*, Cambridge, 1957.
AP	Charles, R. H., (ed.), *The Apocrypha and Pseudepigrapha of the Old Testament*, Oxford, 1913.
BD	Blass, F. and Debrunner, A., *A Greek Grammar of the New Testament and Other Early Christian Literature* (translated by R. W. Funk), Cambridge, 1961.
BJRL	*Bulletin of the John Rylands Library.*
CGTC	*The Cambridge Greek Testament Commentary.*
EB	*Etudes Bibliques.*
EGT	*The Expositor's Greek Testament.*
EQ	*The Evangelical Quarterly.*
ERE	*Encyclopaedia of Religion and Ethics.*
Exp. B	*The Expositor's Bible.*
Exp. T	*The Expository Times.*
HNT	*Handbuch zum Neuen Testament.*
HTK	*Herders Theologischer Kommentar zum Neuen Testament.*
ICC	*The International Critical Commentary.*
JBL	*Journal of Biblical Literature.*
JTS	*Journal of Theological Studies.*
KEK	*Kritisch-Exegetischer Kommentar über das Neue Testament.*
LS	Liddell, H. G., Scott, R., Jones, H. S., and McKenzie, R., (ed.), *A Greek-English Lexicon*, Oxford, 1940.
Macmillan	The unfinished set of New Testament comment-

	aries begun by F. J. A. Hort, J. B. Lightfoot and B. F. Westcott and continued by later scholars.
MH	Moulton, J. H., Howard, W. F. and Turner, N., *A Grammar of New Testament Greek*, Edinburgh, 1908, 1929, 1963.
Moore	Moore, G. F., *Judaism in the First Centuries of the Christian Era*, Cambridge, U.S.A., 1927–1930.
MNTC	*Moffatt New Testament Commentary.*
NBC	Guthrie, D., and Motyer, J. A., (ed.) *The New Bible Commentary Revised*, London, 1970.
NLC	*New London Commentary (New International Commentary).*
NTD	*Das Neue Testament Deutsch.*
NTS	*New Testament Studies.*
PC	Black, M., (ed.), *Peake's Commentary on the Bible*, 1962.
SB	Strack, H. L. and Billerbeck, P., *Kommentar zum Neuen Testament aus Talmud und Midrasch*, München, 1956.[2]
SJT	*Scottish Journal of Theology.*
TDNT	Kittel, G. and Friedrich, G. (ed.), *Theological Dictionary of the New Testament*, Grand Rapids, 1964–74.
TL	*Theologische Literaturzeitung.*
TNTC	*Tyndale New Testament Commentaries.*
TU	*Texte und Untersuchungen zur Geschichte der altchristlichen Literature.*
WC	*Westminster Commentaries.*
WH	Westcott and Hort.
ZTK	*Zeitschrift für Theologie und Kirche.*

Introduction

During recent years there has been a considerable discussion among biblical scholars on the nature of the Christian life as this is presented to us in the New Testament. A number of studies have tackled the problems of Christian initiation, and there has been intense revival of interest in the doctrine of the Church and in Christian ethics. The characteristic feature of most contributions to the contemporary debate has been a concentration of attention on the communal aspects of the Christian life. They have dealt with the life of the Christian from an external, human point of view in terms of his relationships to other Christians within the Body of Christ and to other men in general. It would not be unfair to suggest that study of the life of the Christian in relation to God has been neglected. The titles of only a few works by New Testament scholars come readily to mind, notably V. Taylor, *Forgiveness and Reconciliation* (1941), E. Schweizer, *Lordship and Discipleship* (1960), A. R. George, *Communion with God in the New Testament* (1954), E. J. Tinsley, *The Imitation of God in Christ* (1960), and E. M. B. Green, *The Meaning of Salvation* (1965). Of these, the work of Dr. Taylor is really a study in the nature of the atonement, and that of Prof. Schweizer is much more a study of Christology than of the life of the disciple; it is only in the works of Principal George, Prof. Tinsley, and Mr. Green that we find full-length studies of important aspects of the Christian life. It is not too much to say that the doctrine of the Christian life has been considerably neglected by New Testament scholars. So important a doctrine as sanctification, for example, has been left almost completely to the Church historian and systematic theologian.

The present study is an attempt to explore one part of this largely uncharted field in New Testament studies. The somewhat forbidding title which has been given to it by dogmatic theology is 'the perseverance of the saints.' We may express it more simply as the study of the tension under which the Christian lives his life from his conversion until his entry to the heavenly Kingdom.

On the one hand, the Christian life is a life which is continually sustained by the power of God. It does not merely depend upon a once-for-all gift of God received in the moment of conversion, but is a continual relationship to God in which His gracious gifts are received by faith. On the other hand, the believer is continually faced by temptations which jeopardize his faith. He is thus in a state of tension as he receives the gift of life from God and at the same time faces the forces of temptation which threaten to deprive him of that life. Positively, his duty is to grow in the Christian life towards the goal of sinlessness, i.e. of victory by the power of God over the temptations which assail him. This is the process known as sanctification. Negatively, the believer faces the danger of succumbing to temptation through failure to trust in God. He may be said to *fall away* from his faith in God, and the limit to this process would be *apostasy*, i.e. complete abandonment of faith and surrender to temptation; in such a case the divine life would cease to exist in the man.

Now it would be universally admitted that when a man becomes a Christian he does not immediately reach a state of perfection in which he no longer sins, and, according to the most likely reading of the evidence, he cannot reach a position in which it is impossible for him to sin,[1] although sinlessness is put before him as the ideal after which he ought to seek. In his important book, *Taufe und Sünde im ältesten Christentum bis auf Origenes* (Tübingen, 1908), Hans Windisch had little difficulty in showing that the New Testament does expect Christians to be holy and sinless. He doubtless erred in trying to prove that the New Testament regards this state as normal for every Christian,[2] but he was right in showing that this ideal or norm was not always a reality and that the attempt to relate the perfect ideal to the sinful reality created no small problem for the New Testament writers.

Once this fact is recognized, there is a case for study of the converse of sanctification, what we may call the pathology of the Christian life. Granted that sin is to be found in the Church, can we determine anything about its working in the life of the Christian? In particular, is it possible for temptation and sin to crush and destroy the life of the Christian? If entire sanctification is a dubious possibility, is complete apostasy also an impossibility in the Christian life?

The idea of persistence in faith against temptation is usually expressed in theology by the word 'perseverance'; this word is not used in this sense in the New Testament, the same idea being expressed by the term 'steadfast endurance.'[3] Failure to persist in faith is expressed by words which mean falling away, drifting and stumbling,[4] and the word 'apostasy' is also found with the meaning of clear denial and rejection of Jesus Christ and hence repudiation of the gift of life which He bestows.[5] Although the actual vocabulary is not very common, the ideas themselves are more frequent than might be supposed.

The investigation of these concepts provides our field of study. We must examine the influences which enable a Christian to persevere in his faith and the temptations which endanger that faith. The question then arises whether the Christian can be infallibly certain of final victory in his battle against temptation or is in danger of defeat. We must ask whether Christians are predestined to emerge victoriously from the conflict and whether the nature of the life which is bestowed upon them by God is such that it cannot possibly be lost. On the other hand, if the Christian may possibly suffer defeat, we must ask whether such defeat is permanent in its effects, so that it is impossible to regain faith in Jesus Christ and eternal life, or may be merely temporary with the possibility of restoration of the former relationship with God. If the evidence suggests that a believer is infallibly certain to persevere, an explanation must be found for the various apparent cases of falling away and apostasy which take place in the Church and are described in the New Testament. Finally, some attention must be paid to the Church discipline which is applied in cases of falling away and apostasy.[6]

Through such study it is hoped to clarify an important aspect of the doctrine of the Christian life in the New Testament. At the same time our purpose is not narrowly specialist. The choice of this particular theme for study has been partly dictated by consciousness of a pressing pastoral problem which faces the Church today. This problem is that of the backslider.[7] It has come to the fore as a result of the large-scale evangelistic campaigns of recent years in which many thousands of people have made decisions to accept Jesus Christ as Saviour and Lord. Although many of these decisions have undoubtedly led to genuine conversions with lasting consequences in the lives of the people who made them, it is also true that other decisions have not issued in lives of active Christian discipleship once the period of initial enthusiasm has ended. The number of those who have failed to persevere is not small, and has given rise to a considerable practical problem for the Church.[8]

But the problem is not a new one which has arisen only in these campaigns; it has merely been high-lighted by them. Out of the many examples from the day-to-day life of the Church which might be selected, we draw attention to the official statistics of membership published annually by the Methodist Church. During such a typical year as 1966 there was a loss to the Church of 12,740 members who 'ceased to meet' out of a total membership at the beginning of the year of 690,347. This figure naturally does not include members who died or were transferred to other denominations during the year; it is the number of 'lost sheep.' A loss of roughly 18 members out of every 1,000 is not slight. But whether the loss be regarded as small or great — and it is worth remembering that the New Testament regards one individual sheep out of a hundred as worth restoring to the fold — it inevitably raises a practical pastoral problem of the first importance.

Our concern here is not with the various psychological and sociological data which can be used to elucidate this problem, but with the theology which must underlie our consideration of it. It is being increasingly recognized that no proper solutions to pastoral problems can be found without a thorough understanding of the theological principles which are involved,[10] and the current state of the Church demands that the theologian should examine carefully the question of perseverance in the Christian faith.

It is not, however, only the minister entrusted with the cure of souls who requires the services of the student of the New Testament. There is an unsolved theological problem which has raised its head from time to time in the history of Christian doctrine. This is the question whether it is possible for a man who has truly become a Christian and an heir to the life of heaven to fall away from his faith and be finally lost.

Some groups in the early Church certainly accepted that it was possible for a person to cease to be a Christian through denial of Christ or through some heinous sin, and there grew up a complicated system of penance and excommunication whose aim was to prevent men from falling away or, if the worst happened, to carry out the judgement of God upon them by pronouncing sentence of excommunication. The question which arose was whether it was possible for a person who had been excommunicated to be restored to the fellowship of the Church and the hope of salvation. In some quarters at least it was held that various sins could take a Christian to the point of no return where penance would be of no avail. There was considerable controversy between the supporters of rigorist and lax points of view as regards the cancellation of excommunication, but it was universally recognized that a Christian who did not do penance for his sin or seek readmission to the Church would die in his sin. In other words, the possibility of professing Christians becoming apostate and dying in their sin was fully recognized; the theory that such apostates had never truly been Christians does not seem to have been suggested.[11]

This theory was, however, propounded by Augustine. He enunciated a rigorous doctrine of double predestination to salvation and damnation. God's purpose was to save a certain fixed number of men, the 'elect,' and it was in the nature of things utterly impossible for any of the elect to fall away completely from Him and be finally lost, even if they might fall temporarily into sin. The grace of perseverance guaranteed their ultimate salvation. Any who professed faith and yet fell away into apostasy could not have belonged to the 'elect' and were therefore never truly converted. In effect, then, Augustine distinguished three classes of men: the elect who truly believed and received the grace of perseverance; the non-elect who never even professed belief; and the non-elect who professed belief but were not true believers (because they did not receive the divine gift of faith) and who must inevitably fall away and not receive final salvation because they did not receive the grace of perseverance.[12]

At the Reformation the theology of Augustine acquired a new lease of life through its influence on John Calvin who made Augustinianism the basis of his teaching on the grace of God and election. The final perseverance of the saints was thus a necessary and logical part of his theological system.[13] This view was shared by Martin Luther,[14] although the later Lutherans and the theologians of the Counter-Reformation espoused a non-Augustinian position.[15] Their example was followed by the Arminians, whose theological position was expressed in their rejection of the Calvinist Five Points of Dort, the fifth of which was final perseverance.[16]

In England the Calvinist position was adopted by the Puritans[17] and received a violent and massive defence against the spirited attacks of John Goodwin from John Owen.[18] Since then those who stand in the Calvinist tradition have accepted final perseverance as axiomatic.[19] But Arminius has also had his followers; in the eighteenth century John Wesley opposed the doctrine of final perseverance in his attacks on the hyper-Calvinism of his day,[20] and Methodists have generally accepted his position.[21]

The result would appear to be a theological stalemate, which may be expressed by juxtaposing well-known verses from A. M. Toplady and Charles Wesley. The former expressed the Calvinist certainty:

> The work which His goodness began
> The arm of His strength will complete:
> His promise is Yea and Amen,
> And never was forfeited yet.
> Things future nor things that are now,
> Nor all things below or above,
> Can make Him His purpose forego,
> Or sever my soul from His love.
>
> My name from the palms of His hands
> Eternity will not erase;
> Impressed on His heart it remains
> In marks of indelible grace.
> Yes I to the end shall endure,
> As sure as the earnest is given:
> More happy, but not more secure
> The glorified saints in heaven.[22]

The latter wrote:

> Ah! Lord, with trembling I confess,
> A gracious soul may fall from grace;
> The salt may lose its seasoning power,
> And never; never find it more.[23]

The point which impresses one when reading some Calvinist authors is that they tend to accept the doctrine of final perseverance on philosophical and dogmatic grounds. For the Calvinist the doctrine of perseverance can be regarded as a corollary of the doctrine of the predestination of particular individuals to salvation.[24] The Arminian, for his part, may argue for the possibility of loss of salvation from his doctrine of the freedom of the human will to accept or reject salvation.[25] The only hope of moving beyond these two points of view would appear to lie in a thorough study of the New Testament evidence. It is in an attempt to provide this that the present survey has been undertaken.

CHAPTER ONE

The Old Testament and Jewish Background

Before we consider the doctrine of the Christian life in the New Testament it is necessary for us to examine the background of thought in the Old Testament and in Judaism which may have exercised an influence upon the doctrine of the first Christians. The material to be considered includes the Old Testament, the Dead Sea Scrolls, and the Rabbinic literature.

1. THE OLD TESTAMENT

The theme of the Old Testament is the way in which God chose the people of Israel to be His people and the recipients of His salvation. This people must be regarded as the forerunner of the Christian Church, established under the new covenant, and it will be of value for us to consider the relationship of the old Israel to God for the light which it may shed on the parallel situation of the new Israel.

The Old Testament emphasizes the fact that the individual is part of a community more than the New Testament. The dividing line between the acts of individuals and of communities to which they belong is a very thin one, as the well-known story of Achan and his family testifies. It is not surprising, therefore, that the Old Testament places considerable stress on the relationship of the community to God, and its vocabulary of falling away and apostasy is applied more to the community than to individuals. Any conclusions which may be drawn from the Old Testament about the relation of the community to God must accordingly be applied with caution to the position of the individual under the new covenant.

This does not of course mean that the relationship of the

individual to God is ignored in the Old Testament or is unimportant. The individual lived as a member of a society bound by a system of God-given laws, and disobedience to these laws corresponded to communal apostasy. In order, therefore, to gain a full picture of the situation in the Old Testament, as it would appear to the first Christians, we must consider its teaching about both national apostasy (found principally in the prophets) and individual transgression of the law (found principally in the Pentateuch).

NATIONAL APOSTASY

The Old Testament possesses a very considerable number of words to express the ideas of sin and rebellion against Yahweh, and it would be tedious to consider them individually and in detail here.[1] It has, however, been noted that one of these words, *shûb* ('to turn'), was cultivated with the double sense of 'to turn away from Yahweh' and 'to return to Yahweh' by Jeremiah.[2] This fact suggests that Jeremiah may be a key figure in the Old Testament doctrine of apostasy, and we shall in fact find it possible to use his work as the framework for our investigation, at the same time bringing into view important material from elsewhere in the Old Testament.

The Ideal

Jeremiah stood at the crucial turning point in Israelite history and from his central vantage point he was able to survey the sinful life of the people, which culminated in their exile, and to interpret it with rich insight. The particular viewpoint which governed his interpretation of the life of Israel was his conviction that Yahweh longed for a people who would cleave to Him without turning away and hoped that Israel would fulfil His purpose.

'I thought how I would set you among my sons, and give you a pleasant land, a heritage most beauteous of all nations. And I thought you would call me, My Father, and would not turn from following me' (Jeremiah 3:19). With this we may compare the affirmation of the people in Psalm 44:17f. and the realization of the ideal in the affirmation of the Servant of Yahweh (Isaiah 50:5).

The Reality

The burden of Jeremiah was that, although there had been times when this ideal had been a reality in the life of the people (cf. Psalm 44:17f., 20f.), more often God's people had turned away from Him and been faithless:

'Surely, as a faithless wife leaves her husband, so have you been faithless to me, O house of Israel, says the Lord' (Jeremiah 3:20; cf. 3:1–10).

The same tale is told by other writers. According to the author of Psalm 78, which is a cultic recital of the history of Israel, the life of God's people has been one of continual backsliding despite the repeated mercies of Yahweh. The purpose of its historical reminder is that the new generation 'should not be like their fathers, a stubborn and rebellious generation, a generation whose heart was not steadfast, whose spirit was not faithful to God' (Psalm 78:8). A similar tale is told elsewhere in the Psalter (Psalms 106, 107) and in the Song of Moses (Deuteronomy 32:1–43) where we read of Jeshurun who 'forsook God who made him, and scoffed at the Rock of his salvation' (Deuteronomy 32:15). Many other passages could be cited, Judges 2:11–23 and Nehemiah 9 being good examples of the same pattern. From these passages a general picture of the backsliding situation can be drawn.

Thus we see that backsliding characteristically follows a display of God's mercy and power to His people. The sin of the backsliding nation is made all the more culpable by the fact that it has known the grace of God and has then turned against Him (Psalm 78:7, 11, 32, 35, 42; Deuteronomy 32:7, 18; Jeremiah 2:1–3:6). Its attitude is essentially one of sin against God (Psalm 78:17, 32; cf. 1 Samuel 14:33). The people are faithless towards God (Psalm 78:8, 37), forsaking His covenant (Hosea 6:7; Deuteronomy 29:25 [MT 24]; 31:16), turning aside from His way (Exodus 32:8; Deuteronomy 9:12; Judges 2:17) and no longer keeping His law (Psalms 78:7, 10; 119:85, 158). They turn from God to serve idols (Psalm 78:58; Exodus 32:8; Deuteronomy 32:16f.; Judges 2:12f., 17, 19; 10:10; Isaiah 65:1–5; Jeremiah 1:16; 2:23; Zephaniah 1:4–6). In the end, they persist in stubbornness against God (Hosea 4:16; Jeremiah 6:28; Nehemiah 9:29), and test God to see how far they can go with impunity in disobedience to Him (Psalm 78:18, 41, 56).

There are no doubt degrees of backsliding, but what is characteristic of the situation in the Old Testament is the fact that the sin of the nation is deep-seated, affecting every class in society. If the rulers give the lead, the mass of people are ready to follow them (Jeremiah 2:8; 50:6; Isaiah 1:2–9). Nor is it simply the whole nation which is affected. It is the whole history of that nation which is condemned by the prophets (cf. Jeremiah 8:5).

The Penalty for Backsliders and Apostates

The inevitable reaction of a holy God is to act in judgement against those who fall away and rebel against Him (Jeremiah 5:9). The judgement matches the offence: when God's people forsake Him, then He forsakes them. Because of their sin He refuses to accept them (Jeremiah 14:10; Psalm 78:59–62). He removes His protective presence and allows the enemies of His people to overcome them (cf. Numbers 14:43; 32:15; 1 Chronicles 28:9; Hosea 5:6f).

It is important to observe that in His judgements God is not simply vindicating His own character and law (Jeremiah 5:9). Part of His purpose is to bring His people to their senses by showing them the folly of backsliding. 'Your wickedness will chasten you, and your apostasy will reprove you. Know and see that it is evil and bitter for you to forsake the Lord your God; the fear of me is not in you, says the Lord God of hosts' (Jeremiah 2:19).

Yet, although God's judgement is meant to lead His people back to Him, it may not succeed (Jeremiah 2:30). A point may be reached at which nothing can stop the course of judgement. God's people may indeed cry out to Him to withhold His judgements and to help them, but their cries may be so hypocritical that He is unable to do so. After hearing the cries of His people God can only say: 'You have rejected me, says the Lord, you keep going backward; so I have stretched out my hand against you and destroyed you; I am weary of relenting' (Jeremiah 15:6, after Jeremiah 14:7–15:4; cf. Hosea 5:15–6:6; 11:7). He may even forbid the prophet to pray for the people (Jeremiah 7:16; 11:14; 14:11f.; 15:1).

The outcome of rebellion is thus judgement, but this judgement is designed, in part at least, to show God's people the folly of their ways. There is in fact an element of mercy in judgement. We are being led to see that there is a way back from sin to God; the word *shûb* can also, we remember, refer to return to Yahweh.

Mercy for Backsliders and Apostates

Although sin leads to judgement, God does not always act in judgement. This is made especially clear in Psalm 78: 'Yet he, being compassionate, forgave their iniquity, and did not destroy them; he restrained his anger often, and did not stir up all his wrath. He remembered that they were but flesh, a wind that passes and comes not again. How often they rebelled against him in the wilderness and grieved him in the desert!' (Psalm

78:38–40).[3] This is the great truth which was especially taught by Hosea (Hosea 11:1–4).[4]

From this it is a short step to the assertion that God can cure the backsliding of His people and will heal their faithlessness (Hosea 14:4). The thought is clearly expressed in the later chapters of the book of Isaiah: 'Because of the iniquity of his covetousness I was angry, I smote him, I hid my face and was angry; but he went on backsliding in the way of his own heart. I have seen his ways, but I will heal him; I will lead him and requite him with comfort, creating for his mourners the fruit of the lips' (Isaiah 57:17f.; cf. Isaiah 58–59). Similarly, Ezekiel makes the eschatological promise: 'They shall not defile themselves any more with their idols and their detestable things, or with any of their transgressions; but I will save them from all the backslidings in which they have sinned, and will cleanse them; and they shall be my people, and I will be their God' (Ezekiel 37:23).

So far as Jeremiah himself is concerned, the answer lies in the new covenant. N. H. Snaith writes: 'Even though man himself will not turn to God, yet God Himself can bring this to pass. God's sure, unswerving love will find a way by which even stubborn, unrepentant Israel can turn. It will mean new hearts, but God will accomplish even this. Then there will be a turning to God in all sincerity, and loyal obedience to His Law. Not all Israel will be partakers in this, but only a Remnant.'[5] The thought here appears to be that the display of God's love will cause some of His rebellious people to turn back to Him. God Himself will give them new hearts. But it is never stated that more than a remnant of the people will return to Him in this way.

The Summons to Repentance

There is thus a possibility of return from apostasy. God is willing to forgive the people whom He has chastened if they will return to Him (Hosea 14:1–4). Thus Jeremiah proclaims: 'Return, faithless Israel, says the Lord. I will not look on you in anger, for I am merciful, says the Lord; I will not be angry for ever. Only acknowledge your guilt, that you have rebelled against the Lord your God' (Jeremiah 3:12f.; cf. 3:14, 22; 4:1f., 14). All this is because of the Lord's mercy. He will not make a full end of His people (Jeremiah 5:18), and even though He speaks against Ephraim His heart yearns for him and He will have mercy on him (Jeremiah 31:20).

God takes the initiative in restoring His people to Himself. But the people themselves must take the decisive step of returning to God, even if it is God who in His prevenient grace gives them the opportunity to return and woos them with words of love. God's purpose is that His people may cry out to Him in repentance: I have heard Ephraim bemoaning, 'Thou hast chastened me, and I was chastened, like an untrained calf: bring me back that I may be restored, for thou art the Lord my God. For after I had turned away I repented; and after I was instructed, I smote upon my thigh; I was ashamed, and I was confounded, because I bore the disgrace of my youth" ' (Jeremiah 31:18f.).[6]

Two final points must be noted. First, these promises and appeals (and the consequent act of repentance) applied only to a part of the nation. Although Yahweh's appeals were made in all-embracing terms, it was a remnant of the people which responded. When His hand fell in judgement, many of the people perished, and for them there was no more hope of return;[7] what happened to them was a warning to the rest of the people so that they might repent and return to Yahweh.

Second, we might well ask whether the mercy of God acted in any way to prevent His people from backsliding and apostasy. It is true that God gave His people many warnings, that He promised to them a new heart, and that He protected and kept those who put their trust in Him (cf. Deuteronomy 29–30), but at the same time there are no grounds for supposing that the people as a whole were automatically preserved from falling away. God's promises always appear to be conditional on the faith and obedience of His people.

To summarize: The Old Testament[8] often describes sin in terms of a falling away from God by His people. When this happens and His grace is rejected by them, He deprives them of His presence and blessing and submits them to destruction and exile. Apostasy and its penalty are realities in the Old Testament. But at the same time God longs for His people to return to Him in contrition and repentance and His judgement of the nation as a whole is tempered with mercy. Although individual groups and generations within Israel may fall away from Him and die, it is still possible for the nation to return to Him, and the prophets look forward to the possibility of a time when the people will cease to backslide.

INDIVIDUAL TRANSGRESSIONS AND FORGIVENESS

We must now look more closely at the position of the individual Israelite under the developed legislation of the Old Testament. Having seen how Yahweh treated Israel as a whole in its sin and waywardness, we must inquire how He treated the individual sinner. The vital question for us is whether there was in every case the possibility of forgiveness for the sinner.

As in the previous section, we are not concerned here with the historical development of thought in the Old Testament, but simply to present the teaching of the Old Testament as it would have appeared to the men of the New Testament in order that we may enter into their understanding of the ways of God with men.

Unwitting sins

The basic point which emerges when we glance at the developed sacrificial teaching of the Old Testament contained in the final codification of the pentateuchal law is that a broad distinction was made between two types of sin. One large class of sins was described as *unwitting*: the person who committed such a sin was not aware that he was committing sin. Full provision was made under the sacrificial system for atoning for such sins by means of the sin offering and the guilt offering (Leviticus 4:1–5:13; and Leviticus 5:14–6:7; cf. 22:14).[9] The types of sin for which provision was thus made appear to have been mainly ritual offences — i.e. failure to carry out the rites prescribed by the law or unintentional errors in performance[10] — but at various points sins are listed which would certainly appear to be conscious errors. Thus Leviticus 5:1 refers to failure to give public testimony when a general summons for witnesses is made, and the guilt offering (which involved restitution) was to be offered in atonement for various sins against one's neighbour, viz. deceit in monetary affairs, robbery and failure to restore found property to its owner, which were clearly witting sins (Leviticus 6:1 7).[11] The boundary between unwitting and fitting sins was thus a vague one.

Deliberate sins

From this brief survey we see that the sacrificial system extended to the unwitting sins of the people and that certain types of witting sins were also dealt with in this way. There was, however, a second category of sins, those committed with a high hand, i.e. presumptuously and deliberately.[12] These sins were to be punished by the sinner being cut off from the people, whether by excommunication or by execution.[13] No provision was made for sacrificial atonement for such sins, and in the nature of things there could be no restoration of a man who had paid the supreme penalty for his sin. The person who sinned presumptuously was regarded as reviling Yahweh. He had refused the word of Yahweh and broken His commandments.

His iniquity rested upon him and could not be expiated by sacrifice (Numbers 15:30f.).

There would thus appear to have been the possibility of serious sin for which there was no hope of forgiveness and restoration whatever. The verdict of H. Schultz is typical: 'The later law . . . knows of a reconciliation with God through sacrifices, only in the case of a few comparatively trivial offences . . . For one who sins "with a high hand", that is, with the intention of acting in defiance of God's commandment, there is no sin-offering. He refuses, in fact, to enter the circle within which such a sacrifice has efficacy. Hence that soul must be cut off from among the people, whether God do it Himself by an act of judgement, or commissions the authorities to do it.'[14]

If this were all that there is to be said, we would have to agree with N. H. Snaith that the sacrificial code of the Pentateuch is 'singularly inadequate.'[15] There is, however, some evidence on the other side.

In this connexion the question of the efficacy of the Day of Atonement has been raised. A. R. S. Kennedy, following S. R. Driver, held that its efficacy extended only to unwitting sins,[16] but C. R. Smith held that a ritual carried out for all the sins of Israel must have had some significance to the worshippers who went up yearly to Jerusalem with regard to the sins of which they were aware.[17] It is probably best to think of the sacrifice as being on behalf of Israel as a whole rather than on behalf of individual Israelites, but Smith's suggestion may be regarded as pointing towards the fact that the line of demarcation between witting and unwitting sins was not always clearly drawn.

C. R. Smith further notes that the same offering (the sin offering) which is prescribed in Leviticus 6:1–7 for witting sins was also used in the purification of a leper or after childbirth, and he suggests that Leviticus is concerned with ritual rather than with ethics. Similarly, the high-handed sins in Numbers 15 are sins against ritual rules; the question of ethics is thus not raised.[18] It would thus appear to be true that in general breaking of what we may call the civil law was not covered by this distinction; there were many comparatively minor legal offences which were not punished as drastically as might have been expected if all witting sins received the full penalty.

We are led to the conclusion that the dividing line between witting and unwitting sins was not always clearly defined, and there must have been many offences which could be classified as witting sins for which expiation was possible (provided, of course, that the offender was repentant). The witting sins for which no way of atonement was provided in the sacrificial system other than the death of the offender were ritual offences, apostasy expressed in blasphemy and 'atheism,' and capital crimes such as murder.[19]

The explanation of this system is partly to be found in the Old Testament concept of sin as 'theo-fugal.'[20] Sin is an attitude of rebellion against Yahweh, and the person who sins wittingly is a person who does not wish forgiveness. Having taken up a deliberate stand against Yahweh, he has cut himself off from the source of forgiveness. He is therefore to be cut off from Israel, the people of God, lest his sin contaminate the people as a whole (e.g. Joshua 7; 1 Samuel 14), and his sin is atoned for by his death (cf. Isaiah 22:14).[21]

What the sacrificial system does not provide for is the case of the man who repents after he has sinned deliberately. It is conceivable that his sin is regarded as so great that no act of repentance is sufficient to atone for it. But there is another possibility. At best, the sacrificial system is a legal system and is concerned only with those sins which are open and outward acts; there is a whole range of sins of the mind and heart which it cannot punish and for which it makes no sacrificial provision. It is not surprising, therefore, that there were individuals in Israel who saw beyond the ritual of the sacrificial system and its concern with outward acts to the possibility of personal reconciliation with God.[22] Even the sacrifices themselves were ineffective apart from confession of sin and repentance, and certain of the Psalmists saw that in a sense sacrifices were unnecessary. A number of Psalms (e.g. Psalms 32; 51; 130) contain a pattern of confession of sin and admission of guilt before Yahweh, a plea for forgiveness, and an assurance that forgiveness has been granted by Yahweh. It may be right to associate this pattern with a form of worship in the Temple.[23] In any case, we have here evidence that the individual Israelite could turn to Yahweh in prayer and find assurance of forgiveness for his sins, even without the offering of material sacrifices.[24]

This important conclusion is strengthened by the way in which the prophetic appeals to the nation to repent and turn to Yahweh ultimately break down into appeals to individuals to repent. 'Return, every one from his evil way, and amend your ways and your doings,' is the message of Jeremiah (Jeremiah 18:11, et al.). Even deliberate sin can be forgiven (2 Samuel 24:10). [25] In all these cases repentance and a contrite heart are the inevitable presuppositions for forgiveness.[26] Forgiveness is not bestowed indiscriminately, but is given to the man who submits to God and casts himself upon His mercy. The person who does not repent does not find forgiveness precisely because he is not looking for it.

The sum total of the Old Testament teaching is thus that it is possible for a man to sin deliberately and grievously against God in a fashion which leads to judgement; such a man was cut off from the congregation of Israel by excommunication or death because the manner of his sin made him an apostate. On the other hand, outside the provisions of the sacrificial system, and where a person had not sinned wittingly beyond hope of recovery, forgiveness was a real possibility on condition of repentance, The Old Testament thus knows the possibility and the fact of individual apostasy from which there is no return, but at the same time it emphasizes the great mercy of God in forgiving His people when they repent of their sins.

2. THE DEAD SEA SCROLLS

From the Old Testament we must now turn to the inter-Testamental period and consider those currents of thought in Judaism which may also be held to have influenced the doctrines of the early Church.[27]

There is scarcely anything directly relevant for us in the Apocrypha. 1 and 2 Maccabees bear witness to the rise of apostasy as a national problem during the period when Hellenistic influences were becoming powerful in Judaea (1 Maccabees 2:15; cf. Daniel 11:30). At this time there arose more than one group of men who were determined to preserve the ancient loyalty of the people to Yahweh and to work for the restoration of what they regarded as the true religion. For our understanding of the concept of the apostasy in this period we must turn to the writings of these men who felt so keenly the declension of Israel from its lofty ideals. This means that our interest must be directed to the Qumran sect who produced the Dead Sea Scrolls. Although there is no surviving Pharisee literature from this period to give us an insight into the minds of the other main group of upholders of traditional piety, there is a rich supply of material in the Rabbinic literature which can be used with caution to give us some insight into the orthodox Judaism of the first century A.D.[28]

THE APOSTASY OF ISRAEL

The Dead Sea Scrolls are of direct interest for our study because they depict the life and beliefs of a sect whose very existence was due to their conviction that apostasy had corrupted the life of their nation.[29] In the Admonition which forms the first part of the Zadokite Document the basic interpretation of the history of Israel as a record of apostasy already familiar to us from the Old Testament is repeated. God redeemed the people of Israel out of Egypt and made a covenant with them, requiring them to keep His laws, but they refused to obey Him and renounced Him. He therefore gave them up to be consumed and allowed them to be destroyed. Nevertheless, because of His covenant He did not totally destroy them, but preserved a remnant of faithful men (the sect) who constituted the true Israel, and to them He sent prophets and teachers.

This view is set out succinctly at the beginning of the Admonition: '(God) will execute judgement upon all that despise Him. For when they sinned in that they forsook Him, He hid His face from Israel and from His sanctuary and gave them to the sword. But when He remembered the covenant of the forefathers, He caused a remnant to remain of Israel and gave them not up to be confused.' This is followed by a historical summary of how men went astray and walked in the stubbornness of their hearts.[30]

It was the belief of the men of Qumran that this same pattern of history was being expressed in the events of their own day, and so they exercised their ingenuity in finding hidden predictions of contemporary events in the Old Testament.[31] Whatever be the precise dating of the rise of the sect and of the composition of its writings, it can scarcely be doubted that they would find much in the contemporary life of Israel to justify their view of history. It is indeed the continual backsliding and apostasy of Israel over a period of more than two centuries which makes it difficult to locate the historical references in the scrolls with complete certainty. What is significant is that the sect believed that they were living in the final era of apostasy. They awaited the dawn of God's final intervention in history when He would defeat and punish the wicked and set up a kingdom of peace and righteousness.

During this period before God's decisive intervention, which might be protracted for a long time,[32] the sect believed that they had been raised up by God as the remnant of Israel, just as He had raised up a remnant in the past (CD 1:4f.). They were prepared to admit the sinfulness of Israel, which included their own sins,[33] but they believed that because they had repented and returned to God by making a new covenant with Him they, and through them Israel, would be saved.[34] For them, of course, the 'Israel' which was to be saved consisted exclusively of members of the sect; the rest of apostate Israel would be destroyed.[35]

GOD'S CHOICE OF THE COMMUNITY

The basis of the sect's confidence about their own destiny lay in two facts. First, they believed that they had been specially raised up by God Himself. 'And in the epoch of wrath, "three hundred and ninety" years after "He had given them into the hand of Nebuchadnezzar, king of Babylon," He visited them; and He caused to grow forth from Israel and Aaron "a root of cultivation, to possess His land" and to wax fat in the goodness of His soil . . . And He raised for them "a teacher of righteousness" to lead them in "the way of His heart" . . . "God remembered the covenant of the forefathers," and He raised from Aaron "men of understanding" and from Israel "men of wisdom." '(CD 1:5–8, 11; 6:2f.).

Second, the sect believed that God foreknew all that was to happen:[36] 'For God has not chosen them (the backsliders) "from of old, (from the days of) eternity," and before they were established He knew their works and abhorred the generations when they arose, and He hid His face from the land from their arising (or: and from Israel) until their being consumed. And He knows (or: knew) the years of their existence and the number (or: set times) and exact epochs of all them that come into being in eternity (or: in the worlds) and past events, even unto that which will befall in the epochs of all the years of eternity (or: the world). And in all of them He raised for Himself "*men* called by name," in order "to leave a remnant" for the land . . . And with exactitude He set out their names; but those whom He hated He caused to stray' (CD 2:7–13).[37]

From such a passage as this it might well be concluded that the sect taught a rigid predestination both of good and of evil. A further passage, quoted by J. van der Ploeg, is in the same strain:

> For the way that a man goes is not his own,
> man does not dispose his own steps,
> for God ordains it;
> if one does well, that comes from Him!
> Through His wisdom all things came to pass
> and all that is has been determined by His plan,
> and without Him it does not come to be. (1 QS 11:10f.).

But, as van der Ploeg goes on to say, we may not be entitled to draw rigid logical conclusions from such passages.[38] It may well be that the authors had never considered all the implications of their statements or brought them into relation with other parts of their theology. What they seem concerned to emphasize are the truths that ultimate control of the world is in the hands of God so that nothing can take Him by surprise or overthrow Him, and that the righteous who entrust themselves to Him are guided and empowered by Him. In fact it is implied that man has some control over his actions. In the description of the spirits of truth and perversion who are at work in the hearts of men (1 QS 3:13–4:26) it is said that they are equally opposed to each other in the world, and apparently also in the hearts of men, so that a man can choose which he is going to obey; only at the End will God bring to nought the spirit of perversion and cleanse some of mankind by the Spirit. Thus the act of joining the community is a free choice by a man himself, although a man should attribute whatever good is in himself to the activity of God and His Spirit.

APOSTASY AND DISCIPLINE IN THE COMMUNITY

Those who joined the community lived a life centered upon the Torah and occupied themselves in a minute study of the Old Testament Scriptures (1 QS 6:6–8). In this way they attempted to avoid the errors of the people of Israel generally who had transgressed against the covenant, broken the ordinances of God and persecuted the godly, and were therefore doomed to extinction (CD 1:13–2:1).

Nevertheless, the mere act of joining the community did not preserve a man from the possibility of becoming apostate and falling under God's condemnation. The sect was all too conscious of the fact of sin and apostasy within its midst, and its members took all possible steps to prevent the rise of disobedience to the covenant and to discipline those who went astray. A hierarchical system of different orders of members was instituted, and the penalties for disobedience were minutely prescribed. The general principle was that those who showed themselves to be apostate, although they were members of the community, were to be excluded from the community and its blessings (CD 8:21; 19:33–20:13). Such exclusion from the community was held to bring the curse of God upon the person concerned so that he was consigned to everlasting destruction. At the solemn initiation ceremony for new members of the community a curse against all such backsliders was pronounced in the clearest terms (1 QS 2:11–18).

For lesser offences other punishments were laid down. The members of the sect were organized in various orders and they were promoted or down-graded according to their spiritual progress (1 QS 5:24). A person who told lies about his property and thus held some of it back from the communal fund was deprived of one quarter of his food rations for a period of a year (1 QS 6:25). For other misdemeanours a person might be temporarily suspended from membership of the sect, being excluded from its rites and its common meals.

What is of especial interest from our point of view is that for more serious acts of disobedience involving apostasy both temporary and permanent excommunication were possible. The relevant passage states: 'Whoever goes about calumniating the Many shall be sent away from them and shall not return. And the man who murmurs against the Institution of the Community shall be sent away and shall not return . . . And the man whose spirit fears the Institution of the Community to the point of betraying the Truth and of walking in the stubbornness of his heart, if he returns shall be punished for two years . . . And no man who is in the Council of the Community for more than ten whole years and whose spirit turns back to the point of betraying the Community and who goes out from before the Many to walk in the stubbornness of his heart, shall return again to the Council of the Community' (1 QS 7:16–24, abbreviated). From this passage it appears that the punishment of expulsion was reserved for those who committed apostasy by fundamental disagreement with the principles of the sect or by blasphemy (cf. 1 QS 6:27–7:2). Moreover, the punishment of full and irrevocable expulsion was reserved for men who had been members sufficiently long to realize what they were doing; they would indeed be witting sinners (cf. 1 QS 5:1 lf.; CD 3:14f. for unwitting sins). This is confirmed by the treatment of men who belonged to the highest order of holiness within the community. Even a single transgression against the Torah by such a person was to be punished with complete expulsion; but if his one transgression could be regarded as inadvertent, he was to be demoted and put on probation for a period of two years, only after which could he be restored to his original grade (1 QS 8:20–9:2).

We thus see that sin, if witting and high-handed, was regarded as being beyond pardon. There was no hope of return. It is not unfair to say that in this respect the sect showed a rigour which went beyond anything else in Judaism.[39]

CONCLUSION

From this survey of the teaching of the sect on apostasy two apparently contradictory facts will have become apparent. On the one hand, the Qumran sect believed firmly in divine predestination and had a strong conviction of His protective power (e.g. IQH 2:22f., 25, 31–37; 5:11ff.). But on the other hand, they devoted much attention to the possibility of sin and apostasy within their ranks. Evidently, therefore, they did not hold to a doctrine of perseverance or predestination which precluded the possibility of apostasy.[40] Even men who had been in the community for more than ten years might apostatize. It becomes plain that God's grace was for the man who bound himself to the covenant. The consciousness of the power of such grace was strong, but it did not exclude the fear of falling away. It is not surprising, therefore, that the Overseers of the various communities were expected to exert a pastoral influence over their members (CD 13:7–10).

3. THE TEACHING OF THE RABBIS

We have considered the teaching of the Qumran sect before that of the Rabbis since the sources for it are certainly earlier and come directly from the sect itself. But the Qumran sect represented only a minority in Judaea and the main stream of Jewish religious thought is to be found in the Rabbinic writings. We must now attempt, with all due caution, to use these writings as a guide to first-century Jewish thought.[41]

ENTRY INTO THE WORLD TO COME

In the Old Testament salvation consisted in membership of the people of Israel who enjoyed fellowship with God in the land which He gave to them, and the effect of apostasy was to exclude a man, or the nation as a whole, from these earthly blessings. Since there was little real hope of a future life, the problem of who would share in it did not arise.

In the Rabbinic literature, however, the concept of salvation was understood more in terms of the future and in particular of life after death. It was realized that the questions of retribution and reward cannot be fully answered within the bounds of this life, and the new world must be called in to redress the balance of the old. A complex doctrine of the future life developed from the seeds sown in the writings of the inter-Testamental period. Broadly speaking, the Rabbis looked forward to the Messianic

Age during which the heathen enemies of Israel would be defeated and destroyed; then would follow the resurrection of the dead and God's final judgement of all mankind, after which would begin the life of the World to Come.[42]

While there was considerable interest in the Messianic Age and who would share in it, the main interest in Jewish eschatology was in the final judgement and who would be judged worthy by God to participate in the World to Come. Thanks to what R. A. Stewart has called 'the unblushing juxtaposition of incompatible teachings'[43] in the literature on this matter, as on every other, it is not easy to find a consistent strain of thought on the problem. But since it was generally thought that there was no place for the Gentiles in the World to Come — circumcision being an indispensable qualification, though not a final guarantee, for entry[44] — our concern is with the way in which a Jew might obtain entry to the World to Come and with the factors which might exclude him.

THE EFFICACY OF REPENTANCE

Although some Jewish teaching might appear to suggest that circumcision was a mechanical or magical guarantee of salvation, the teaching of the Rabbis at its best was undoubtedly moral and spiritual. They started from the fact that all men (apart from a few negligible exceptions) are sinners and need to seek forgiveness from God. There were many ways in which forgiveness might be sought, but common to all of them was the need for repentance. Repentance was named as one of the seven things created before the world, a fact which invested it with a special dignity and importance.[45] The operative factor in sacrifice was the repentance of the sinner. While certain sins might need the sacrifices of the Day of Atonement or even the death of the sinner to atone for them, it was laid down very early that both the Day of Atonement and the death of the sinner were ineffective if not accompanied by repentance.[46] For the Rabbis repentance included both confession of sin with remorse and the abandonment of sin for the future.[47]

THE LIMITS OF REPENTANCE

In certain circumstances repentance might be regarded as ineffectual, with the result that the sinner could not obtain divine forgiveness. Thus it was laid down that although a man might certainly repent and find forgiveness more than once for his sin, God would not receive the man whose repentance was hypocritical or who persisted in sin with the thought that he would be able to repent at some time in the future. 'If a man said, "I will sin and repent, and sin again and repent," he will be given no change to repent. (If he said,) "I will sin and the Day of Atonement will effect atonement," then the Day of Atonement effects no atonement.'[48]

The Rabbis also maintained the Old Testament distinction between unwitting and presumptuous sins and linked it to a distinction between lesser and greater commandments and transgressions.[49] As a result, means of atonement through punishment and forgiveness were provided even for deliberate sins. A broad distinction was drawn between transgressions against lesser commandments, for which atonement was possible simply by repentance, and those against greater commandments, for which atonement was possible only through extirpation or capital punishment. The Day of Atonement atoned for sins of which the transgressor was completely unaware. By these means it was theoretically possible to atone for all kinds of sins.[50]

These considerations show that, while a limit was set to the possibility of forgiveness through the need for genuine repentance, there was in theory no limit to the gravity of the sin which might be atoned for by the repentant sinner. But we must now ask whether it was always possible for the sinner to repent.

One principle which is frequently affirmed is that: 'He that leads the many to sin, to him shall be given no means for repentance' (Pirqe Aboth 5:18). Of particular interest is the ascription of this sentiment to Jesus, in order that He might be condemned from His own lips: 'Rabbi Joshua ben Perahyah said to him (Jesus, in Egypt), Repent! He replied to him, This is what I have received from you: If a man sins and leads many into sin, he is no longer given the opportunity to repent.' The story is unhistorical, but the saying is typically Rabbinic.[51]

Similarly, God withholds repentance from a man who refuses the opportunities of repentance which are given to him. This is implicit in the teaching already quoted, although the passages explicitly developing this doctrine are late, coming from the fourth century. One example will suffice: 'After God has waited for the godless to repent and they have not done so, he finally accepts their heart (their placid deliberation) not to repent, even if they may wish to repent . . . Even when they wish to turn to God (in repentance) and set about to busy themselves with prayer, they are unable to do so, because he hinders them: for he has closed (the door of repentance and prayer) before them' (Exodus Rabbah 11, (74c)).[52] It is clear that a man can fall so completely into sin that he is not allowed by God to repent.

APOSTASY AND REPENTANCE

Is the apostate in this category? Clearly the unrepentant apostate could not be forgiven and find entry to the World to Come, but the evidence is divided about the possibility of the apostate being able to repent.

(1) A well-known list in Sanhedrin 10:1–3 gives a list of people to be excluded from the World to Come. While 'all Israelites have a share in the world to come,' those who deny the resurrection of the dead, those who deny the divine origin of the Torah, and Epicureans are specifically excluded. Rabbi Akiba added to this list readers of heretical books and workers of magic, and Abba Saul added blasphemers who used the sacred name. There is no mention of repentance in this context, and we cannot be sure whether this passage denies the possibility of it to the various kinds of apostate mentioned. Elsewhere, however, this denial is made explicit: 'If a man from among you wishes to bring an offering, Leviticus 1:2. "From among you" is meant to exclude the apostates (for they no longer belong to the congregation of Israel). Why do you say then? — Say (rather) "a man" (quite general) is meant to include the apostates; "from among you" is meant to exclude the proselytes . . . The Scripture teaches, Say to the children of Israel, Leviticus 1:2; as the children of Israel are those who have accepted the covenant, so also the proselytes are those who have accepted the covenant. Thus the apostates are excluded who have not accepted the covenant' (Siphra Leviticus 1:2 (11a)).[53]

This evidence suggests that the earlier Rabbinic teaching excluded apostates from repentance and so from the World to Come.

(2) But there is also evidence which points in the opposite direction. A saying attributed to Rabbi Simeon ben Yohai (*c.* A.D. 150) states that if a man has been wicked all his life and yet repents at the end God will receive him.[54] It is true that the saying does not make clear whether or not the wicked man was an apostate, but one classic story does tell how an apostate was summoned to repent. Rabbi Elisha ben Abuya (*c.* A.D. 120) was an apostate who (according to one story) visited heaven in a vision and cut down the plants of paradise, and (according to another story) expressed disbelief in future reward and resurrection from the dead.[55] During his last illness Rabbi Meir asked

him: ' "Although you possess all this wisdom, are you not willing to repent?" He replied, "I cannot!" He said to him, "Why?" He said to him, "Once I was riding on my horse on the Day of Atonement, which fell on a Sabbath, in front of the Holy of Holies, and I heard a heavenly voice which came from the Holy of Holies and cried, Turn back, children, except for Elisha ben Abuya, for he knew my power and has raised himself up against me." '[56] The story is quoted up to this point by Billerbeck in illustration of the impossibility of second repentance, but in fact it does not end there: 'To Meir's exhortation to repent, Elisha replied, Would I be received even now? Meir answered by quoting Psalm 90:3, to which he gave the turn, "Thou lettest man return (repent) even unto crushing — that is, until life is crushed out of him — and sayest repent, ye children of men." '[57] Finally, when Rabbi Meir received news that the grave of his teacher was in flames, he went out, 'and took his mantle and spread it out over it, and said, (quoting Ruth 3:13), "Remain here this night," remain in this world which resembles night; "and in the morning," that is the World to Come, which is all morning; "if the Good One wishes to redeem you, he will redeem you" (Midrash), that refers to God who is good, see Psalm 145:9: Yahweh is good to all. "But if he has no desire to redeem you, then, as Yahweh lives, I will redeem you." Then the fire was extinguished.'[58]

The story shows that while the generally accepted opinion was against the possibility of an apostate repenting the view did establish itself that even an apostate could repent. This was certainly the case in very much later Jewish texts; although, for example, Manasseh was excluded from the World to Come in the Mishnah (Sanhedrin 10:2), later Rabbis allotted a place in it to him.[59]

The conclusion which we are permitted to draw from this evidence is that an opinion did exist among the Rabbis that even an apostate could repent and find favour with God. But, although the Rabbis were thus prepared to admit the great mercy of God, there was also the possibility in individual cases that God's sentence might be spoken against a man long before his death.[60]

THE APPLICATION OF DISCIPLINE

It is difficult to know exactly what was the practice of the Rabbis with regard to the disciplining of apostates. A detailed picture of a developed system is given by P. Billerbeck.[61]

In Rabbinic legislation sinners were disciplined by the

imposition of the 'ban,' a breaking off of relations with a sinner until such time as he should repent and seek forgiveness. The simplest form was a personal reprimand (*n*[e]*ziphāh*), which was simply breaking off of relations by an offended person for seven days and did not affect the relation of the offender to the rest of the community.

A more drastic treatment was known as *niddûy* or *shammattā"*; this was a ban normally imposed for a period of 30 days by an individual Rabbi or, more usually, by a court of three men upon an offender who was guilty of blasphemy or 'Epicureanism' or for monetary offences such as failure to pay debts. The ban was ceremonially imposed to the accompaniment of curses upon the guilty man; its effect was to cut him off from all human relationships, except with his family, and the man was expected to go about as if he were in mourning. He was, however, permitted to go to worship. From this it is clear that the purpose of the ban was to lead the person to repentance, and that when he showed penitence the ban was regarded as having been effective and he was freed from it.

If imposition of the ban produced no effect, it could be reimposed for another 30 days, and if this additional period also failed in its purpose, recourse was had to a more severe form of ban, *ḥerem*. This was similar to the simple ban, but had the effect of severing the individual from all relationships with the community and his family. Its duration was uncertain, but it could be cancelled if the offender showed signs of penitence. Its purpose was not to exclude rebels from the synagogue, but rather to lead them to obedience.

This detailed procedure, however, belongs to a period well after the close of NT times.[62] During the first century AD the *niddûy* was the only type of communal ban which was practised; the ḥerem is not mentioned until the third century AD. Originally the *niddûy* was imposed for at least 30 days, and was of unlimited duration, i.e. until death or repentance. Its use was largely restricted to Pharisaic teachers and it was directed against those who failed to conform to Pharisaic traditions. It would appear to have excluded deviant individuals from participation in Pharisaic groups, and was not used to discipline ordinary members of the synagogue. Some form of total exclusion (expressed by *dāḥāh*) also appears to have been used. But owing to the scarceness of the sources it is difficult to form a clear picture of first century practice.[63] We may suspect that Pharisaic practice was not unlike that at Qumran where both temporary and permanent excommunication of individuals from the community was practised.[64]

PREDESTINATION AND DIVINE PROTECTION

So far in this section we have been concerned simply to deal with the actual occurrence of apostasy according to Rabbinic teaching and have seen that the fact of apostasy is taken for granted by the Rabbis. One final question which must now be raised is whether those who become apostate do so of their own free will or because their action has been predestined by God. The general nature of the answer given to this question by the Rabbis is well known, and will not be found to affect in any material way the conclusions already reached.

Although there were differences of opinion about details, in general the Rabbis held that the course of the world was already foreseen by God. Thus Rabbi Akiba could say: 'All is foreseen, but freedom of choice is given' (Pirqe Aboth 3:16).[65] At the most, however, the Rabbinic teaching gives 'merely a statement of divine foreknowledge, without any necessary implication of predestination.'[66] In fact, one distinct exception is made in any formulation of a divine determinism: as indicated in the quotation from Rabbi Akiba above, man is free to choose between good and evil. This view, which rests ultimately upon the teaching of the Old Testament, is found in such early sources as Ecclesiasticus 15:11–17, Psalms of Solomon 9:7, and 2 Esdras 8:55ff., and persists throughout Rabbinic teaching. One late example will suffice: Rabbi Hanina ben Papa (*c.* A.D. 300) said, 'The angel who is appointed over conception . . . takes the drop of semen and brings it before God, and says before him, Lord of the world, what shall come from this drop? A strong man or a weak, a wise man or a fool, a rich man or a poor? And see, he does not say, "A godless man or a righteous man?" ' (Niddah 16b).[67] As Moore states: 'It is unnecessary to multiply examples further; there are no dissentient voices.'[68] There is, consequently, no suggestion that certain men are foreordained to be righteous or to be apostates.

God, however, does not leave men entirely alone. His task is to lead men on in the way which they have chosen for themselves.

'Hearing will you hear, Exodus 15:26. On the basis of this text it has been said, If a man hears a command, (God) allows him to hear many commands, as it says, Hearing you will hear. If a man forgets a command, (God) lets him forget many commands, as it says, Forgetting you will forget, Deuteronomy 8:19 . . . These are words of Rabbi Joshua (*c.* A.D. 90). Simeon ben Azzai (*c.* A.D. 110) said, . . . If a man heard freely, he is made to hear against his will; if he wished to forget freely, he is also made to forget against his will. The freedom is preserved. As God mocks the mockers, he gives grace to the humble, Proverbs 3:34' (Mekilta Exodus 15:26 (53b))[69] This is consonant with what we have established earlier, that God takes away the opportunity of repentance from those who refuse to repent.

According to Josephus there was considerable dispute over the place to be assigned to 'fate' (εἱμαρμένη) in human action. Only the Essenes attempted to regulate everything by fate, the Sadducees denied its influence, and the Pharisees held that the human will was operative along with destiny.[70] Hence for the Pharisees everything really depended upon the course in life which a man himself decided to follow. No attempt was made to work out philosophically the relation between divine foreknowledge and human action; it was enough to state the fact of a human freedom which might lead to righteousness or apostasy.

CHAPTER TWO

The Synoptic Gospels

Any study of the New Testament teaching on a particular theme must inevitably begin with a consideration of the teaching of Jesus, and accordingly our attention must now be directed to the report of His ministry given in the Synoptic Gospels. For our present purpose, which is the study of a theological concept, the question of what Jesus actually said — His *ipsissima verba* — is not as important as the question of what the early Church thought that He had said. This means that a minute study of the authenticity of each saying ascribed to Him is not demanded in this book, although our aim will certainly be to go back, as far as possible, to His actual words as distinct from what may be regarded as later expansions of His teaching. Our conviction, however, is that the differences between what Jesus actually said and what the Gospels report on this topic are not so significant as to require us to spend much time on questions of authenticity.[1]

1. THE KINGDOM OF GOD

There is now no doubt among scholars that the principal way in which Jesus described the salvation which He came to offer to men was in terms of the kingdom of God. This means that our understanding of the ideas of perseverance and apostasy must be related to the teaching of Jesus about the kingdom. The concept of the kingdom has been the subject of much scholarly attention in recent years and, while it would certainly be wrong to speak of a complete consensus of opinion, there is now a fair amount of unanimity on some of the most important problems which arise in connexion with it.[2]

From our particular point of view two facts are of importance. The first is that the kingdom of God is a term which refers both to the saving act of God in exercising His kingship over the world in order that He might be ruler of a community redeemed from the power of Satan and to the realm or community which is set up as a result of God's action. It is precisely at this point that one of the distinctive features in the teaching of Jesus over against that of Judaism is clearly visible. For the Jews, especially the Rabbis, the kingdom was to be conceived in terms of human responsibility rather than of divine grace, and salvation was a consequence of the eschatological kingdom rather than a part of the kingdom itself.[3] In the teaching of Jesus the kingship of God as an act of grace and salvation comes to the fore. Consequently, alongside the apocalyptic concept of the kingdom as God's final manifestation of His kingly power, and the Rabbinic concept of the kingdom as God's eternal sovereignty operating within the hearts of men must be placed Jesus' concept of the kingdom as the act and sphere of divine salvation. Through the act of God a redeemed community is constituted, which may legitimately be termed His kingdom.[4]

The second point is concerned with the time of God's kingly action. For the Jews this was of course to be placed in the future, and their longing for God to act is clearly reflected in the Gospels (Mark 11:10; 15:43; Matthew 20:21; Luke 1:33; 14:15; 17:20).[5] This accent on the future was shared by Jesus who spoke of the kingdom as coming at some future time (Mark 9:1; 14:25; Matthew 6:10; 13:43; 20:1–16; 22:2; Luke 19:11; 21:31; 22:30; 23:42).[6] He also spoke of men entering the kingdom, and, while the qualifications for entry are couched in the present tense, it is of importance to note that the time of entry is often either explicitly future or may be reasonably understood as future (Mark 9:47; 10:15; Matthew 5:20; 7:21; 8:11f.; 25:34).[7] A number of other texts speak of men taking action for the sake of the kingdom, and these imply that they live now in such a way as to be fit to enter the kingdom when it comes (Matthew 6:33; 13:52; 19:12; Luke 18:29).[8] Finally, the blessings associated with the kingdom are to be regarded as essentially future, although they may be experienced in part here and now; the Beatitudes refer primarily to the future, although they can also describe the present experience of men who have come in contact with Jesus.[9]

This means that Jesus shared to a considerable extent the view of His contemporaries that the kingdom was a future entity. What made His message distinctive was His proclamation that the coming of the kingdom was imminent and that in some sense it was already present; the Jewish 'Kaddish' prayer, 'May He set up His reign in your days,' was replaced by the good news that the kingdom was at hand. It has been argued by C. H. Dodd and others that this proclamation of Jesus is to be understood to mean that the coming of the kingdom was wholly fulfilled in His own advent and ministry. But it now seems certain that this is a wrong interpretation of the evidence[10] and that we must distinguish in the teaching of Jesus between (i) His proclamation that the kingdom would come in the future and (ii) His assertion that the kingdom was already come in His own ministry. A number of texts (Matthew 4:14–16; 11:2–6, 12f.; 12:28; 13:16f.; Luke 17:21)[11] indicate unmistakably that the ministry of Jesus was a time of fulfillment in which the good news of the advent of the kingdom was being proclaimed, God was active in Jesus to save men from the power of Satan, and men could take upon themselves the yoke of the kingdom which was the yoke of Jesus. But, while it is thus legitimate to speak of the kingdom as present in the ministry of Jesus, this does not exclude the fact of its future consummation. God's saving power was fully, but not finally revealed. This is confirmed by the teaching of the rest of the New Testament where the kingdom of God is conceived as a future realm to be set up at the parousia; where the kingdom is spoken of as present, the reference is to the kingdom of Christ which was inaugurated at His ascension.[12] The importance of this conclusion for our study will become obvious in the next section.

2. HUMAN RESPONSE TO THE GOSPEL OF THE KINGDOM

ENTRY TO THE KINGDOM

If the conclusion reached in the previous section is a sound one, it follows that, as far as the outlook of Jesus is concerned, entry to the kingdom of God is something which takes place in the future, although men can already qualify for entrance to the kingdom and participate in its blessings. Thus, on the one hand, men cannot now enter into the future bliss to which there is no end; that would be to anticipate the final judgement of God. On the other hand, it is the present time which is decisive in fixing a man's final destiny, since the qualifications for future entry into the kingdom are uniformly stated in the present tense. If this is so, we are bound to ask what is the present condition and status of those who seek to enter the kingdom of God. Is their entry automatically guaranteed to them, or are they set upon a path of pilgrimage from which they may turn aside? Is it possible for a person to enjoy the blessings of the kingdom here and now in this life, and yet to fail to obtain entry to the kingdom in the end?[13] In order to answer these questions we must begin with an examination of the characteristics of the followers of Jesus.

THE BENEFITS OF THE KINGDOM

Since the message of Jesus is primarily an offer and only secondarily a demand, the basic characteristic of the men who seek the kingdom is that they have received the grace of God. Although, as we have seen, the visible manifestation of the power of God to which the designation of the kingdom is properly applied lay in the future, yet the saving intervention of God was already taking place in the ministry of Jesus, and the blessings of the kingdom were truly and really available to men.

This was especially obvious on the physical plane in the mighty works performed by Jesus which were evidence that the arm of God was being bared for the salvation of men. The physical disabilities characteristic of the age of Satan were being overcome. A woman, held captive by Satan, was set free (Luke 13:16). The lepers were cleansed, the blind, the deaf, and the dumb were healed, and even the dead were raised to life. The demons which infested human life were expelled. All these curses of sin and evil were overcome. Men and women were in utter reality recipients of the blessings of God.

These more physical blessings were accompanied by the spiritual blessings of the kingdom. Thus, although the Beatitudes had primarily a future reference, they undoubtedly spoke also of the present blessings given by the One through whom God summoned men to find rest and ease from their burdens. Again, despite the infrequency of its mention, Jesus undoubtedly forgave sins (Mark 2:1–12; Luke 7:36–50).[14] Such forgiveness was probably purely retrospective (for past sins), since elsewhere Jesus commanded His disciples to pray daily for forgiveness (Matthew 6:11–12). It is likely, therefore, that it was not regarded as a once-for-all act, incapable of repetition. The lack of evidence makes it difficult to give a precise formulation, but we may well be justified in concluding that to all who become His disciples Jesus offered forgiveness in the name of God, but that this forgiveness was not necessarily regarded as a once-for-all act involving an automatic entry to the kingdom. We remember that the disciples were commanded to rejoice because their names were written in heaven (Luke 10:20), but the warning in Revelation 3:5 reminds us that discipleship did not automatically find its appointed consummation in admission to the heavenly kingdom.

REPENTANCE AND FAITH

There is a certain difficulty in determining what was the basic response demanded by Jesus to the message which He proclaimed. One obvious form in which this response was to be made was repentance (Mark 1:15; Matthew 11:20f.). It is now generally agreed that the Greek word μετανοέω expresses the same idea as the Hebrew *shûb*, whose significance we noted earlier. It therefore expresses not so much sorrow and remorse for sin as the intention to make a clean-cut break with it. The man who seeks the kingdom is resolved to turn to God with his whole heart and to turn his back upon sin.

A similar idea is expressed by the word 'conversion.' Thus the word 'convert' is used to translate *shûb* in the passage from Isaiah 6:10 quoted in Mark 4:12. It is especially characteristic of Luke (1:16f.; 22:32; Acts 3:19, et al.) and is found in one passage in Matthew (18:3), where, however, the meaning is in dispute: 'Unless you turn and become like children, you will never enter the kingdom of heaven.' P. Joüon has suggested that στρέφω is used here as an auxiliary verb meaning 'again' — 'unless you become *again* like children.'[15] But the supposition (on which this conjecture rests) that the original Aramaic has been mistranslated is unnecessary; the Greek gives perfectly good sense; and even Joüon admits that the Semitism is 'un peu gros.' We prefer, therefore, to take the verb here to mean 'to be converted.'[16]

In any case the weight of emphasis falls on the words 'become like children.' J. Jeremias thinks that the reference is to the childlike trust which calls God 'Abba,'[17] but there is nothing in the context to suggest that the saying would have conveyed this meaning to Jesus' hearers, and it seems more likely that in accordance with Matthew 18:4 the reference is to humility. There will be no place for pride in the kingdom and therefore the man who turns back to God must be like a little child in becoming humble and receptive before God.[18]

If 'Repent!' was the negative side of the message of Jesus, the positive side was expressed by 'Believe!' Such belief was, to be sure, an acceptance of the gospel of the kingdom (Mark 1:15),[19] but it is clear that basically the kind of belief indicated in the Gospels was a trust in the power and grace of the God whom Jesus proclaimed (Mark 11:22–24). Although the idea of faith in *Jesus* is rarely expressed in the Gospels in so many words, we must agree with A. M. Hunter that the idea is one that is often present.[20] Again, the relationship between faith and the kingdom (as in Mark 1:15) is one that is not developed in the Gospels in explicit manner. The link is to be seen in the fact that faith is in the God whose grace and power are evident in His kingly acts, and that without the receptive faith of men Jesus is unable to convey to them the blessings associated with the kingdom. On the whole, however, there is less emphasis in the Gospels on faith than might have been expected in view of the great prominence given to the idea in the rest of the New Testament.[21] It is plain that we have not yet found the concept which is most characteristic of the teaching of Jesus about men's response to the gospel of the kingdom.

DISCIPLESHIP

The most characteristic name for the men who are seeking to enter the kingdom in the Gospels is that of 'disciples.' This is all the more clear when we remember that the name completely drops out of use outside the Gospels, with the single and important exception of Acts which continues to use this title to describe members of the Church.[22]

The word μαθητής means a learner in a general sense. In practice it was nearly always used of the pupil of some particular teacher and implied a special relationship to him.[23] We may compare the specialized way in which the English 'pupil' or 'student' is used to mean one who not merely learns from a certain teacher but also accepts for himself the distinctive outlook and teaching of the master. When we are told that the Pharisees were disciples of Moses (John 9:28), the meaning is that they accepted his teaching as their rule of life.[24]

When John the Baptist came and proclaimed a new way of life as preparation for the coming of the Messiah, it is not surprising that his adherents were known as his disciples. To be baptized by John and to become a disciple of his were one and the same thing.[25] Nevertheless, it is hard to believe that all who were baptized by him became members of the band of close followers which is referred to several times in the Gospels; we may perhaps compare the way in which the Essenes had members living in separate communities and also as ordinary citizens throughout Palestine.[26] It is more likely that within the larger group of those who submitted to his baptism there was a smaller group who formed his personal friends and helpers in his work. This larger company of his disciples no doubt practised prayer and fasting as they had been taught by John (Mark 2:18; Luke 5:33; 11:1), but it is probably the smaller group that is meant when we read about the company of men who accompanied John and regarded him as their Rabbi, who later remained with him even while he was in prison and who finally cared for his dead body (John 1:35, 37; 3:26; Luke 7:18–24; Mark 6:29).

When Jesus began His ministry, He also appeared to His contemporaries like a rabbinic teacher, though admittedly as an eccentric one who was unlearned in the rabbinic schools (John 7:14f.), and was regularly addressed as 'teacher' or 'rabbi'; those who listened to Him and followed Him were known as His disciples.[27] We may roughly distinguish four groups of people related to Him in various ways. (1). The most general term applied to His hearers is 'multitude,' a word which, whatever be its theological undertones in the individual Gospels, does not imply any close attachment to the person of Jesus. (2). The word 'disciples' is used to indicate those who listened to the message of Jesus and accepted it, and on occasion a large number of people may be meant (Luke 6:17; 19:37). (3). But the disciples are sometimes described as a smaller company, capable of being transported in one or two boats (Mark 6:45; 8:10). In this case we must think of a group of companions who accompanied Jesus on His travels; according to Luke it must have included at least seventy people at one stage, among whom were women (Luke 10:1; 8:2f.). We thus have the same distinction between a large company of disciples and a small group of companions as in the case of John the Baptist. (4). Finally, out of this group of companions Jesus chose twelve men, apparently to be permanently with Him and to do special tasks for Him (Mark 3:14).

The point which we wish to draw out of this analysis is that the followers of Jesus were all known as His disciples, whether they continued at their normal work and in their normal residence or followed Him in His travels.[28] There is no distinction drawn between these two groups which would suggest that there were different levels of discipleship.[29]

The basic fact about discipleship was that it was due to a calling by Jesus Himself (Mark 1:16–20; 2:13f.). Although we hear about this only in connexion with members of the Twelve, there is no doubt that the call of Jesus was the decisive preliminary to discipleship. Personal allegiance to Jesus was the distinctive mark of His followers (Mark 8:34–38; Luke 14:26ff. — these sayings are addressed to the multitudes and it is unlikely that they necessarily refer to a literal following of Jesus on His travels). It is thoroughly in keeping with this that the disciples addressed Jesus not merely as 'teacher' but also as 'lord.'[30] Thus V. Taylor writes: 'The distinguishing feature of the disciples of Jesus was their utter devotion to Him and not simply to His teaching,' and quotes the dictum of K. H. Rengstorf: 'Er ist für sie kein Rabbi / διδάσκαλος sondern ihr Herr.'[31]

Two main facts about the functions of disciples may be gathered from the description of the Twelve. (1). Their primary task was to be with Jesus, no doubt in order that He might teach them (Mark 3:14).[32] Although there were different levels of teaching, we may presume that this was basically true for all His disciples. (2). They were given authority, as the representatives of Jesus, to preach the kingdom of God, to cast out demons and to heal the sick (Mark 3:14f.; 6:13). There is evidence that these tasks were by no means confined to the Twelve (Mark 5:19; 9:38, 41; Matthew 10:42; 25:31ff.; Luke 10:9).

These two activities show the relationship of disciples to the kingdom. They heard the message of the kingdom from Jesus, and they shared with Him in preaching it and in manifesting the signs of the saving power of God. Response to the message of the kingdom was expressed in discipleship. The way to the kingdom consisted in following Jesus and being ready to follow the pattern of His life whatever the cost.[33] This also implies that discipleship is a continuous relationship with Jesus. Response to Him is not simply a once-for-all acceptance of His call; it is a life which consists in following Him, learning from Him, and doing the will of His Father. Consequently, an initial conversion, vital though this is, is not sufficient to guarantee entrance into the kingdom; perseverance in the new life of discipleship is necessary.

Before we proceed to examine more closely some of the other characteristics of the life of discipleship it may be worth asking whether material derived from the Gospels about the relationship of disciples to Jesus during His earthly life can legitimately be drawn into a study of the relationship of Christians to the risen Lord. For there is no doubt that the death and resurrection of Jesus radically affected the relationship between Him and His followers. After the resurrection the disciples became completely convinced that Jesus was the Messiah and that His death had been no tragic accident but was 'for sins.'[34] Moreover, it is clear that after the resurrection the disciples became conscious of the gift of the Holy Spirit. The history of the Church thus really begins at Pentecost. Can we therefore use material from the Gospels which describes the life of disciples before the birth of the Church in a theology of the Christian life? And, in particular, can we use any conclusions which we may draw from the teaching about apostasy from discipleship in a discussion of apostasy from the Christian life?

In order to accentuate the problem, we may remind ourselves that the New Testament concept of a Christian is of a person who has been baptized into Christ and accepted Him as Lord, who has received forgiveness from God through Him, who has been united with Christ by faith in Him, and who has received the gift of the Spirit. Since all of this would be radically anachronistic in the Gospels, would it not be true to say that there is such a difference between discipleship and the Christian life as to make comparison theologically unsound?

But is the difference really so far-reaching? The very fact that the Gospel teaching about discipleship was preserved and recorded at a comparatively mature stage in the life of the Church indicates that no such inconsistency was felt, although the Church perhaps showed its consciousness that here there were two complementary points of view by the way in which it did not depict discipleship with the aid of later theological concepts. Luke's use of the word 'disciples' to describe members of the Church indicates that he felt no inconsistency between the two stages, but rather organic development.

In fact, the basic characteristics of Christians were already present in the disciples. They had accepted the challenge to repent, had put their faith in God, and given their allegiance to Jesus; we have seen that it is probable that they had received forgiveness from Jesus. There is no compelling evidence for their baptism by Jesus, which would in any case have been a water baptism and not a Spirit baptism; but it must be remembered that several of them had been baptized by John (John 1:35–42; cf. Matthew 21:31f.) and that there is good evidence that at an early stage in His ministry Jesus permitted His disciples to baptize (John 3:26; 4:1f.).[35] On the other hand, there is no evidence that all of the 120 disciples who shared in the Pentecostal gift were baptized with water, at Pentecost or before. It is also true that the disciples did not possess the Holy Spirit, but it must be remembered that during the period of discipleship Jesus was visibly present with at least some of His disciples and that He promised to them the gift of the Spirit in time of need. Finally, although the birth of the Church is best set at Pentecost, the disciples undoubtedly formed a community bound together by their faith in God and allegiance to Jesus.[36]

We are thus led to conclude that the differences between disciples and Christians can be greatly exaggerated and that there is sufficient continuity present for us to use the evidence of the Gospels in our study.[37]

THE LAW OF GOD

Two further characteristics of the life of disciples require to be briefly investigated before we come to the main theme of our study. The first of these characteristics is that the disciples were required to obey the will of God, and our particular problem is to discover the way in which this law, as expounded by Jesus, was to be regarded. The content of the ethic of Jesus is well known; its applicability is still a matter for discussion.

The theory of A. Schweitzer and J. Weiss on this point is well known in its general outline. They held that the ethic of Jesus was an interim or crisis ethic, meant for the special conditions during the brief period preceding the parousia which was regarded, mainly on the basis of Matthew 10:23, as imminent. It was never meant to apply to the continuing life of ordinary society but was a set of special provisions for the interim period before the catastrophic arrival of the kingdom. Since it demanded an impossible heroism, and since in fact the anticipated parousia did not take place, the ethic of Jesus in this radical form is not binding upon Christians.

The point which is worth preserving out of this theory is that the ethic of Jesus is an interim ethic meant for the time before the full coming of the kingdom at the parousia. Where the Schweitzer-Weiss theory went wrong was in depicting the end as an imminent catastrophe,[38] and in regarding the ethic as an almost impossible ideal to be practised in a time of crisis.[39] The truth is rather that this ethic is meant for all of Jesus' disciples in the period before the coming of the kingdom.[40] It is an interim ethic, but not a crisis ethic.

Hence, in the words of R. Bultmann, 'Fulfilment of God's will is the condition for participation in the salvation of His reign.'[41] Those who would enter the coming kingdom of God must show that they seek it by their continued fulfilment of the ethic of Jesus. For the ethic of Jesus is the detailed exposition of what it means to accept God as king. Those who would live under the rule of God in His consummated kingdom must also accept His rule here and now.

Nothing in what has just been said should be taken to imply that fulfilment of the ethic of Jesus is to be taken as a condition for entry to the kingdom in the sense that men must show themselves worthy of the kingdom or work to seek a place in it. The ethic is simply the detailed portrayal of the way of life of those who accept the good news of the kingdom. We owe to J. Jeremias the extremely important insight that the ethic is preceded by the Gospel.[42] It is an ethic of grace and consequently can be fulfilled only by disciples who have responded to the gracious offer of Jesus. Even if we search with difficulty in the Gospels for the concept of a divine power working in the lives of the disciples to enable them to obey the will of God, as is taught in the Epistles, nevertheless the basic fact that the ethic is an ethic of response to the grace of the kingdom is certainly part of the teaching of Jesus.

Hence we conclude that discipleship is a way of life which is expressed in ready obedience to the will of God as expounded in the teaching of Jesus. It is a continuing life in which disciples seek to live on earth the life of heaven. Perseverance in this life is the way of entry into the future kingdom.

THE NEW COMMUNITY

For our present purpose it is unnecessary to discuss at any length the question whether Jesus is to be regarded as the founder of the Church. It is sufficient for us to note that there is evidence that Jesus did create a new community composed of the disciples who responded to His call and gave Him their allegiance. It is true that, as far as the evidence available shows, the greater number of His followers were not organized into a community with any kind of set constitution and order. But the fact of their discipleship distinguished them from Israel at large and so formed them into a definite group which was the forerunner of the Church. It is surely legitimate to talk about membership of this group, even if we hesitate to go further than this.[43]

Although the formation of the Church belongs to the period after the death of Jesus, we should no doubt see a definite continuity between the group of disciples and the Church. Not only did the group of disciples become the Church, but also the development would appear to have been entirely in line with the purpose of Jesus.[44] We may, therefore, legitimately utilize teaching about the group of disciples in the Gospels in our general understanding of the Church and its membership.

3. A MIXED COMMUNITY

Our discussion so far has shown that in the Gospels, entry to the coming Kingdom of God is promised to those who become disciples of Jesus and are prepared to show their acceptance of the Gospel by a life lived in accordance with His teaching. It is now possible for us to look in more detail at the problems associated with persevering in discipleship and falling away from discipleship. The first question which must occupy us is whether the Gospels regard it as possible for a man to make a false profession of discipleship, so that his 'falling away' is in reality a falling away from a status which he never truly possessed, and whether this would be a full explanation of the cases of falling away in the Gospels. A number of passages require consideration:

THE PARABLE OF THE SOWER
(Mark 4:3–9, 14–20)

A good case can be made out for the view that this parable of Jesus is addressed to the crowds and inculcates the lesson 'Be careful how you hear the gospel of the kingdom,' rather than that it depicts the harvest of God which is already under way in the ministry of Jesus.[45] On this view, the 'interpretation' of the parable correctly represents the intention of Jesus, and there are good reasons for ascribing it to Him rather than to the hand of the Evangelist.[46]

The parable distinguishes four ways in which men may hear the Gospel. The fourth group of men described plainly consists of those who become real disciples. The first group hear the Word but it is snatched away from them before it can take root. Matthew (13:19) explains that they do not understand the Word,[47] and Luke (8:12) states that the result of Satan's activity is that they do not believe and so are not saved. Consequently, these men do not come into the category of professing disciples.

The second group are in the same situation as seed which struggles to survive on rocky ground; they receive the Word with joy but have no deep roots, and when harsh circumstances arise they 'fall away' (NEB for σκανδαλίζονται). The language used here certainly implies that these men became professed disciples for a time;[48] the question is whether their profession was genuine at the time.

According to Luke's interpretation (Luke 8:13), 'they believe for a time and in a time of temptation they desert.' [49] The use of 'believe' here (as also in Luke 8:12) may represent Church usage, but the interpretation is surely an unobjectionable one. Faith is attributed to these men, but they have 'no root.' Their faith may not have been securely based and may not have been a total act of commitment. But there is no indication that it was unsound other than the evidence of how the men failed in a crisis. There is no evidence that they failed to belong to a secret company of 'the elect,' and no explanation of their fall is offered. We can conclude only that the character of faith is shown up by testing, and that in this case a lack of steadfastness is evident. But there is no evidence to suggest that it would have been possible to tell in advance that these men would not endure. One might press the details of the parable and argue that the men did not bring forth fruit, which is the evidence of inward character (Matthew 7:16–20; Luke 6:43f.), but this procedure is unwarrantable. To describe the men as hypocrites would be plainly unjustifiable.

The third group are those who hear the Word but allow its growth to be stifled by the cares of this world, just as a young plant can be choked by weeds. These appear to be people who receive the Word and make some apparent growth in discipleship, but never reach the stage of producing the fruit which is the evidence of maturity. They yield to worldly temptations and so fall away from whatever faith they had professed.

From this parable, then, we may conclude that the group of disciples will include some who do not persevere in their faith. They lack the ability to withstand testing and temptation. Their faith is real, so far as it goes, but it is overcome by temptation. It lacks the quality of persistence (Luke 8:15).

SAYING AND DOING
(Matthew 7:21–23; Luke 6:46; 13:26f.)

In the Lucan form of this saying Jesus expresses His despair over those who are ready to call Him Master without treating Him as a master who is entitled to obedience. The Matthaean form,[50] stresses that such people will not enter the kingdom; entry is reserved for those who do the Father's will, a thought which is implicit in Mark 3:35. Thus it is possible to claim to be a disciple and yet not to enter the kingdom. A man may even prophesy, cast out demons, and do mighty works in the name of Jesus, and yet be finally rejected by God.[51]

Here, therefore, we have evidence of the possibility of claiming to be a disciple without actually being one. Matthew in particular knows that the company of Jesus' disciples is a mixed group in which true and false disciples are to be found side by side.[52] Such false disciples cannot be said to fall away from discipleship because they never were true disciples.

THE PARABLE OF THE TARES (Matthew 13:24–30, 36–43)

A similar lesson is indicated in the parable of the tares in its Matthaean form.[53] In this present world good and evil will flourish together and will be separated from each other only at the harvest of God.

It is generally thought that the parable teaches the presence of wheat and tares in the kingdom of the Son of man, i.e. in the Church; cf. v. 41, 'they will gather out of his kingdom all causes of sin and all evildoers.'[54] But in this form the interpretation is at least questionable. The parable does not teach that the kingdom is like a field,[55] and the interpretation expressly states that the field is the world. Further, the 'sons of the kingdom' are surely these who will inherit the kingdom when it comes rather than present dwellers in it.[56] As for verse 41, it would seem to be better to interpret it of the time when 'the kingdoms of this world have become the kingdom of our God'; the world is destined to be the kingdom of God, and at the judgement He will clear His realm of all evil.[57]

But if the tares do not appear in the kingdom, it is certainly true that they are found among the wheat and the servants wish to root them out. We cannot escape seeing here the band of disciples or the Church with an admixture of evildoers. As in the passage previously considered they are not regarded as lapsed disciples but as invaders from outside into the Church. The same point is repeated in the parable of the dragnet (Matthew 13:47–50). J. Jeremias comments, '(Jesus) repeatedly emphasizes the warning that the company of the disciples is not a purified community, and that at the end their ranks must undergo the process of separation (Matthew 7: 21–23, 24–27; 22:11–14).'[58] Mere membership of the group of disciples or of the Church does not constitute a passport for entry into the kingdom.

THE PARABLE OF THE MARRIAGE FEAST
(Matthew 22:1–14)

In the first part of this parable (verses 1–10)[59] we find the characteristic teaching of Jesus that when those for whom the Gospel was first intended refused it the invitation was extended to others who apparently did not deserve it. The point which interests us here is that in the parabolic narrative the servants went beyond the letter of their instructions to *invite* the second set of guests to the feast and actually *gathered* in all whom they found, *both bad and good*. It is unlikely that this means simply that the Gospel comes to all kinds of men. The words point forward to what follows in the second part of the story and indicate that the company of those who responded to the teaching of Jesus was composed of both bad and good men. Once again, the Church is seen to be a mixed community. At the day of judgement, so the second part of the parable tells us, a process of separation will take place in the ranks of the disciples. The person who has failed to provide himself with a wedding garment — no doubt a symbol of divine forgiveness and salvation[60] — will be cast out of the messianic banquet into Gehenna. For although many are called, not all finally enter the company of the elect.[61]

THE PARABLE OF THE TEN VIRGINS
(Matthew 25:1–13)

The parable of the ten virgins is meant to inculcate the lesson of readiness at any time for the onset of a future crisis; the general content of the parable and its position in Matthew's Gospel indicate that the crisis in question is the parousia and the coming of the kingdom, although some scholars prefer a vaguer reference.[62] The problem which concerns us is the people to whom the parable is applied. All of the ten virgins were awaiting the coming of the bridegroom. Were they then meant to portray the people of Israel in general who looked for the coming of the kingdom, in which case the five wise virgins would symbolize the disciples? Or were they meant to portray the professing disciples of Jesus, in which case the wise virgins would symbolize those who were real disciples and not simply outward professors? Certainly the second interpretation is that understood by Matthew, and it would be unwise to insist on the first interpretation when there is no clear evidence in the parable itself in favour of it.[63] The warning given in verse 12 is parallel to that in Matthew 7:23, and we are justified in seeing a similar situation presented. R. V. G. Tasker concludes: 'The Church contains, it is implied, both those who are prepared and those who are unprepared, though not necessarily in equal proportion.'[64]

THE PARABLE OF THE TALENTS
(Matthew 25:14–30)

Although it has been suggested that this parable was originally addressed to the scribes, who had been bad stewards of the Word of God,[65] in its present context it is addressed to the disciples and is meant to warn them of the coming of a day of judgement and reckoning. Those who have served their Master faithfully on earth have nothing to fear on that day, but will find that He is pleased with them. The third servant typifies those who are unfaithful and have no affection for their Master, and their fate is to be cast into Gehenna. The point of the parable is thus the same as that of the virgins. The professed followers of Jesus include those who turn out to be unfaithful and who will have no share in the coming kingdom. It may be that they never believed or that they lapsed from belief: the parable simply does not say.[66]

THE LAST JUDGEMENT
(Matthew 25:31–46)

The third parable in Matthew 25 describes the judgement of the nations of the world, and more than one scholar has emphasized that it is the judgement of *all* men which is being described.[67] It follows that although the disciples of Jesus are among those judged, the parable describes not a 'mixed Church' but a 'mixed world,' and consequently nothing can be deduced about the nature of the Church from this parable.

If we may now summarize the conclusions of this section, we see that Matthew certainly regarded the group of disciples or the Church as being of mixed composition, and that it is very likely that he is faithfully reflecting the teaching of Jesus Himself. The group of disciples contained those whose profession was not matched by a true conversion, and this was seen in their lack of 'fruit.' A person who has responded gladly to the Gospel may fail to last the course, but it is not as yet clear whether we are entitled to say that such a person was a lapsed believer or that he had never really possessed faith.

It is, however, precisely this question which interests us and to which we must seek an answer. Certainly those who never really believed will not find entry to the kingdom despite their protestations of discipleship; the day of judgement will be a day of surprises. But can we ascertain whether the group of those who lapse includes those who at one time were true disciples in addition to those who were never anything other than wolves in sheep's clothing? Do the Gospels draw a distinction of this kind, or is the attempt to draw such a distinction an indication that too static a concept of faith and discipleship is being presupposed? Is the fact of perseverance to be seen precisely in the fact of perseverance, that a person actually does reach the end of the course, rather than in some particular quality which has always inhered in his faith?

In order to answer these questions we must make a more detailed examination of the teaching in the Gospels about the temptations which face disciples and the divine resources which are at their disposal.

4. TEMPTATION AND CONFLICT

Our examination of the parable of the sower has already shown us that disciples have to face temptations and trials which may jeopardize their faith in God and their obedience to Jesus. The day-to-day life of the godly has never been a bed of roses. Jesus also shared the conviction found in the apocalyptic writings that the End would be preceded by a time of unparalleled distress; evil would make its last fling against God, and His people would suffer much before the End came, and with the End the victory of God over His enemies.[68] He therefore warned His disciples against the period of woes which was to ensue before the parousia. Consequently, we shall find in His teaching warnings in general terms and warnings more specifically related to the distresses of the End-time, but in both cases the same essential principles of attack and defence are to be found.

SUFFERING AND PERSECUTION

The most general word used to describe the lot of disciples under the attacks of evil is 'tribulation,' a word which indicates the suffering to be experienced in the last days (Mark 13:19, 24; Matthew 24:9). It is a sufficiently unpleasant experience to be compared to the pangs of travail (Mark 13:8), but the use of this metaphor may perhaps indicate that a hopeful future is foreshadowed (cf. Luke 21:28).[69] From the point of view of those who inflict this suffering upon disciples it is to be regarded as 'persecution' (Mark 4:17; 10:30; Matthew 5:10–12, 44; 10:23; 23:34; Luke 21:12), and its purpose is either to force the disciples to give up their faith or else to liquidate them. It is not exclusively eschatological (Luke 21:12; cf. Matthew 10:23), but is the normal lot of disciples,[70] and may take the form of hatred, reproaches, slanders, excommunication, betrayal and killing.[71]

TEMPTATION

Since the purpose of the persecutors is the forcible conversion of the persecuted, it follows that their activity appears to the persecuted in the form of temptation.

It is sometimes asserted that in the Gospels the word 'temptation' is a technical term descriptive of the last great eschatological crisis (cf. Revelation 3:10) but a brief review of the texts will show that the meaning is more general and that temptation is characteristic of the life of the disciple at all points.

An eschatological reference has been found in the Lord's Prayer, 'Lead us not into temptation' (Matthew 6:13; Luke 11:4).[72] But the absence of the article speaks against the interpretation, 'Grant that we may escape *the* great tribulation.' Moreover, an eschatological reference is likely here only if it is supported by the context, but the reasons for taking 'daily bread' purely eschatologically are not compelling. The traditional understanding of the prayer would therefore appear to be justified, provided that we qualify it by admitting that since the coming of Jesus the End is 'at hand' and His disciples do form the eschatological community.[73] Hence all their temptations have an eschatological 'flavour.'

The warning given by Jesus in Gethsemane, 'Pray that you may not enter into temptation' (Mark 14:38; Matthew 26:41; Luke 22:40, 46), has similarly been interpreted to mean that Jesus expected the eschatological crisis with the final great temptation to break out in connexion with His death.[74] The argument in favour of this view is that the vocabulary — watch, hour, temptation — is eschatological. But there is no compelling reason for taking 'watch' eschatologically, and in its eschatological use it refers to waiting for the parousia rather than for the advent of Satan;[75] the qualification of 'hour' by 'one' is hardly consistent with the idea of the eschatological hour as a point in time rather than a period; and, finally, 'temptation' (which is again used without the article) is the word whose meaning is in question. The main argument which remains is that Jesus expected the End in connexion with His death, but this is extremely questionable.[76] The text, therefore, must refer to the crisis that evening when the disciples all forsook Jesus, or to the general experiences of temptation which awaited them in the future, and of these the former is the more likely alternative.

The two remaining occurrences are in Luke 8:13, where the reference is quite general, and Luke 22:28 where the reference is to trials already shared by the disciples with Jesus.[77]

It may, therefore, be concluded that 'temptation' has a general meaning in the Gospels. The experiences of trial and persecution which may befall the disciples at any time constitute a temptation to them to give up their faith and fall into sin. The closing petition in the Lord's Prayer may well be regarded as a prayer for protection from apostasy.[78]

STUMBLING-BLOCKS

The thought of causing somebody to stumble is closely allied to the concept of temptation. The verb conveys the idea of catching somebody in a trap in order that he may fall, and is used metaphorically in two ways. First, the idea may be simply that of causing offence and annoyance to somebody (e.g. Matthew 17:27). Twice we hear of people taking offence at Jesus (Mark 6:3; Matthew 15:12); they could not accept what He said because of His humble origins or because it ran contrary to their way of thinking. Hence the meaning is that they rejected Jesus and the way of discipleship. 'To reject Jesus is to turn away from God.'[79] On the other hand, Jesus pronounced a benediction upon those who accepted Him: 'Blessed is he who takes no offence at me' (Matthew 11:6; Luke 7:23).

Second, the idea may be that of causing a person to sin; he is forced to stumble instead of doing what is right. Not only may one's own bodily desires lead to sin (Mark 9:43–47; Matthew 5:29f.; 18:8f.), but one person may lead another into sin. Thus Peter was a stumbling-block to Jesus because he suggested to Him doing earthly things rather than obeying the will of God (Matthew 16:23).[80] Similarly, men may attempt to lead the little ones who believe in Jesus into sin (Mark 9:42; Matthew 18:6f.; Luke 17:1f.). It would be better for such tempters to be drowned in the depths of the sea before they can get the chance to exercise their powers of temptation, for (it is implied) in that case a dreadful fate awaits them; they will certainly have no place in the Kingdom (Matthew 13:41).

We are bound to ask, What is the fate of those who are caused to stumble? In the case of the 'little ones' it is not clear whether isolated acts of sin are meant or something much more radical, namely apostasy. C. E. B. Cranfield supports the latter alternative: 'The verb here means to cause someone to stumble in his faith, to destroy someone's faith, to cause to fall away from God.'[81] This view finds support in the solemnity of the saying itself, and also in the following verses which speak of loss of eternal life for those who cause themselves to stumble.[82]

According to Matthew 24:10 the final tribulation will cause many to stumble (NEB — 'to lose their faith'). This, however, is true not only of the final tribulation, but also of tribulation in general. We have already met in the interpretation of the parable of the sower those who stumble in time of persecution (Mark 4:17; Matthew 13:21; Luke 8:13 has 'to fall away').

From this section we see that the possibility of men being led away from Jesus is present in His teaching. It is true that the expressions used are sometimes hypothetical, but this is not always the case. The possibility is a real one. Further, those who are in danger are described as believers, and there is nothing in the context to determine whether or not their faith is real. The evidence is accumulating that faith is proved to be persevering faith only by the fact that it actually does persevere. Yet, lest we come to a one-sided conclusion, we are reminded that one of the passages about stumbling goes on to state that it is not the will of the Father that one of the little ones should perish (Matthew 18:14).

ERROR AND DECEPTION

Another threat to believers arises through the possibility of error and deception, especially in connexion with the events of the End.

This possibility is particularly prominent in Mark 13.[84] There is a considerable number of specific warnings to the disciples to take heed and watch (Mark 13:5, 9, 23, 33, 35, 37). There are dangers from false prophets and Messiahs; they will show signs and wonders, and lead many men astray. Can believers be led astray by their machinations? It may well be argued that the presence of so many warnings is a clear indication that a danger exists. There is also no point in warning people against dangers that cannot harm them. The chief consideration, however, must be the meaning of Mark 13:22: 'False Christs and false prophets will arise and show wonders, to lead astray, if possible, the elect.' Does this text mean that it is possible for the elect to be led astray.?

Our first task is to decide who 'the elect' are. The name (ἐκλεκτοί) appears quite suddenly in Mark at this point (Mark 13:20, 22, 27), and elsewhere in the Gospels it occurs only twice as a designation of men (Matthew 22:14; Luke 18:7). We are thus given little evidence on which to base a verdict as to usage in the Gospels.

In the Old Testament the word is used to indicate people who have been chosen by God for salvation (Psalm 105:6, 43) and who are regarded as His servants (Isaiah 65:9, 15, 22). It is one of the many titles applied to the people of God and indicates that their existence as His people, their reception of His salvation, and their enrollment in His service all rest upon His prior choice of them. Yet this choice by God is not independent of the willingness of the individual to receive it, nor is its nature such that a man cannot renounce it. After a detailed study H. H. Rowley concludes that for the Church, as the heir of Israel's election, her election is conditional upon her desire to retain it.[85]

The use of the title for the people of God developed in the inter-Testamental period, and is especially characteristic of 1 Enoch and the Dead Sea Scrolls. It was thus prevalent in sectarian and apocalyptic circles, and this may have been the route by which it entered the Gospels.

In his comment on Colossians 3:12 J. B. Lightfoot observed that in the Gospels there is a distinction between κλητοί and ἐκλεκτοί, the former word meaning those summoned to the privileges of the Gospel and the latter those appointed to final salvation, but in St. Paul no such distinction can be traced.[86] Lightfoot was certainly correct in his estimate of Pauline usage, but we may well wonder whether he has correctly assessed the Gospel evidence. Only one text supports a contrast between the two words: 'Many are called, but few are chosen' (Matthew 22:14). K. L. Schmidt argues that we should not perhaps make too much of the difference between the two words: the saying is to be taken dialectically and means 'Many are called and yet few are called; many are elected and yet few are elected.'[87] This seems to complicate the text unnecessarily. The saying should be seen in the light of the preceding parable, where the invitation or 'call' went out to many, but not all were in the end found worthy and therefore chosen to sit down at the banquet. The reason, however, why one man (presumably typical of several) was rejected was not because he was not appointed by some secret choice of the king (representing God) but because he had failed to provide himself with a wedding garment. The contrast is thus between the large number of men (both Jews and Gentiles) who hear the call of God and the smaller number who respond to the invitation with faith and obedience, and the saying is therefore a summons to a right response to the gospel message.[88] To read predestination into the verse is unwarranted; there is nothing to suggest that there is a predestined group of people who are unable to disobey God's call (and a corresponding group whom God has determined shall not obey the call).

The other saying which must be considered is Luke 18:7f.: 'Will not God vindicate his elect who cry to him day and night? Will he delay long over them? I tell you, he will vindicate them speedily. Nevertheless, when the Son of man comes, will he find faith on earth?' The parable which concludes with these verses[89] promises that God will vindicate His elect without delay; then comes the qualifying thought, but will the Son of man find faithful men upon the earth at His parousia? In other words, it is problematic whether there will be any elect at that time; perhaps they may have succumbed to persecution. It is not, therefore, the faithfulness of God in answering prayer which is doubtful but the perseverance of disciples in continuing to pray. Consequently G. Schrenk finds in this verse the possibility of apostasy by the elect.[90]

This brief survey shows that the word ἐκλεκτός does not contain in itself the certainty of perseverance. The idea of election as such does not exclude the possibility of apostasy. Is, then, this possibility to be found in Mark 13:22?

The answer will depend on the meaning assigned to 'to lead astray.' The construction here, πρός with the articular infinitive, is used in New Testament Greek to indicate purpose or contemplated result, and there are no cases where it is used to indicate an actual result (except perhaps Matthew 5:28).[91] It is, therefore, the result aimed at by the false Christs and prophets which is described here, and we are not told whether their purpose will be accomplished.[92]

We must ask, however, whether the purpose is regarded as one that is in principle capable of fulfilment. What is the force of 'if possible'? This phrase can be taken in two ways. (i). It may express the thought in the mind of the deceivers: 'Let us lead them astray if we can.' On this view a real condition is expressed, and the question of possibility is left open. (ii). It may express the comment of the speaker (Jesus): 'They will try to lead the elect astray, if such a thing is possible.' In this case, the words are most naturally taken as an unfulfilled condition, and it is denied that the possibility exists.

The evidence from New Testament usage is not very conclusive, but on the whole there is some support for the former alternative.[93] If so, the possibility that the elect may be led astray cannot be ruled out. Although the form of expression suggests that the possibility is a remote one,[94] it is significant that the saying is immediately followed by a warning to watch (Mark 13:23).

OTHER TEACHING IN MATTHEW

In order to complete the picture of the trials to be endured by disciples we must glance at the apocalyptic teaching of Jesus as it is presented by Matthew. Matthew has transferred material from Mark 13:9–13 to his mission discourse in ch. 10, and has thereby shown the link between the trials and persecutions of the disciples and their work of mission. Nevertheless, the eschatological consciousness is not lost, for in Matthew 10:23 the mission is brought into relation with the parousia of the Son of man in a saying whose meaning (for Jesus and for Matthew) is still uncertain.[95]

As compensation for the omission of this section from the apocalyptic discourse Matthew has inserted verses 10–12 in ch. 24. Although these verses are generally regarded as a Matthaean composition, there is some possibility that they contain a fragment from the apocalyptic teaching of Jesus which has not been preserved in Mark or Q.[96] The distinctive emphasis of the section is that it speaks of the danger of hatred and betrayal, which will be found in the world at large in the last days, also being present in the community of the disciples. In the light of what we have already discovered about a 'mixed community' in Matthew, it would be possible to regard verses 10 and 11 as a description of mere professors of the faith: their so-called faith will be found wanting, and their sufferings under persecution will cause them to abandon it. They accept the teaching of the false prophets, and they save their own skins by betraying other members of the Church.

The difficulty is to extend this interpretation to verse 12: with the increase of lawlessness the love of the majority will grow cold. It is difficult to see in this description as a whole how any other than real believers can be meant. The danger is thus one that may affect any member of the Church, and point is given to the warnings about enduring to the end.

THE WORK OF THE HOLY SPIRIT

From the forces which are arrayed against disciples we must now turn to those which stand in their defence. For it is not to be supposed that God leaves His people to their own devices in the tribulation of the last day. On the contrary, He is active in their defence.

Yet the teaching of Jesus on this point is surprisingly reticent.[97] He teaches that the Holy Spirit will enable disciples to stand up to persecution. They do not need to fear being put on trial in the courts because what they must say will be given to them by God; it will not be they who speak but the Holy Spirit (Mark 13:11; Matthew 10:19f.).[98] Help is thus given by God to the disciples of Jesus in their hour of need. Yet this help is not given in such a manner that a disciple may not rebel against the Spirit; there is a sin against the Holy Spirit which must be discussed presently.

THE NEED FOR ENDURANCE

If Jesus says little about the work of the Spirit in aiding disciples, He does emphasize the importance of their endurance in the persecution of the last days: 'He who endures to the end shall be saved' (Mark 13:13).

The meaning of 'saved' must first be determined. Although the verb is used principally in Mark with the physical meaning 'to preserve life,' whether from illness or death, it seems to be necessary to accept a 'spiritual' meaning here, 'to receive salvation.'[99] For the preceding verse (Mark 13:12) definitely states that death will take place among the ranks of the disciples. Again, a physical sense would give a tautology: he who endures to the end shall not die before the end. Rather the verse teaches that the disciple who endures will be saved for the kingdom of God.[100] The similar clause in Luke 21:19, 'By your endurance you will gain your lives,' suggests a thought not so very far removed from that of Mark 8:35 — by endurance, even to death, you will be preserved in the deepest sense, i.e. for God's kingdom. The thought is thus of salvation from the messianic judgement and preservation for life in the coming Kingdom.

The condition for salvation is that 'steadfast endurance' which does not give way under temptation but remains loyal to God and His will. This is accented by the phrase 'to the end.' It probably indicates not so much endurance to the very end of the period of tribulation but rather endurance to the very limit, even to the point of death. According to G. R. Beasley-Murray, 'the "endurance" cannot signify mere continuance to the end of the age, as though that would automatically secure entrance into the next; it is endurance in the confession of the Name.'[101]

In the Lucan version of the apocalyptic discourse[102] there is a tone of confidence, which stands in a certain contrast with the teaching in Matthew. Although the disciples will be hated by all men and some of them will be put to death, yet 'not a hair of your head will perish. By your endurance you will gain your lives' (Luke 21:18f.). The point of the saying is that persecution cannot really separate the disciples from the care of God.[103] Consequently, if they show endurance they will preserve themselves. Alongside the promise of divine protection there is thus placed the demand for the endurance of God's people. Through watchfulness and prayer they will have strength to come safely through all that is going to happen and then to stand in the presence of the Son of man at His parousia (Luke 21:36).

Throughout this apocalyptic teaching we see that there is a constant emphasis on the need for the disciple to hold fast to the end. There will be no salvation for the person who gives up or does not avail himself of the power of the Spirit. Although this possibility is a slight one on the whole, nevertheless it is a real possibility, and we have no right to deny its existence in the interests of a preconceived theory.

We find here, therefore, a clear presentation of the paradox of the promise of divine protection and the demand for human faith and steadfastness. Nothing is said which would resolve this paradox. The believer is simply promised divine aid and exhorted to endure. His faith is thus not a human achievement — there is no trace of Pelagianism here — but a continuing trust in God. But neither is this faith to be regarded as something given by God independently of human volition: i.e. there is no suggestion that the reason why some men endure and others do not endure lies in a different treatment meted out to them by God. Nor finally is it suggested that the faith which endures to the end possesses some kind of *virtus perseverantiae*.

THE POSSIBILITY OF JUDGEMENT

Before we conclude this section, mention should be made of two passages which may be relevant to the question of the fate of disciples who fail to endure.

(1) A saying of Jesus about salt is applied by Matthew to the disciples (Matthew 5:13): 'You are the salt of the earth; but if salt has lost its taste, how shall its saltness be restored? It is no longer good for anything except to be thrown out and trodden under foot by men.' The meaning is that once salt has become flavourless it is of no further use and is fit only to be thrown out.[104] The application to the disciples is that if they become 'insipid,' if the Gospel no longer has power in their lives, then they will be cast out. Thus the responsibility of the disciples is emphasized, and at the same time the possibility of judgement is held over them. The saying may originally have been applied to the Jewish leaders who said, 'We are the bearers of revelation: God can never take this honour from us,' but it is now applied to disciples: they can be lost just like Israel.[105]

(2) A second passage is Luke 12:35–48. Here the parables of the watching servants and of the burglar are specifically applied to the disciples. Those who fail in the responsibilities entrusted to them and act like unbelievers will share the fate of unbelievers or hypocrites.[106] But the fate of disobedient disciples will be in some way worse than that of unbelievers because they knew what their duty was and sinned wittingly. In its present form, therefore, this passage warns the disciples against the judgement which will fall on the unfaithful.

There is some uncertainty as to whether this was the original meaning of the parables in the mouth of Jesus. A strong case has been presented by J. Jeremias for regarding the passage as being originally addressed to the leaders of the Jewish nation, warning them of their fate if they failed to fulfil their responsibilities.[107] This reconstruction is necessarily hypothetical, but it does attempt to do justice to certain difficulties in the passage as it stands. In any case, however, there would seem to be no reason in principle why Jesus may not have warned His disciples in the same way as the leaders of Israel about the dangers of abusing their privileged position, and, whether or not Jeremias's suggestion be accepted, there is no doubt that in their present form the parables are applied to the disciples. Falling away from discipleship leads to judgement. It is possible for those who have received great privileges to be lost in the end because they proved unfaithful.

5. THE UNFORGIVABLE SIN

One particular category of sin must now be looked at more carefully because of its close connexion with our subject. This is the so-called unforgivable sin against the Holy Spirit, and our aim is to discover whether this sin is in fact apostasy, that is to say, whether it is a sin which can be committed by true disciples of Jesus. If an affirmative answer is given to this question, we shall have some confirmation of our previous argument that the teaching of Jesus in the Gospels does recognize the possibility of apostasy from among the ranks of the disciples.[108]

THE TWO TRADITIONS OF THE SAYING

Our task at this point is rendered extremely difficult by the fact that we possess two distinct versions of a saying about an unforgivable sin; it is far from certain which version is original and which, if any, can be regarded as a genuine saying of Jesus. The presence of references to the Son of man and to the Holy Spirit makes the saying very suspect to many scholars.

In Mark the saying appears in the context of the Beelzebul controversy in the form: 'Truly, I say to you, all sins will be forgiven the sons of men, and whatever blasphemies they utter; but whoever blasphemes against the Holy Spirit never has forgiveness, but is guilty of an eternal sin' (Mark 3:28f.). Luke has nothing corresponding in his account of the Beelzebul controversy, but includes the saying in a passage containing exhortations to fearlessness in confession (Luke 12:2–10; cf. Matthew 10:26–33); here it reads, 'And everyone who speaks a word against the Son of man will be forgiven; but he who blasphemes against the Holy Spirit will not be forgiven' (Luke 12:10). Matthew gives the saying in its Marcan context, but his wording appears to be a conflation of the Marcan and Lucan (Q) forms.[109]

Both forms of the saying contain features which suggest an original formulation in Aramaic, and thus guarantee its Palestinian origin. The principal difference is that Mark speaks of forgiveness *for the sons* of men but Luke of speaking a word *against* the *Son* of man. J. Wellhausen made the obvious suggestion that the original form of the saying had forgiveness for the 'son of man' in the generic sense of 'man'; this was altered to the plural in Mark to avoid ambiguity with the titular use, and was misunderstood in a messianic sense in the reformulation of the saying in Q.[110] Wellhausen's suggestion in its original form has been increasingly subject to criticism, but there has been no great degree of unanimity in proposing an alternative. The authenticity of the saying is generally denied, although F. H. Borsch raises a number of objections to this common assumption. E. Schweizer and H. E. Tödt support the originality of the Q form as an early Church creation distinguishing between opposition to the earthly Son of man and to the manifest activity of the Spirit in the Church, and a similar view is adopted by A. J. B. Higgins. C. Colpe, however, argues that a saying about blasphemy against the Son of man would not be softened to one about blasphemy against men, and holds that an original saying about blasphemy against the Spirit was enlarged by the contrast with the forgivable sin of blasphemy against men. Later, the saying was messianically interpreted to give the form in Q. Colpe is prepared to admit the authenticity of the saying in something like its Marcan form without reference to the Son of man.[111]

In the present state of scholarly debate it would be temerarious to offer any firm conclusions on the saying. With all due caution, however, we would submit that it is still not certain that the two forms of the saying must go back to one original saying. It is not irrelevant that Matthew evidently regarded both forms of the saying as distinct and meaningful, since he quotes them both. Further, the contexts of the Marcan and Q forms of the saying are different. In Mark the saying forms an integral part of the Beelzebul controversy in which Jesus replies to the accusation that His exorcisms were wrought by the power of Beelzebul. In saying that Jesus was possessed by an unclean spirit, the Jews were in effect denying that the Holy Spirit was at work in Jesus and in danger of blaspheming against the Spirit.[112] The saying is, therefore, an effective *ad hominem* reply. The context of the saying in Q is harder to define. The omission of the saying in the Q form of the Beelzebul controversy (Matthew 12:22–37; Luke 11:14–23) by Luke strongly suggests that it did not originally belong to it in Q.[113] In Luke the saying forms part of the section Luke 12:8–12, and it is possible that this was its original context in Q, although we cannot be sure that each one of this particular group of sayings was spoken on the same occasion.[114]

A third point is that it is difficult to see how the Marcan and Q forms of the saying could have been derived from each other or from a common source. The differences in expression and vocabulary are sufficiently great to make it unlikely that misunderstanding of the original wording was the cause. In particular, there is in our opinion no certain case where an original 'Son of man' has been misunderstood in a messianic sense.[115]

These considerations suggest that we may in fact have to do with two separate sayings in the tradition rather than variants of one original saying.[116] Each must therefore be interpreted individually.

THE SAYING IN MARK

There would appear to be no compelling argument against the authenticity of the saying in the general form in which it appears in Mark. As we have seen, it fits excellently into its context. It is introduced by ἀμήν which is a prima facie indication of authenticity.[117] The only real objection, therefore, is to the mention of the Holy Spirit, but there is sufficient evidence in our opinion to show that Jesus was conscious of being the bearer of the Spirit and that a reference to the Spirit as a reply to the scribes' accusation of demonic activity would be fully in place.[118]

The saying is addressed to the scribes and expresses the fact that all sins may be forgiven by God except blasphemy against the Spirit.[119] The suggestion that this means that all other sins will in fact be forgiven[120] is baseless in view of the Jewish stress on the need for repentance as a condition of forgiveness. Nor, on the other hand, should the saying be taken as an oriental hyperbole which simply asserts that blasphemy against the Spirit is a very terrible sin.[121] Rather, Jesus says that to attribute the good working of God's Spirit to the devil and thus consciously to call good evil is unforgivable. The person who does this is rejecting the grace of God through which forgiveness is offered to men, and hence cutting himself off from the source of forgiveness.[122] Such a sin is surely a persistent attitude rather than a single act.

It is not suggested that the sin had been committed by Jesus' hearers, and the question whether disciples may commit it is not raised in the context. Nor is the problem raised whether God may bring the recalcitrant sinner to repentance; a contrast between human readiness to repent and a divine constraint to repent is quite foreign to the saying. Nor finally is it the Church's business to decide who has or has not committed this sin; it is God who forgives and condemns, not man.[123] The saying is meant as a fearful warning to the opponents of Jesus.

THE SAYING IN LUKE

In Luke the saying forms part of a passage addressed to the disciples, encouraging them to trust in the providence of God and not to fear what men may do to them. The person who confesses Jesus faithfully before men, even if he has to suffer for it, will be acknowledged by Him in heaven; the person who denies Jesus will not be acknowledged by Him. Then comes our saying that blasphemy against the Son of man will be forgiven, but not blasphemy against the Spirit. Finally, there is a promise that the Spirit will assist those who do confess Jesus faithfully.

Most interpretations of the saying assume that it arose or gained its present form in the early Church. A. Fridrichsen interpreted it from the Jewish mission of the Church. Jews could be forgiven for their sins of ignorance against Jesus in His lifetime, who was active but not for their disobedience to the Spirit in the apostolic preaching. In the context of Luke the saying became an ecclesiastical rule defining different degrees of apostasy among Christians.[124]

Each of the two parts of this suggestion has been taken up by later scholars. According to G. Bornkamm, the saying gives us the theory of the early Church that blasphemy before Pentecost against the Son of man is forgivable, but blasphemy after Pentecost against the Holy Spirit is unforgivable, since it was only after Pentecost that it became obvious who Jesus really was.[125] This view reads into the text a great deal which is not there. Above all, there is no distinction of tenses to support this temporal scheme.[126]

An interpretation closely akin to the second part of Fridrichsen's suggestion was offered by C. K. Barrett, who noted that the patristic interpretation of the text sees in blasphemy against the Son of man pre-baptismal sin committed by the heathen in their ignorance, whereas blasphemy against the Spirit is a sin of the baptized, an act of apostasy for which there is no remission.[127] The evidence which Barrett adduces in favour of this theory is not very strong, but his view may help us towards an understanding of the saying. J. Weiss suggested that the saying expresses a contrast between blasphemy against the Son of man, meaning Jesus as a private person, and blasphemy against the Holy Spirit, meaning the divine power at work in Him.[129] Similarly, M.-J. Lagrange held that 'it is excusable to a point to fail to recognize the dignity of the One who hides Himself under the humble appearance of a man, but not to disparge works manifestly salutary which reveal the action of the Divine Spirit.'[130]

Can a saying in this form be regarded as going back to Jesus Himself? If the term 'Son of man' were, as E. Stauffer put it, 'just about the most pretentious piece of self-description that any man in the ancient East could possibly have used,'[131] a contrast between the Son of man and the Holy Spirit would be most improbable. It is, however, highly unlikely that 'Son of man' was either a widely known title or one which had this impressive content. It is uncertain when the Similitudes of Enoch (1 Enoch 37–71), in which the Son of man plays a leading role, were composed; they may well have existed in the time of Jesus, but it is fairly certain that they were not widely known among the people at large.[132] The title 'Son of man' is not attested in the Dead Sea Scrolls, and the Rabbinic material is very scanty. P. Billerbeck's opinion that the title was used for the Messiah in apocalyptic circles but was unknown to the mass of the people is probably still a fair summary of the situation.[133] It is, therefore, not impossible that 'Son of man' could be used to express the desired contrast.

The greatest doubt, however, surrounds the use of the title by Jesus to refer to Himself. While some scholars deny that Jesus used the title at all or allow the authenticity of only a few sayings referring to the future coming of the Son of man, it is our belief that there is sufficient evidence that Jesus did use the title to express the humiliation and the hiddenness of His ministry on earth. He contrasted the humble life of the Son of man on earth with the heavenly glory which ought to be His lot.[134] It was possible for a person to fail to see through the lowly appearance of the Son of man and thus to reject His claims to be the messenger of God to men.

From this point of view it does not seem impossible that Jesus may have uttered the saying about unforgivable sin in its Lucan form. Such a view of the saying is not surrounded by any greater difficulties than those which attempt to explain it as a creation of the early Church. The question of its original context remains obscure. The tradition taken over by Luke applies it to the disciples,[135] and emphasizes the danger of witting denial of Jesus especially when the power of the Spirit is available to help them to bear witness. Thus the saying in Luke definitely allows for the possibility of apostasy by the disciples under persecution and states that apostasy is unforgivable, but at the same time the surrounding sayings emphasize that there is no need for disciples to fall into this danger, since the Spirit will teach them what to say in the hour of trial. Even though the threat of death hangs over them, they are not to be afraid, but to trust in the power of the God who cares even for the birds.

Whether the saying was spoken by Jesus in this precise context is doubtful. Luke's formulation of it, however, does not go against the general tenor of the teaching of Jesus, but rather fits in with it. It seems most likely that Jesus did speak of a sin against the Holy Spirit, whatever may have been the precise form of His words, and that the warning contained in His utterance is directed to all who turn away from the source of divine forgiveness by a deliberate act of will.

Thus the saying is in accord with the teaching of Jesus which we already have discussed; He warned His disciples against the possibility of apostasy, but at the same time He assured them that they could persevere in faith through the power of the Spirit.[136]

6. DISCIPLINE AND EXCOMMUNICATION

Earlier in this chapter we saw that there was good reason to believe that Jesus gathered together a group of disciples who later formed the nucleus of the Christian Church. We may therefore expect that if our conclusions so far are sound we shall find some confirmation of them in the character of the communal life of the group of disciples; at the same time we shall see what measures were taken to preserve disciples from falling away and to win back or discipline any who did fall away.

In this aspect of our subject particularly it is often hard to distinguish between the authentic teaching of Jesus and the way in which that teaching has been preserved and adapted for the situation of life in the Church after Pentecost. It follows that what is discussed in this section may perhaps be the life of the early Palestinian Church rather than that of the disciples during the lifetime of Jesus, but there is no good reason to suspect that the early Church flagrantly misrepresented the teaching of its Lord.

The main source for the teaching of Jesus on this theme is to be found in Matthew 18. This chapter is no doubt composite in form; it uses teaching from Mark 9 as a framework into which are inserted some material from Q and in all probability material from the Matthaean special source M.[137] The teaching forms a kind of Church 'halakah' on the question of forgiveness in which the teaching of Jesus is applied to the practical needs of the Church.[138]

PASTORAL CARE FOR THE LITTLE ONES

In the first section of the chapter (Matthew 18:1–14) Jesus develops the theme of care for the little ones in the Church. The chapter begins by referring to little children (vs. 2–5), but in vs. 10–14 it would seem that disciples are in mind, and in v. 6 the interpretation is uncertain. On the whole it is probable that from v. 6 onwards disciples are in mind.[139] Two attitudes towards them are contrasted: despising them and leading them into sin, and pastoral care for them.

Something has been said earlier about the first of these attitudes; we have seen that the passage means that the fate which will attend a person who leads a little one into sin is so dreadful that it would be preferable for him to suffer death by drowning before he gets a chance to work havoc among the disciples. Thus the attitude condemned is that of leading helpless disciples into sin, with, as we saw above, the possibility of apostasy from their faith. Those responsible for such temptations will themselves suffer exclusion from the kingdom. Since the saying is put in a churchly context it is meant here as a warning to disciples.

The opposite attitude is now inculcated. Who dare despise the little ones since their heavenly angels actually stand in the presence of God? At any time the angels can report on their charges to God.[140] Whatever be the difficulties in interpreting this statement, the idea present is clearly that of divine protection. Nevertheless, such protection does not inevitably save a person from falling into sin.

There then follows the parable of the lost sheep which in this context teaches that, if God cares for His people like a shepherd, the disciples of Jesus ought to shepherd one other. The stronger disciples must exercise a constant vigilance and care on behalf of the little ones. It is not God's will that the little ones should perish. But is it possible that His will may be frustrated if men fail to follow his example?[141] The question is not answered. Equally it is not made clear whether those who lead little ones astray suffer punishment in place of the little ones whom they deceive. If the thought of the possibility of terrible consequences for those who go astray and above all for those who lead others astray cannot be excluded from the teaching of Jesus, it is also true that we have no right to deny the boundlessness of the mercy which is revealed to us here also. The secret things belong to the Lord our God and His mercy is to be trusted.

THE DANGER OF SIN AGAINST A BROTHER

Already in Matthew 5:25f. the possibility of sin against one's brother has been raised in the little parable which exhorts a man to come to terms with his adversary before it is too late. It is frequently said that Matthew has missed the point of this parable, turning what was originally an eschatological warning, as in the parallel passage in Luke 12:57–9, into a moral precept.[142] But J. Schniewind has shown that the parable warns against the danger of some wronged person rising up to sue us at God's judgement seat, so that we are cast into hell. It is, therefore, dangerous to go through life with a sin against a fellow man on our conscience. We must hasten to seek forgiveness before it is too late.[143] Hence the parable is thoroughly eschatological in the sanction which it invokes. Its significance for our purpose is that it warns men not to live in a state of alienation from their fellows because of some sin which they refuse to admit. The life of the unrepentant sinner is fraught with eternal danger.

It is this possibility of sin by one disciple against another which is the presupposition of the teaching in the second part of Matthew 18. The disciples must be ready to forgive their erring brethren. The lesson is enforced, as in the first part of the chapter with an *a fortiori* argument: if God forgives freely, men must do likewise. The 'seventy times seven' signifies the boundless readiness to forgive shown supremely by God Himself.

From the similar saying in Luke 17:4 it appears that what Jesus has in mind repeatedly asks for is the brother who sins repeatedly, and forgiveness in an attitude of repentance. Such a situation may well try patience to the limit, but the teaching of Jesus is that forgiveness must be unlimited. In Matthew, there is no mention of repentance (although it is implied in v. 15) and all the stress is on the need for an unconditional readiness to forgive, even as God is ready forgive.

At this point there comes the parable of the unmerciful debtor. Its relevance to the point at issue has sometimes been questioned. Thus J. Jeremias states that the parable itself says nothing about *repeated* forgiveness, and that the connexion with the preceding verses is a secondary one made by Matthew. Since Luke does not know of the connexion between Luke 17:3f. and the parable the connexion cannot be original.[144] Neither of these arguments is weighty. If Matthew is drawing at this point from M and not from Q, the second argument ceases to be relevant.[145] And it is a sufficient reply to the first argument to say that teaching about repeated forgiveness may well need to be buttressed by teaching about readiness to forgive *even once*.

It is important to note that the parable is addressed to believers and speaks of them extending 'to others the divine forgiveness which they have experienced.'[146] If such a person refuses to forgive his brother, then his own forgiveness is forfeited. This is confirmed by Matthew 6:14f. and Mark 11:25. If men forgive their brethren, God will forgive them; if they do not do so, then God will not forgive them. Matthew places this teaching in the context of the prayer which Jesus taught to His disciples. The version of the saying in Mark — 'Whenever you stand praying, forgive, if you have anything against anyone; so that your Father also who is in heaven may forgive you your trespasses' — has no firm context.[147] Matthew has probably taken it over from Mark, but the context in which he has placed it is entirely appropriate. If a person is not ready to forgive others, then he does not continue to receive the divine forgiveness for which he should daily pray. Earlier it was suggested that there is no clear evidence that Jesus regarded forgiveness as a once-for-all act when a person becomes a disciple. This view is now confirmed. Forgiveness is seen to be part of a continuing relationship with God, and it can be forfeited by the man who does not share the forgiveness which he has obtained from God with other men. Such an attitude, if persisted in, can lead to exclusion from the kingdom.

THE APPLICATION OF DISCIPLINE

In a community which is, as we have now seen, governed by the idea of forgiveness the question arises of how to treat a person who refuses to accept forgiveness. Teaching about this situation is given in Matthew 18:15–20. The situation is that of a brother (i.e. a disciple) who sins against another disciple[148] and does not come to him seeking forgiveness. In these circumstances a sequence of treatment with three possible stages is laid down.

The first stage is that the offended person privately reproves the offender (cf. Leviticus 19:17). According to Luke, if the man repents of the fault he is to be forgiven. Matthew expresses this by saying that if the offender listens to (i.e. obeys) the reproof, then the offended person has 'gained' his brother. The fellowship has been restored, and the brother is no longer in danger of being lost. For by his act he had put a barrier between himself and his brother and had begun to separate himself from the company of disciples and from God, whose will he had disobeyed. The fault is thus nipped in the bud, and it is probably to be regarded as an unwitting sin which the offender was willing to repent of as soon as he realized that he had committed it.

The further treatment to be used, if this approach should fail, is described by Matthew only. There is to be a further appeal to the man, this time in the presence of two or three witnesses (Deuteronomy 19:15). This has a twofold purpose. It is implied that a further opportunity of repentance is given to the offender. At the same time it is realized that the alleged offence is no longer a private matter between individuals, and the presence of the witnesses enables a reliable account of the dispute to be established in case it should be necessary to proceed any further.

The third stage is when the matter is reported to the 'church.' If the man again fails to listen — it being assumed that he has been shown to be in the wrong — then he is to be regarded as a Gentile or tax collector. In other words, he is to be excluded from the people of Israel.

Three comments may be permitted on this account. First, although the form of expression is not precise, we are probably to understand that excommunication is the result of this third stage of discipline.[149] It is true that a formal act is not described, but it is difficult to see what else can be meant. Thus the church has the right to exclude from its membership those who openly refuse to live as its members and whose sin has become deliberate and witting.

Second, we must note that the authenticity of Matthew's account as genuine teaching of Jesus is suspect. It is certainly true that the background of the passage is Jewish and not Hellenistic,[150] but the use of the terms 'Gentile and tax collector' and also of 'church' has created difficulties. The former phrase, which is paralleled in Matthew 5:46f., is strange upon the lips of Jesus, unless one supposes that He was saying in effect, 'You must treat these people in the same way as the Jews treat the Gentiles and tax collectors.' The sin of those who disrupt the fellowship of the disciples is as heinous as the Jews imagined that of their enemies to be. As for the use of 'church,' there is no doubt that Matthew himself thought that the Christian Church was meant here. The possibility that Jesus really meant the Old Testament 'congregation' has been suggested by K. L. Schmidt,[151] but this is unlikely since 'church' here fairly plainly means the group of the disciples. We must be prepared for the possibility that an authentic saying of Jesus has been recast in the Palestinian Church in the course of transmission.

Third, the meaning of Matthew 18:18 must be taken into account: 'Whatever you bind on earth will be bound in heaven, and whatever you loosen on earth will be loosened in heaven.' The traditional interpretation of this verse is that certain decisions of the disciples will be ratified in heaven, but the fact that the Greek text here makes use of a perfect participle with reference to the divine action suggests that the meaning is not so simple, and we may have to seek an interpretation along the lines suggested by J. B. Phillips who thinks that 'Jesus' true disciples will be so led by the Spirit that they will be following the Heavenly pattern.'[152] Which decisions are meant here? One view is that the reference is to the application or remission of excommunication;[153] this gives a close link with the previous verse. A second view is that the reference is a more general one to decisions made by the Church on the analogy of rabbinic legal decisions.[154] The identical saying in Matthew 16:19 addressed to Peter is brought into connexion with a saying about the keys of the kingdom, and a similar saying in John 20:23 speaks of forgiving and retaining sins. These two verses thus strongly support the first possibility of interpretation, in which case the saying refers to the authority of the disciples to pronounce or withhold forgiveness in the name of God. The person whom the Church excommunicates under divine guidance is rejected by Him.

Since, however, this verse speaks of both binding and loosing, we may well be correct in assuming that the excommunicated member could be readmitted to the community of disciples upon repentance.[155]

Matthew 18 as a whole, therefore, shows us the danger which confronted members of the Church who failed to forgive each other and also those who refused to repent and accept forgiveness. In each case the person who refused to be reconciled with God was in danger of exclusion from salvation. Persistent refusal to submit to the discipline of the kingdom could lead to an excommunication which, although designed to bring a man to his senses, might be permanent in effect. Thus the practice of discipline which the Church developed on the basis of the teaching of Jesus shows that the possibility of disciples failing to endure was a real one.

7. TWO HISTORICAL EXAMPLES — JUDAS AND PETER

We may sum up this lengthy discussion of the teaching of Jesus by glancing finally at the careers of two disciples who are paradigm cases of apostasy and perseverance respectively.

Judas was one of the inner circle of twelve disciples of Jesus and shared in all the privileges of discipleship which came to them. Yet just before the Last Supper it was he who went to the chief priests and offered to betray Jesus to them, and after the supper he led the band of men to Jesus and made the act of betrayal the more dreadful by his traitorous kiss.

We are not concerned here with the psychology of this deed — an area where in any case we are reduced to pure guess-work — but with the theology of it. According to Mark the betrayal was foretold by Jesus at the last supper (Mark 14:17–21). His remark caused the disciples to wonder which of them individually might do this. Then He commented: 'The Son of man goes as it is written of him, but woe to that man by whom the Son of man is betrayed! It would have been better for that man if he had not been born.' There is no indication here that Judas was predestined to carry out this act of betrayal.[156] The verse teaches on the one hand the fact that Jesus' passion was in fulfilment of Scripture, and on the other hand the responsibility of the man who betrayed Him. The warning is reminiscent of that already found in Mark 9:42. Nothing is said to indicate whether Judas was a real or a feigned disciple from the start.[157]

In Acts 1:17, 25 Judas is spoken of as a man numbered with the twelve and sharing in their ministry; he had a place in an apostleship and ministry from which he turned aside to go to his own place. The words occur in a passage ascribed to Peter, but the final formulation is by Luke himself and may be taken to represent the Church's verdict. Judas is thus again clearly regarded as one who shared in discipleship at the choice of Jesus Himself. His act of betrayal was thus an act of apostasy from discipleship.

The story of Peter's denial of Jesus is certain to be historical; so shabby a story about the leading disciple would not have been preserved if it had not been true.[158] Three times Peter denied that he was a disciple of Jesus. He ought to have known what he was doing, for Jesus had foretold the fact of his denial. Yet the fact that it needed the cock-crow to bring him to his senses indicates that he probably hardly knew what he was doing. He was allowed to fall in order that his self-confidence might receive a hard lesson. He does not, therefore, emerge from this story as an apostate, although his action, like that of the other disciples, is described as a 'falling away' (Mark 14:27, 29).

The story is elaborated in Luke 22:31–34. There we are told that Satan desired to sift the disciples,[159] but Jesus had prayed for Peter that he might not fail in his faith; when he was restored, it would be his task to strengthen his brethren. This brief saying reveals that the falling away of the disciples was regarded as due to temptation by Satan. Yet as a result of prayer by Jesus Peter's faith did not fail; he continued to believe, and so he could repent and be restored.[160]

The narrative raises difficult questions. Does Jesus pray for all His disciples? Did He pray for Judas? Can His prayers go unanswered? We remember that the Gospels certainly record unfulfilled longings of Jesus (Mark 14:36; Luke 13:34; 19:42). We must frankly face the fact that these questions seem to be unanswerable. All that we can draw from the story is that a man may go far in denial of Jesus and yet not be an apostate. Against the power of Satan is matched the prayer of Jesus. We cannot deny the efficacy of the divine protection thus extended to a disciple, but at the same time we cannot use the story to prove that disciples are inevitably and automatically preserved from the possibility of falling away; Judas was also a disciple.

J. Schniewind has suggested that there is a certain parallelism between the stories of Judas and Peter: 'The narrative (sc. about Judas) is inserted in the account of the second trial, just as the denial by Peter is put in the previous trial (sc. in Matthew's narrative). The sin of the man who ended in such doubt is probably meant to appear unforgiven and unforgivable (Matthew 12:31f.); this is different from the guilt of the denier, Peter, who remembered the word of Jesus and was brought through this condemnatory word to repentance (2 Corinthians 7:9, 10). The difference between the sorrow bringing life and death has often been shown with regard to the two apostles (2 Corinthians 7:10).'[161]

8. CONCLUSION

Our survey of the teaching of Jesus according to the record in the Synoptic Gospels has shown that He called men to a life of discipleship in which they received the blessings of the coming kingdom of God. In theory, therefore, it is possible to be a disciple and yet to fail to attain to the kingdom when it comes. This is certainly true of those whose discipleship was purely nominal and not accompanied by a readiness to own Jesus as Lord in their hearts, depart from iniquity and do the will of God. But is it also true of those who do own Jesus as Lord and do the will of God? What we have discovered is that the life of the disciple is one of testing and temptation, and the only proof offered that faith is real is that it proves itself by endurance to the end. Such endurance depends upon trust in God and the help of His Spirit. The danger caused by temptation is shown to be a very real one by the presence of numerous warnings addressed to the disciples. Even the sayings about unforgivable sin do not exclude the disciples from view.

It is, however, extremely difficult to say whether any true disciples did actually fall away in this manner. Judas may have belonged (some would say he certainly belonged) from the outset to the class of nominal disciples, and in the case of Peter (and the other ten disciples) who fell away before the crucifixion we are expressly told that the falling away was only temporary.

What is important is that there is no way of distinguishing between those who will fall away and those who will persevere. If we exclude the nominal disciples from consideration, we find that the reality of true discipleship is demonstrated only at the end of the day by their continued perseverance. Moreover, the warnings addressed to disciples are warnings *not to fall away from faith*, and not exhortations to consider whether one is or is not a disciple. In other words, there is no mysterious quality about the faith of certain disciples which enables us to guarantee in advance that they will persevere.

Does, then, the doctrine of predestination afford any guarantee that some disciples are certain to persevere and receive a special grace of perseverance which is not granted to the non-elect? It seems safe to say that there is no hint of this in the teaching of Jesus. There is only one saying which might be thought to suggest it (Matthew 22:14), and it is unlikely that this is the meaning of the saying. To assert that God gives some men such grace and refuses it to others would be to attribute an intolerable arbitrariness to the mercy of God. In any case, it is difficult to see how this doctrine would help the individual believer, since there is no way in which he can know for certain what is the secret will of God concerning himself; he can know that he is one of the 'elect' only by the evidence of his own faith and 'fruitfulness,' and the condition of final salvation is precisely that he goes on showing this evidence. So far, then, as the Gospels are concerned, the mystery of why some disciples persevere and others do not is not to be explained in terms of an inscrutable will of God; it is beyond explanation, and all that we may do is to speak of the mystery of evil — a mystery which, it seems, perplexed even Jesus.

Lest, however, a pessimistic impression be gained, it must be strongly emphasized that falling away is by no means inevitable. It is no easy thing to deceive the people of God, and every assurance is given to those who put their trust in God that He will protect them. This does not mean that effort is not required, but the effort is that of faith which draws its strength from God and His promises and not from itself. Moreover, in general there is hope of restoration for the person who falls. This must not be taken as minimizing the fearful danger in which the sinner finds himself — one may go to Gehenna for causing another person to sin, and there is no forgiveness for the man who sins against the Holy Spirit — indeed it emphasizes the tremendous responsibility of the faithful in seeking to bring the sinner to repentance and renewed faith.

In the end, then, the Gospels do not encourage us to speculate about who will and who will not persevere. They simply urge us to trust in God and to obey His will in the confidence that He will protect those who trust in Him. Our perseverance will be seen in the fact that we persevere. Such perseverance is expected by Jesus of His disciples; to one and all He says, 'Watch and pray that you may not enter into temptation.'

CHAPTER THREE

The Acts of the Apostles

In the life of the early Church described in the second part of Luke's two-volume work[1] the fundamental experience of the followers of Jesus may be described as salvation.[2] The idea of the kingdom remains basically a future one, but in the idea of salvation we have something which is received by believers here and now.[3] This is shown by the way in which the early Christians were conscious of having received the gift of forgiveness of sins and the presence of the Holy Spirit in their midst. Through hearing the Gospel and believing in Jesus — an experience which included repentance and found expression in submission to baptism — men received salvation and became members of the nascent Church. Thus through the experiences of Easter and Pentecost the disciples of Jesus felt themselves to be much more the possessors of salvation than when they had been His earthly disciples.

It is particularly stressed in Acts that these experiences took place at God's direction. Both the coming of Jesus and the consequent mission of the Church happened according to God's plan and purpose. The course of saving history was already known to the Old Testament prophets in broad outline (e.g. Acts 1:20; 2:17–21, 30f.; 3:17ff.; 4:25–8)[4] and it is perhaps not accidental that δεῖ, indicating a divine necessity, is particularly common in the writings of Luke. Hence the mission of the Church takes place at God's direct command and instruction (e.g. Acts 1:8; 5:19f.; 13:2; 15:7), and it is God who continually guides His apostles and servants in their journeyings with the Gospel (e.g. Acts 8:26; 9:10ff.; 10:19f.; 16:6–10).[5]

Luke, however, goes even further than this and shows that it is God who takes the initiative in bringing salvation to individual men. It was God who sent Philip to the Ethiopian eunuch, who revealed His Son to Saul of Tarsus, and who sent Peter to Cornelius. When men come to belief it is because the hand of the Lord is with the preachers (Acts 11:21).

If salvation has thus become a present experience, and if it is received by men through the initiative of God, the question now arises whether it is regarded as an inalienable possession which is guaranteed to men by God. The problem of perseverance is consequently a more pressing one than in the Gospels.

1. PREDESTINATION TO SALVATION

We must begin by asking whether the fact that God takes the initiative in salvation implies that those who receive the gift have been predestined never to lose it. It would seem unlikely that predestination to salvation is merely predestination to a temporary salvation, although Calvin was forced by the biblical evidence to admit that God could bestow some experience of grace even on the reprobate.[6] Five passages in Acts raise the question of predestination.

ACTS 13:48

In his description of Paul's mission in Pisidian Antioch Luke relates how Paul turned from the Jews, who rejected the gospel, to the Gentiles: the latter 'were glad and glorified the word of the Lord; and as many as were ordained to eternal life believed.' This language sounds strongly predestinarian,[7] but it is unlikely that we should press it to mean that the people in question believed and received eternal life because they had been individually predestined to do so.

For, first, the previous verses speak of the free rejection of the Gospel by the Jews who disbelieved; the passage says nothing about their being predestined to do so. It is certainly the case that the Jewish hardness of heart was foretold by Isaiah (6:9–10) in a passage expressly quoted in Acts 28:25–28, but this quotation refers to the nation as a whole; in the very same passage we hear of some Jews who did believe the Gospel preached by Paul and in whose case, therefore, the prophecy was not fulfilled (Acts 28:24).

Second, it may be that those who are described as being ordained to eternal life were Gentiles who were already proselytes and worshippers of God. Earlier in Acts Cornelius was already a religious man when God took the initiative in bringing a preacher of the good news of Jesus to him, and the same is true of the Ethiopian eunuch who had come to Jerusalem in order to worship. In both cases we are concerned with people who were already seeking salvation and had gone as far as the Jewish religion could take them. Now in Acts 13:43 we are told that 'many Jews and devout converts to Judaism followed Paul and Barnabas, who spoke to them and urged them to continue in the grace of God.' Was it these men who were already 'in the grace of God' who were enrolled for eternal life and now were led to believe in the good news of Jesus?[8]

Third, whether or not the preceding suggestion is correct, the context of the verse shows that it is concerned with the transition in the plan of God from the Jews to the Gentiles. The divine plan required that the Gospel be preached first to the Jews, but also, when they as a community rejected it, to the Gentiles in accordance with Isaiah 49:6. For God's purpose included the gathering of the Gentiles into the kingdom. It was this prophecy which was fulfilled in the response of the Gentiles in Antioch. It was because the Gentiles as such had been ordained to eternal life — on condition of faith — that now they believed. Luke's statement, therefore, is not concerned to delimit a particular group of Gentiles who, in distinction from other people, were specially ordained to believe, but to demonstrate that when God took the initiative and offered salvation to the Gentiles, in accordance with His purpose to call a people for Himself out of the Gentiles, they responded with faith. The Gentiles have as much right in God's plan to eternal life as the Jews.

ACTS 16:14

The narrative of the conversion of Lydia tells us that 'the Lord opened her heart to give heed to what was said by Paul.' It is thus God who makes human hearts receptive to His Gospel; apart from His act the preaching of Paul would have consisted of ineffective words. Here again, however, it is noteworthy that Lydia was already a worshipper of God.

ACTS 18:10

When Paul was working in Corinth he was counselled by God not to be afraid, for, said God in a vision, 'I am with you . . . I have many people in this city.' The 'many people' are usually and rightly regarded as people who would form Paul's field for evangelism and not as the many who had already believed (Acts

18:8). Hence the forces of evil would not prevent Paul from accomplishing the work given to him by God. Divine foreknowledge of the situation is thus indicated, but it is going too far to find in the verse the predestination of individuals to salvation.[9]

ACTS 18:27

In this verse the mission of Apollos has as its aim to help 'those who through grace had believed.' These words show that faith in God is due to the grace of God. They may be linked with Acts 16:14 in proving that salvation is always due to the work of God. It would also be possible to construe the words to mean 'to help through grace those who had believed,' in which case the thought is of the divine grace which operates throughout the Christian life. In any case, there is no mention of predestination in this verse.

ACTS 26:19

In the final verse to be considered in this section Paul states that at the time of his conversion he was 'not disobedient to the heavenly vision.' Does this mean that he was free to have chosen to act otherwise? Could he have refused the divine offer of salvation? It is true that the verse deals not so much with Paul's conversion as with his commission to preach the Gospel, but for Paul the two were no doubt closely bound up with each other. More important is the fact that the expression is probably a litotes; it is, comments E. Haenchen, 'a strengthened "I obeyed" . . . It was impossible for Paul (cf. σκληρόν κτλ. v. 14!) to withstand the heavenly command.'[10] Elsewhere in Acts Paul is spoken of as a chosen vessel of God for the preaching of the Gospel (Acts 9:15), and this agrees with his own testimony that he was set apart from his mother's womb to receive a revelation of the Son of God in order that he might preach Him to the Gentiles (Galatians 1:15f.). Thus the language of choice and election is certainly used of Paul, and he certainly responded to the election of God with a determined obedience. Nevertheless, we are bound to ask whether the possibility of his disobedience could be totally excluded. At one stage in his life he was certainly in open rebellion against God and resisting the goads (Acts 8:1, 3; 9:1, 4–6).

The result of this study would seem to be that while the initiative of God in salvation is strongly stressed in Acts Luke does not teach that individuals are predestined to salvation so that a secret divine plan is fulfilled in their acceptance or rejection of the gospel. When men reject the Gospel it is of their own choice. Nor have we found anything in Luke's teaching which guarantees that those who are elected to salvation will necessarily and inevitably be preserved from falling away. Continual perseverance in faith is required.

2. THE POSSIBILITY OF FALLING AWAY

Luke does not say much in Acts about the danger of individuals failing to persevere,[11] but in at least one passage Christians are warned against the danger of falling away. In his speech to the elders of the Ephesian Church at Miletus Paul warned them about the danger that, 'From among your own selves will arise men speaking perverse things, to draw away the disciples after them' (Acts 20:30). This passage predicts the rise of false teachers in the Church along with the danger of 'fierce wolves' from outside, whose purpose is to draw away the disciples after them. The danger is a real one, and therefore Paul has to warn the Church against it. We are not told how great the danger is, and whether it will in fact lead to apostasy within the Church, but the fact of danger for the disciples is clearly emphasized.

In two other passages there may be reference to actual cases of lapse from the faith.

ANANIAS AND SAPPHIRA

Acts 5:1–11 describes the grave sin of two members of the Church. F. F. Bruce writes, 'It is idle to ask if Ananias and Sapphira were genuine believers or not. Certainly they did not behave as if they were. But we cannot be sure that they were not, unless we are prepared to say that no one who is guilty of an act of deliberate deceit can be a true Christian.'[12] More probably the point is that the reality of Christian belief has to be continually demonstrated by turning from iniquity. The couple's sin consisted in lying to the Spirit and so to God about the price of the property which they were handing over to the church (Acts. 5:3f.).[13] It was an attempt to try the Spirit, the sin committed by Israel in the wilderness (cf. Exodus 17:2; Deuteronomy 6:16, and also 1 Corinthians 10:9; Ephesians 4:30). When they were accused of their sin, both man and wife fell down dead, and their death was no doubt regarded as a punishment for their sin.

It is uncertain whether we are to identify this sin with the unforgivable sin described in the Gospels, although both are sins against the Holy Spirit. Nor is the meaning of the penalty certain. We do not know whether the penalty of physical death also involved eternal exclusion from the Kingdom of God, although this may be the case in the examples mentioned by Paul which will be discussed later.[14] The narrative is not concerned with this point, nor does it raise the question whether the couple were given the opportunity of repentance for their sin. Its point is to indicate by the magnitude of the penalty the deadly seriousness of sin in the Church (cf. Acts 5:5, 11).

SIMON MAGUS

In the story of the conversion of the Samaritans (Acts 8) after we have been told that the people believed the good news preached by Philip and were baptized, we learn that even a man called Simon 'himself believed and (was) baptized' (Acts 8:13). But at this stage the people had not yet received the Spirit, and this gift was granted to them only when the apostles came down and laid hands upon them. It is to be presumed that Simon was among those who had hands laid upon him. Thereafter he sought to obtain by bribery the gift of being able to confer the Spirit on others.

The indications are thus that Simon became a believer, at least outwardly, and would be treated as such.[15] When, therefore, he overreached himself and sought apostolic powers, Peter uttered a curse against him, 'Your silver perish with you,' or, as J. B. Phillips colourfully translates it, 'To hell with you and your money!' It is a strong threat, for Peter goes on to tell him that he has no part or lot in this matter, i.e. in the Christian faith; his heart is not right with God and he is either in or liable to fall in the gall of bitterness and the bond of iniquity. These words may be equivalent to an excommunication.[16] Such an irreverent attitude to the Spirit of God is inconsistent with being a true believer. Yet there remains hope for such a sinner; let him repent and pray that the Lord will forgive the purpose of his heart. The story concludes with Simon's request for the apostles to pray for him lest the threatened punishment come upon him.[17]

The story suggests the beginnings of a practice of summary discipline within the Church. Simon is plainly in danger of perdition, and it is the threat of this coupled with the suggestion of excommunication which leads to his real or feigned repentance. We must conclude that there was a possibility of serious sin by members of the Church which could lead to their exclusion from eternal life, but at the same time there was the possibility of their repentance and restoration. The accent here is different from that in the story of Ananias and Sapphira; here it is upon the individual while there it was upon the effects of the action on the community. The manner of treatment is also different, perhaps to be explained by the different circumstances in Jerusalem and Samaria.

Here, then, we see the possibilities of deadly sin after baptism and of forgiveness for such sin, whether or not we regard Simon's faith as being real.[18]

3. THE NEED FOR PERSEVERANCE

If Luke, then, is optimistic in his view of salvation as a work initiated by God, he is also prepared to allow the possibility of serious sin within the Church. There thus arises the need for human perseverance in the faith and for repentance for sin committed by believers. The various sayings which speak of God giving faith and repentance (Acts 11:18; 14:27) do not mean that these are purely divine gifts but rather that God gives men the opportunity of repentance and faith through the preaching of the Gospel and shows that he accepts their repentance by bestowing the gift of the Spirit. Hence men need to be encouraged to remain in the faith.

We may not be prepared to go all the way with E. Haenchen in describing Acts as an *Erbauungsbuch* or piece of edification for its readers,[19] but there is no doubt that this is a part of Luke's purpose. The Church is to be built up by the word of grace (Acts 11:23; 13:43; 14:22). Divine grace thus does not rule out the need for human perseverance or make it unnecessary for commands and injunctions to be given.[20]

CHAPTER FOUR

The Epistles of Paul

In Paul we meet the most influential figure in the theology of the early Church. Although he is not the most voluminous of the New Testament writers, he ranges as a creative theologian over nearly every aspect of Christian thought, and his doctrine of the Christian life is of central importance for our study.[1]

1. PAUL'S CONCEPT OF SALVATION

Although Paul frequently uses the concept of salvation in a future sense to indicate the content of the Christian's hope at the parousia,[2] it is equally true that he thinks of God's saving work as something which has already begun in the believer. A Christian is a person who is already a new creature, who has been justified, redeemed, and sanctified, who is 'in Christ' and possesses the gift of the Spirit, and whose nature is being transformed from day to day. Through God's act of cleansing and forgiveness and his own act of faith, both of which are symbolized in baptism, he has entered the Church and enjoys fellowship with God. He enjoys what Charles Wesley has termed an 'antepast of heaven.'

The problem is whether this present salvation will inevitably lead to future salvation. Paul's statements are sufficiently paradoxical to make this a real problem. Thus one and the same writer, J. Weiss, can write: 'The experiences of grace through which he had already passed are too powerful for him [Paul] to question the certainty of his salvation'; and, on the other hand, 'Salvation can always be lost again if Christians do not "continue in God's goodness" (Romans 11:22) and "continue steadfast in the faith" (Colossians 1:23). . . . Christians should not be too sure of their possession of salvation; it might happen quite otherwise to them as it did to the generation in the wilderness.'[3] H. Lietzmann is even more emphatic with regard to the negative possibility: 'The Apostle threatened sinful Christians with death and therefore with final rejection such as faced every non-Christian. He reckons with the possibilities that even a Christian who has been baptized and endowed with the Spirit can turn once more to the flesh and to sinfulness in such a way that God will withdraw His grace and hand him over to damnation.'[4] Finally, W. G. Kümmel holds that 'the saved' and 'the lost' (1 Corinthians 1:18) 'designate non-Christians and Christians as a matter of fact, but with a clear eschatological reserve which reckons with the possibility of becoming a believer or of falling.'[5]

What we wish to determine is whether the present possession of salvation is in fact conditioned by this 'eschatological reserve.' Does the verdict that we have been justified by grace through faith mean that we are certain to be justified on the day of judgement or must there remain an element of doubt until the final sentence of acquittal or of guilt is passed?[6] In order to answer this question we must consider in turn the action of God in salvation, the various temptations which assail the believer, the different possibilities of failure to persevere, and the aids given to the believer in his life of faith.

2. DIVINE CHOICE AND PREDESTINATION

1 AND 2 THESSALONIANS

In these two early writings Paul affirms his fundamental belief that the salvation of men is due to the initiative of God. The church is a company of people beloved by God (1 Thessalonians 1:4; cf. 2 Thessalonians 2:13; Romans 1:7; Jude 1). Paul knows that the Thessalonians belong to this company and form part of God's elect people[7] because (*or* in that)[8] the Gospel had been preached to them in the power of the Spirit and had been accepted by them (1 Thessalonians 1:4f.). As a result of this they are destined for salvation and not for wrath at the last day (1 Thessalonians 5:9). From these verses it is apparent that the proof that a person belongs to the elect is to be seen in the response of faith to the Gospel and in the resulting new life. How the process of election takes place is not explained; Paul does not say that the human response of faith takes place in some men as a result of a divine decree but only that God calls men powerfully by the Gospel. Nor does Paul state that God's purpose must inevitably lead to final salvation.

These thoughts are repeated in 2 Thessalonians 2:13f. Here we note that God's calling comes to men through the preaching of the Gospel and is not something which takes place in past eternity. But what of the words 'God chose you from the beginning to be saved'? If the correct reading here is ἀπ' ἀρχῆς, as is assumed by the majority of scholars,[9] the divine choice of the Thessalonians must be set either at the beginning of the preaching in Thessalonica or else in past eternity. There is a reference in Philippians 4:15 to the time 'in the beginning of the gospel,' and it could be that in both of these verses Paul is referring to his work in Macedonia as in some special sense the beginning of his mission.[10] But the use of the phrase in Matthew 19:4 and 1 John 2:13 and the fact that God's call (v. 14) appears to have followed His choice support the other interpretation. The point is then that the Thessalonians belong to the people whose ultimate destiny planned by God is to partake in salvation at the last day; they are contrasted with the unbelievers and persecutors whose fate is judgment (2 Thessalonians 2:3–12). But although this has been God's purpose all along for them,[11] it depends upon their sanctification and faith, and the statement of their planned destiny is made the basis for a command to stand fast, coupled with a promise of divine strengthening (2 Thessalonians 2:15, 16–17). They will not reach their intended goal without persevering in the faith and being strengthened by God.[12]

While, therefore, Paul teaches that divine choice is the basis of salvation, he does not teach that this choice reaches its goal without the faith of those called by the Gospel and their steadfast perseverance.

ROMANS

In the Epistle to the Romans there is a strong emphasis upon the election of believers to salvation. This teaching does not exclude the possibility of believers falling into sin (chs. 6–8),[13] but we must ask whether the nature of the election described is such as to exclude the possibility of complete backsliding.

The passages which interest us particularly are found towards the end of ch. 8 and in chs. 9–11.[14]

In the passage which begins at Romans 8:28 Paul states that everything works for good for those who love God, i.e. those who are called according to His purpose. God has a purpose of salvation for men, in accordance with which He calls them by the Gospel, and the persons described in this verse are those who have answered this call, as is plain from the fact that they now love God. Salvation thus depends upon God's purpose and call and upon human response to that call. The following verse (29) gives the grounds for the statement that we know that all things work together for good. We know this because God's plan for us is one that stretches as far as glorification.

The process, which is now described in detail, begins before God's calling with His foreknowing and predestining. God has set Christians apart beforehand for the purpose of glorification. Predestination in this message therefore refers strictly to God's *final* aim for His people.

The traditional idea of foreordination to salvation is to be found, if anywhere, therefore, in the verb προγινώσκω. The verb means 'to know at a former time' and hence 'to know beforehand.' The 'knowing' here is generally understood in the Hebraic sense of fixing one's loving regard upon a person. But although the Hebrew verb *yāda'* comes close in meaning to *bāḥar*, 'to choose,' it has rather the sense of an intimate knowledge of the person in question.[15] The prefix προ- has been traditionally understood of God's purpose formulated in past eternity, but F. J. Leenhardt claims that it implies simply that God's loving regard rests upon men before they are aware of it.[16] The context gives some support to this interpretation. Paul's concern is with believers who are looking forward to the 'redemption of the body' but are tempted to despair of ever reaching the goal because of their present sufferings. He therefore emphasizes that the plan which God has formed for His people, those whom He already knows to be His, is that they should ultimately be like His Son and share His image (cf. 1 Corinthians 15:49). His readers can be sure that this plan will be fulfilled because God has already begun to carry it out by calling them. The verb thus refers to the loving knowledge which God already has of His people. It does not refer to the separation of the elect and consequent rejection of the reprobate, a thought which is not present in the context.[17]

The purpose, then, which God has already formed for those whom He 'knows' as His people is glorification.[18] The intervening steps are now set out. God called them, He justified them, He glorified them. At every point it is God who has acted. The past tenses, especially ἐδόξασεν, may be thought to indicate the certainty of the process, but it is more likely that they refer to what has already in fact happened in the lives of Paul's readers; while 'glorification' is normally to be regarded as something future, Paul may here be thinking of the anticipation of final glorification which takes place partially and proleptically in this life (2 Corinthians 3:18).[19]

But the continuation of this process requires a human response. Justification in Paul is always *by faith*, so that the completion of the whole chain of blessings is dependent upon faith. Thus in v. 17 future glorification is dependent upon the believer's readiness to suffer now. This is emphasized by J. Wesley who comments: '*And whom he justified* — provided they "continue in his goodness," Romans 11:22, *he* in the end *glorified* — St. Paul does not affirm, either here or in any other part of his writings, that precisely the same number of men are called, justified and glorified. He does not deny that a believer may fall away and be cut off between his special calling and his glorification, Romans 11:22. Neither does he deny that many are called who are never justified. He only affirms that this is the method whereby God leads us step by step towards Heaven.'[20]

While, then, this passage is concerned to emphasize that it is God who is at work in the believer and that consequently suffering cannot separate the believer from God, nothing is said which would eliminate the need for faith or which would suggest that faith is a gift of God only to a predestined group of the elect. The purpose of the section as a whole is to strengthen faith in the face of suffering and opposition, and its conclusion is full of assurance for faith. If God is on the side of the believer, then nothing conceivable can separate him from the love of God (Romans 8:31–39). For the person who will receive them all the resources of God are available. We may be permitted to ask whether a person may fail to make use of these resources, but nothing can disguise the fact that here Paul's tone is one of exalted optimism and assurance.

We now turn to Romans 9–11. The general theme of this section of the Epistle is the problem of Israel's unbelief (Romans 9:1–5). In the course of Paul's grappling with this tremendous problem of theodicy, he makes clear that it is Israel which has rejected God and not God who has rejected Israel (Romans 9:6–29); that in so far as God has rejected Israel it is because Israel has sought Him by the way of works of the law instead of by the righteousness of faith (Romans 9:30–10:21); and that in the future when the full number of Gentiles have been saved then Israel as a whole will also be saved (Romans 11:1–36).

It is clear throughout this section that Paul teaches the fact of a special predestination or election of the people of Israel to salvation, but it is equally clear that this predestination by no means guarantees the salvation of every Israelite or even of all who hear the Gospel and respond to it.

Looking at the salient facts in more detail we note, first, that although God chose Israel as His people this did not mean that the nation as a whole accepted His grace.[21] Many failed to attain to salvation. On the other hand, the fact that God had hardened the nation did not prevent Paul from praying for Israel to be saved and seeking to win Israelites through jealousy of God's mercy shown to the Gentiles (Romans 10:1; 11:13f.); the hardening was only 'in part' (Romans 11:25). The fact of a divine decree did not rule out either of these possibilities.

Second, the reason why Israel failed to obtain salvation was not that God had rejected them. It is true that He did bring a spirit of hardness upon the people, but this was because they themselves had rejected salvation by seeking it in the wrong way. This misguided zeal for the works of the law was not something predestined by God. What God had done was to send the good news of salvation by faith to Israel, but Israel had failed to obey it.

Third, we note that Paul's doctrine of the grafting in of the Gentiles contains a warning lest the Gentiles be cut off because of unbelief. They stand fast only because of faith, and if they become boastful and cease to rely on faith they will be cut off just as Israel was cut off because of unbelief.[22] Loss of faith will mean loss of salvation.[23]

Two points might be raised in opposition to the line of thought which has just been suggested. Does not the phrase which speaks about the 'remnant chosen by grace' (Romans 11:5, cf. 7) imply that God chooses certain people for salvation apart from the question of their response to the Gospel? In other words, does He predetermine their response? This is surely a wrong inference. No doubt divine election does not rest upon human merit or upon divine foreknowledge of human merit, but this is not to say that human response is predetermined by God. Grace was shown to a number of Israelites and they accepted it and so joined the company of the elect, but it is never said that their response was predetermined by God, or that the offer of God's grace was limited to the number of those who actually responded to it.[24]

The second point that arises is whether Paul's revelation that 'all Israel will be saved' (Romans 11:26) does not imply a divine predestination which would cause every Israelite to respond to the Gospel. May it not even be that a doctrine of universal acceptance of the Gospel is enunciated here?[25] We must observe, however, that, as has been frequently pointed out, Paul is thinking here of the nation rather than of the complete total of individuals who compose it. In the Rabbinic literature references to the salvation of 'all Israel' always exclude certain classes of men who have sinned beyond hope of recovery,[26] and we may safely assume that Paul would have made a similar qualification. The fact that Paul is prepared to limit Israel in Romans — 9:6 'not all who are descended from Israel belong to Israel' — may be held to show that a limitation is implicit here also. Above all, the statement in Romans 11:32 that 'God has consigned all men to disobedience, that he may have mercy upon all' cannot be read as an unqualified assertion of universalism or of the ultimate predestination of all to salvation; it must unquestionably be understood in the light of the parallel in Galatians 3:22: 'The Scripture consigned all things to sin, that what was promised *to faith* in Jesus Christ might be given to those who believe,' where the need for faith is explicitly stated.[27] There is no reason to suppose that election excludes the need for faith or that election automatically produces faith.

We conclude that Romans 9–11 does not teach a divine predestination which guarantees final salvation to those who respond to the Gospel. On the contrary, side by side with the stress on the divine initiative in election and salvation there is a warning to show awe in the sight of God lest anyone should be cut off for failing to continue in His kindness.

EPHESIANS

The third place where ideas of predestination and election come to the fore in the writings of Paul is in Ephesians, the principal passage being Ephesians 1:3–14 where a long and complex sentence sums up the Christian experience of a salvation prepared by God in past eternity. We must ask, as we did in the case of Romans, whether God's premundane plan included the predestination of certain individuals to an inevitable final salvation or simply outlined His purpose for all who would respond to His grace.

In order to answer this question it is important to observe that the passage contains two sets of contrasts, one between the divine acts which accomplish human salvation and the human acts of hearing the Word of God and believing, and the other between 'we' (Ephesians 1:3–12, 14) and 'you' (v. 13). The divine acts are spoken of in connexion with 'we' and the human acts in connexion with 'you.' Now it has been shown by

M. Dibelius that 'we' refers to the Church as a whole and 'you' refers to the once pagan readers of the Epistle who have now been added to the Church.[28] If follows that, although nothing is said about the predestination of the readers to salvation, what is said about 'we' must also apply to them since they are now members of the Church. But similarly, although nothing is said about the predestined 'we' hearing and believing, what is said about 'you' must also apply to them; they too must have heard and believed in the Gospel. Both the divine election and the human response are thus necessary in all cases, and hence the passage means simply that the Church of which 'we' and 'you' are members was part of God's premundane plan: His free choice was to make men His sons. Nothing is said which would deny that certain people heard the Gospel and did not believe, and it is not suggested that such people did not believe because they were not predestinated to believe. All that we are told is that God foreordains those who believe to become holy and to be His sons.

In the second chapter of Ephesians the use of the metaphor of raising dead men to life might be thought to rule out any place for human response to the Gospel; all would then be due to the sovereign act of God in graciously giving life to those whom He chooses. But this would be a false conclusion. The point of Paul's argument is that men are in such a state that they cannot save themselves by works, but when God calls them by the Gospel they can make the response of faith. The whole process is described as a gift of God (Ephesians 2:8),[29] but it is a gift which men must receive. It is not thrust upon men. If their trust in God is impossible apart from God's prevenient grace and call, neither is it due to an orientation of their wills by some secret divine causation. Nothing suggests that men are placed by God upon a predestined path to final salvation from which there is no possibility of falling, and elsewhere in Ephesians the possibility of sin in the believer is clearly recognized (Ephesians 4:14, 17–22, 30).

The Pauline doctrine of election and predestination[30] is thus seen to emphasize God's gracious purposes for those whom He chooses and calls by the preaching of the Gospel. It does not automatically guarantee the response of those called or the final salvation of those who do respond. We may not, therefore, use the doctrine as a means of proving the fact of final perseverance. Nevertheless, it is a doctrine which affords great comfort to the believer, because he knows that God's purpose for him is his sanctification and glorification, and that there is nothing which can separate him from the love of God. This assurance is further strengthened by Paul's teaching about the continuing work of God in the believer, to which we now turn.

3. GOD'S CARE FOR THE BELIEVER

One of the most characteristic facets of Paul's teaching is his emphasis upon the faithfulness of God in fulfilling the promises which He has made to His people.[31]

On the one hand, Paul speaks repeatedly of the fact that God will faithfully watch over His people until the parousia. His prayer in 1 Thessalonians 5:23 for the entire sanctification of the Thessalonians and their preservation at the parousia concludes with the words: 'He who calls you is faithful and he will do it' (1 Thessalonians 5:24). The God who calls men to His kingdom will not fail to prepare them for entry by making them holy.[32] Having begun a good work in His people, He will complete it at the day of Christ Jesus (Philippians 1:6). Again, in 1 Corinthians Paul states that after divine grace has been richly bestowed upon the members of the Church Christ will also[33] confirm them to the end so as to be unblamable in the day of the Lord Jesus; and God, who began by calling them into fellowship with His Son, is faithful to fulfil His promises (1 Corinthians 1:4–9).

On the other hand, Paul also emphasizes God's faithfulness in keeping His people from evil here and now. He will strengthen and keep the Thessalonians from evil, i.e. from the evil one who seeks to thwart the apostolic mission (2 Thessalonians 3:3), and therefore Paul is confident in the Lord of their obedience to his instruction (2 Thessalonians 3:4; cf. Galatians 5:10). When temptations do come to men, God is faithful and will not let them be tempted beyond their strength but will provide a way for them to endure (1 Corinthians 10:13). He will establish and strengthen them.[34]

These promises are great and far-reaching, but they do not rule out the possibility that a person may rebel against God and refuse His protection. The faithfulness of God does not rule out the possibility of the faithlessness of men. The fact that He does not permit men to be tempted above what they ought to be able to bear does not prevent them from being tempted or from succumbing to temptation, and it is compatible with grave warnings against the danger of falling into temptation. Divine protection does not rule out the need for human vigilance.

Similarly, we should not find anything automatic, still less anything magical, in the fact that a divine seal is placed upon believers (2 Corinthians 1:18–22; Ephesians 1:13f.; 4:30). The metaphor of a seal conveys the two ideas that the thing sealed is marked off as belonging to somebody and that it comes under his protection. Hence the reception of the Spirit is the mark that believers belong to God. A further idea is linked with this by the use of the concept of the earnest, or first instalment put down in payment for an object. God in sealing believers and anointing them with His Spirit has given them the first instalment of salvation, and this implies that in due time He will make full payment to them (2 Corinthians 5:5). That this process is not an automatic one is shown by the fact that it is possible for the believer to grieve the Spirit by whom he was sealed for the day of redemption (Ephesians 4:30; cf. 1 Thessalonians 4:8) and so to incur God's displeasure (cf. Isaiah 63:10).

4. THE HINDRANCES TO PERSEVERANCE

From the divine care for the believer we must now turn to consider the various ways in which the faith of the Christian is tested and tempted.

THE FINAL APOSTASY

Only the briefest mention needs to be made of the final apostasy preceding the parousia described in 2 *Thessalonians* 2. It is quite clear that what Paul is describing here has nothing to do with believers. The rebellion or apostasy led by the man of lawlessness takes place in the non-Christian world among those who did not believe the truth but had pleasure in unrighteousness; the men who are deceived are those who will perish because they refused to love the truth and be saved (2 Thessalonians 2:1–12). An emphatic contrast is drawn between such unbelievers and those beloved by God who were chosen for salvation and believed the truth (2 Thessalonians 2:13). Hence in the writings of Paul the final apostasy is not due to a massive defection among believers, but is a stage in the downfall of the non-Christian world.[35]

PERSECUTION

The fear of tribulation and persecution is particularly prominent in the *Epistles to the Thessalonians*, although Paul's other churches were by no means free from this fear. The Thessalonians had received the Gospel amid much affliction and suffered much from their compatriots (1 Thessalonians 1:6; 2: 14–16). Paul consequently longed to revisit them, but it was part of the Satanic plan directed against the Church that his visit should be hindered. He therefore sent Timothy instead to establish them in the faith and to exhort them lest anybody be moved by these afflictions. His fear was lest the tempter had tempted them, so that his labours would prove to have been in vain. Fortunately Timothy was able to reassure him that the Thessalonians had persisted in their faith (1 Thessalonians 2:17–3:10).

This passage shows that Paul had a real fear lest the faith of his converts might have been disturbed and reckoned with this as a genuine possibility, although he was able to rejoice that in this case they had shown perseverance and faith (2 Thessalonians 1:4). Although the believer may rejoice in persecution as a means of promoting Christian character, and although it cannot separate him from the love of God (Romans 5:3f.; 8:35ff.; 12:12), nevertheless it is a danger to his continuance in the faith.

Paul rarely if ever refers to people who have actually fallen away as a result of persecution. The possibility is perhaps to be found in Galatians 6:12, if this passage refers to men who once were believers and had fallen from grace. E. Lohmeyer has suggested that the 'enemies of the cross' in Philippians 3:18f. are people who fell away under fear of persecution.[36]

RELAPSE INTO JUDAISM

The main theme of the *Epistle to the Galatians* is a warning to its readers against turning back to Judaism as a means of salvation. A die-hard Judaizing party had arisen which denied the possibility of table fellowship in the Christian Church between circumcised and uncircumcised and held indeed that circumcision was necessary for salvation. Such teaching was being promulgated in the Galatian churches, and it is certain that some Christians were observing Jewish festivals and sacred seasons (Galatians 4:9f.). It is less certain whether any Gentile converts had actually submitted to circumcision. Although Galatians 6:13 may imply that some had done so,[37] the general tone of the letter is one of warning rather than of condemnation; the false teaching was making headway, but the churches had not wholly succumbed to it.

In itself circumcision was a matter of complete indifference to Paul — except when the physical act was regarded as an indispensable means to salvation. A Gentile who was circumcised was in effect seeking salvation by the law, and his act logically committed him to keeping the whole Mosaic law as his way to favour with God (Galatians 5:3). Now if a man were able to keep the law, his circumcision might have been reckoned to have some value (Romans 2:25), but in fact nobody could keep the whole law. Such people would fall into condemnation (Galatians 3:10f., 21f.).

At the same time, submission to circumcision indicated a cessation of faith in Christ. It implied that even after trusting in Christ a man was still not completely justified from his sins; he was still a transgressor, and Christ's death had been in vain. Christ had become an agent of sin (Galatians 2:17–21). Submission to circumcision was not, therefore, a meaningless piece of empty ritual. It was the expression of an act of repudiation of God's grace manifested in Christ. The person who was circumcised severed himself from Christ and His saving power (Galatians 5:2); he had fallen away from grace (Galatians 5:4).[38] Those who advocated such views would incur judgement (Galatians 5:10).

Paul, therefore, appeals to his converts with all the force of which he is capable, resorting both to threats and to tender exhortation, and arguing from logic and the facts of Christian experience. He writes as one who is startled by the onset of danger and surprised that his converts are taking up such an attitude. His forceful language can be explained only by the fact that a real danger was present. Yet he says that he has confidence in the Lord that they will follow his views, although he sees judgement ahead for those who are unsettling them (Galatians 5:10).

The *Epistle to the Colossians* should also be mentioned at this point. The Colossian church was likewise menaced by a new teaching which detracted from Christ's supreme and sole position as Saviour and Lord, but in this case incipient gnostic tendencies were added to the Judaistic ideas of Paul's opponents. The danger was not so much complete apostasy from the faith as perversion of it by alien elements, which could of course lead ultimately to the ruination of faith. Paul, therefore, wrote to Colossae lest any members of the church might be deluded with beguiling words, and he warned the members not to let anyone make a prey of them by philosophy and empty deceit (Colossians 2:4–8). The tone is less urgent than in Galatians; evidently the danger was not so pressing, and he was writing to more mature Christians who were less likely to be led astray (Colossians 2:5–7).[39]

FALLING INTO SIN

There is no doubt that Paul was conscious of the power which sin could exert in the life of the believer, and we must now ask whether sin can cause the believer to fall away completely from faith in Christ and the hope of salvation.

1 Thessalonians

In 1 Thessalonians 4:3–8 Paul warns believers against the danger of sexual sin, lest any person should wrong his Christian brother in any way. Such sin was not merely against a brother but also against God who had called His people to holiness and given to them His Spirit. There may be a hint here of sin against the Spirit. In any case the sin would be a witting one in view of Paul's express command, and the Lord would take vengeance upon it. It is uncertain whether such vengeance would take the form of exclusion from the kingdom or of a temporal punishment. In the case of an attitude of impenitence the former possibility cannot be ruled out.[40]

2 Thessalonians

A less serious trouble also arose at Thessalonica. Certain people were living in idleness upon their fellow-Christians, possibly while they awaited the parousia (2 Thessalonians 3:6–15; cf. 1 Thessalonians 4: 10f.; 5:14).[41] In addition to repeating his command that such people should work, Paul gave instructions for dealing with the recalcitrant. They were to be left to themselves by the Church; they were still to be treated as brothers and not as enemies, and given the chance to be ashamed and repent. Nothing is said about complete excommunication, and it is unlikely that this extreme resort would have been needed.[42]

Galatians

The Epistle to the Galatians has an important section on the possibility of sin in believers. Paul realizes that Christians might misunderstand their freedom from the law (Galatians 5:1) to mean a licence to follow the inclinations of the flesh (Galatians 5:13–26) instead of the possibility of living under the guidance of the Spirit and following the law of love. Two possibilities thus lie before Christians, walking by the Spirit and gratifying the flesh. Two opposing sets of desires are at conflict within them, and it is possible that the believer may follow either of them. Either set may act to prevent a man from following the other (Galatians 5:17), so that there is a real danger that a man may live by the flesh instead of by the Spirit. Such people will not inherit the kingdom of God; they will reap what they sow, and those who sow to the flesh will reap corruption (Galatians 5:21; 6:8). Here is a plain warning that if a Christian lives according to the flesh he may in the end be excluded from the kingdom. 'Even as a believer man stands both under the promise of grace and also under the threat of apostasy . . . (the flesh) can seize control and threaten him.'[43]

Paul goes on to make provision for the restoration of a person who falls into sin and urges the rest of the church to restore him gently (Galatians 6:1). The other church members must remember that they too may be tempted; nobody is free from temptation and the possibility of sin.

Nothing, however, is said about the possibility of proceeding as far as excommunication. Moreover, for Paul the balance is heavily weighted on the side of the Spirit. The grave sins of which Paul speaks are abnormalities. For in his view the believer is one who has crucified the flesh with its passions and desires (Galatians 5:24).[44]

1 Corinthians

The problem of sin in the life of the Christian arises most acutely in the correspondence of Paul with the Church at Corinth.

Our starting point is *1 Corinthians 6:9–11* where Paul warns the members of the Church against going to law with each other before pagan judges, men who are unrighteous and not heirs of the kingdom. Is this a fit procedure for persons who ought to be living on a different plane, men who have been washed, justified and sanctified? At first sight it might appear that those who are not heirs of the kingdom are the non-believers outside the Church. But we note that in verse 8 Paul complains that members of the Church are wronging and defrauding each other, and then he asks his pointed question, 'Do you not know that *wrong-doers* will not inherit the kingdom?' It is plain that he is here issuing a stern warning to the members of the Church about the possible ultimate outcome of their actions. They may go so far in wrong-doing that they are liable to exclusion from the kingdom.

A second passage which stresses the danger of the sinner is 1 *Corinthians 8:7–13*. In his discussion of the attitude of the believer to food offered to idols, Paul expresses his fear lest the freedom of the 'strong' believer to eat may become a stumbling-lock to a 'weak' believer and cause him to sin. The weak believer is thus in danger of destruction; he has committed a witting sin and is in danger of perishing as an idolater because he does not share the knowledge of the stronger believer that the idol really is nothing.[45] Not only does he suffer the pangs of conscience; he is also in spiritual danger. Moreover, the stronger brother is guilty of sinning against him and so of sinning against Christ.

The stronger believer is thus in danger of destruction as befits one who leads others into sin. The weaker brother is also in danger. It would be wrong to think that a single act of sin is going to cost him his soul, and it is reasonable to assume that Paul is pressing his point the limit when he speaks of destruction in order to stress the enormity of the act, but this does not mean that the ultimate possibility is an unreal one. Sin is to be regarded as a fearful danger in the life of the Church.

The fearfulness of sin is made particularly evident in the third passage which concerns us. In *1 Corinthians 5* we hear of a member of the Church who was living in gross immorality with his step-mother. Paul commanded that this wicked person was to be driven out from their midst (1 Corinthians 5:2, 13). The act was one of excommunication, and is perhaps to be regarded as more severe than that described in 1 Corinthians 5:9 11.[46] The description, however, may imply that something more than excommunication is meant, for Paul states that the man was to be handed over to Satan for the destruction of his flesh in order that the spirit might be saved on the day of the Lord.[47]

It is difficult to be certain about the meaning of 'flesh' in this statement. Origen held that the purpose of the chastisement by Satan was to destroy the man's sinful lusts.[48] If it be objected that Satan is a strange person to have this task assigned to him, a defence of his employment may be erected on the basis of 2 Corinthians 12:7, where he is used by God to curb Paul's pride.

This explanation is not completely satisfactory. It is not certain that flesh means 'lower nature' in 2 Corinthians 12:7, and a physical sense is perhaps required there (cf. 2 Corinthians 12:10). The dominant view today, therefore, is that 'flesh' is meant physically, and that Paul is thinking of Satan inflicting death on the man. After the man has been excommunicated and possibly subjected to a curse, he comes into the domain of Satan who destroys him.[49] Although his body is killed, his spirit may be saved at the last day.

An insuperable objection to this particular theory is that no place is left for the man to repent in order that his spirit may be saved on the day of judgement. That repentance is necessary for forgiveness is a basic assumption in Judaism and in the New Testament; it is shared by Paul, as is seen in 2 Corinthians 12:20f. where the same kind of immorality is in question. Moreover, while it would be wrong to build an argument on the identity of the offender here in 1 Corinthians 5 with the offender in 2 Corinthians 2 and 7 who was to be restored to fellowship when he repented,[50] it is right to draw attention to the fact that these passages from 2 Corinthians also show that discipline was regarded as remedial and meant to lead to the repentance of the sinner. In the similar case in 1 Timothy 1:20 repentance is also envisaged and immediate death is consequently ruled out.[51]

It would, then, be surprising if Paul did not allow for repentance here. Is it possible that death was not regarded as the inevitable issue of the act of excommunication and that the reference is primarily to some other physical hardship, such as illness?[52] Illness figures as a form of chastisement in 1 Corinthians 11:30. On this view, the man would be subject to the progressive destruction of his physical life by illness in order that his spirit might be saved in the day of the Lord.

This interpretation of the flesh is not without its difficulties. A. C. Thiselton has drawn renewed attention to the fact that flesh and spirit can hardly mean the body and soul of the man respectively. What needs to be destroyed is not the body of the man, but his pride and lust, the characteristics of his lower nature. He therefore suggests that Paul's language is deliberately vague and open-ended, but appears to prefer the view that the excommunication of the man would be a severe blow to his pride and so lead to his repentance.[53] Taking up this suggestion, we would propose that for Paul the physical nature and the sinful character of a man were closely connected in his use of the word 'flesh'; the bringing of the man low physically might well lead to his repentance and to the destruction of his lower nature in order that as a spiritual being he might ultimately be saved.

It is most important to note, finally, that the passage does not imply that the man's ultimate salvation was assured.[54] His sin would be forgiven only if he repented. Until that point he was outside the church and under the rule of Satan. It is possible that if the man died as a result of his chastisement this was regarded as a sign that it had been in vain; having failed to repent, he would be excluded from the kingdom (1 Corinthians 6:9f.); if, however, he did repent, he would recover from his illness (cf. James 5:14–16).

A similar problem arises in the fourth passage, *1 Corinthians 11:17–34*. Certain members of the Church were making a mockery of the Lord's Supper by profaning the body and blood of the Lord as represented in the bread and wine of the meal, and Paul states that this is why many of the Church were weak and ill and why some had even fallen asleep in death. This was a chastisement by the Lord upon them so that they should not be finally condemned along with the world (1 Corinthians 11:27–32).

We are not told whether this chastisement was regarded as effective in accomplishing its purpose when it took the form of death. Did the fact of death imply that the sinner had refused to repent? And what kind of a punishment or chastisement was death in these circumstances? One suggestion is that death before the parousia is in mind.[55] This would be a possible hypothesis if we were correct in assuming that Christians were expected to live until the parousia in normal circumstances, but the teaching of 1 Corinthians 15 is against this assumption. But the suggestion is shipwrecked on the fact that Paul taught those who were still living at the parousia would not precede those who had fallen asleep (1 Thessalonians 4:13–16; 1 Corinthians 15:52). Christians who had already died would not be at a disadvantage at the parousia. It is true that the suggestion might have some weight if Paul believed in a state of nakedness between death and the parousia which a man might fear to experience, but this hypothesis is unlikely.[56]

The two possibilities which remain are that death in itself was regarded as something unpleasant to endure, so that death itself is a punishment for sin, or that, as in 1 Corinthians 5, death is the ultimate stage in an unsuccessful process of discipline. The former possibility is ruled out because it implies that sin can be atoned for by the physical death of the sinner, a view which is contrary to Paul's teaching about salvation. We are left with the latter possibility. If the discipline was successful and the person repented, he recovered from his sickness; if it was unsuccessful, the person died, and his physical death was a sign of his spiritual death (unless the possibility of a deathbed repentance is allowed for).[57]

If this is the correct explanation, then we would have here definite examples of people who 'fell asleep' and thus forfeited their salvation.

Finally, we come to the fifth passage about sin in believers, *1 Corinthians 10:1–13*. The Old Testament narrative of God's displeasure with the people of Israel in the wilderness after they had passed through the Red Sea and feasted on the manna and drunk the water from the rock is regarded as a typological warning to the Church not to act in the same way by trusting in the efficacy of baptism and the Lord's Supper. Those who think that they are standing firmly must pay heed lest they fall. The nature of the fate which may befall them is not stated explicitly, but the sins which are mentioned (idolatry and partnership with demons) are those which provoke the Lord to jealousy and cause Him to spurn His people.[58]

It has been suggested that Paul is thinking here also of death before the parousia; this would give a parallel with the death of the Israelites in the wilderness before they reached the promised land. But the objections already mentioned against this theory still stand. Exclusion from the kingdom and salvation may well be meant; this would fit in with 1 Corinthians 6:9f., and would also give the required parallel with the wilderness generation who were excluded from entry to the promised land. There may also be reference to some form of divine chastening, even resulting in death, which is meant to lead to repentance and so preserve Christians from total apostasy and loss of salvation.

The teaching of 1 Corinthians on sin in the life of the believer is thus seen to be a unified whole in which the fearfulness of sin and its consequences are brought home to the Church. There is a divine discipline upon offenders within the Church and the possibility of exclusion from the kingdom and of death if the offender fails to repent.

2 Corinthians and Colossians

The main passages where Paul discusses the disastrous effects which sin may have upon the perseverance of the believer have now been discussed. But to complete our survey we must note that in 2 Corinthians 2:5–11 there is a warning lest the over-rigid application of discipline may have unfortunate effects in causing the disciplined person to be overwhelmed by excessive sorrow; he is to be forgiven, an act regarded by Paul as done 'in the presence of Christ, to keep Satan from gaining the advantage over us.

Finally in the Epistle to the Colossians there is considerable stress on the need for sanctification. The readers are to put to death what is earthly and sinful in their lives, because it is on account of these things that the wrath of God is coming; it would appear to be implied that this wrath threatens believers who persist in their old ways (Colossians 3:5f.; cf. Ephesians 5:2ff.).

5. THE POSSIBILITY OF FAILURE TO PERSEVERE

Our survey of Pauline teaching has shown us that the believer is exposed to a considerable number of temptations which may weaken and even destroy his faith in Christ. The picture must now be completed by examination of a number of ways in which the possibility of such temptations proving effective in their evil purpose is envisaged by Paul. More than once he speaks of the possibility of believers failing in the end to achieve salvation.

Two passages may be dismissed from the reckoning at the start. The one is *Romans 9:3* where Paul expresses his wish that he himself could be cut off from Christ for the sake of his Jewish brethren in order that they might be saved. The wish made here is one that God did not accept, and in any case it would have been entirely against Paul's understanding of the death of Jesus for him to suggest himself as an offering for Israel. The wish is rather couched in words reminiscent of those of Moses (Exodus 32:32) and serves to express with strong hyperbole the depth of Paul's love for his brethren. There is no question of Paul's own salvation hanging in the balance here.

The other passage is *1 Corinthians 3:10–17* with its stern teaching about the judgement which faces Christians whose work is found faulty when it is tested 'by fire' at the last day. Here Paul states explicitly that although the work will be 'burned' and the man concerned will suffer loss,[59] yet the man himself will be saved 'by the skin of his teeth.' On the other hand, we note that in the same context Paul asserts that another class of people — those who attempt to destroy the temple of God — will themselves be destroyed. Here Paul presumably has in mind unbelievers who persecute the Church, those who lead others into sin and perhaps those who eat the Lord's Supper without 'discerning the body'; this list may include those who have been members of the Church.[60]

We now turn to three sets of passages in which the possibility of failure to persevere may be in Paul's mind.

FAILURE TO PERSIST IN FAITH

In 1 Corinthians 15:1f. Paul is concerned to remind his readers of the Gospel which he preached to them and they received. The sentence is not easy to construe, but the most probable rendering of it is: 'I make known to you, brethren, the gospel which I preached to you, which you also received and in which you stand, by which you are saved if you are holding fast the word with which I preached it to you; otherwise you believed in vain.'[61]

The meaning of the last clause which states that the Corinthians may have believed in vain is not certain. The phrase 'in vain' may yield two meanings. First, it may mean 'you believed rashly or thoughtlessly.' On this view, the conversion of the Corinthians was an experience upon which they had entered without fully realizing what they were doing, so that their faith was an empty thing from the start. This view would require taking the opening words of the clause to mean 'unless.' But if we take these words to mean 'otherwise' a second possibility arises with regard to 'in vain,' and the clause will mean 'otherwise you believed in vain, i.e. to no purpose.'[62] Decision between these two alternatives is not easy. If we adopt the former view, then Paul is implying that the Corinthians' belief would be groundless and rash since the resurrection had not in fact occurred and provided a foundation for faith (cf. 1 Corinthians 15:14, 17). If we adopt the latter view, then Paul is stating that if the Corinthians have not held fast to the apostolic message then their original act of faith has been to no purpose. Since Paul goes on in the following verses to show that the validity of faith depends upon the fact of the resurrection, there is something to be said for preferring the first interpretation of the clause. But whatever be our decision on this point, there is no doubt that the warning which would be inculcated by this last clause of the sentence on the second interpretation is clearly expressed in the preceding clause: 'if you are holding fast the word.' Salvation depends upon continuing to hold fast to the apostolic message, and to give up belief in one essential item of it, viz. the resurrection, as some of them apparently had done, was to give up hope of final salvation. Paul's principal point here is that attainment of salvation depends upon continuance in the apostolic faith.

Similarly, a faith which fails to keep hold of the grace of God may prove to be in vain. In 2 Corinthians 6:1 Paul addresses an appeal to his readers 'not to accept the grace of God in vain.' Although the preceding verses (2 Corinthians 5) contain an expression of the Christian message for unbelievers, it would seem that Paul is here stating this in general terms as the content of the apostolic preaching rather than addressing it specifically to his readers as if they were unconverted. We should then take 2 Corinthians 6:1 closely with the following verses, in which case it will form an appeal to the readers to follow up their initial act of belief and acceptance of the grace of God with a consistent Christian life, and in particular by taking Paul to their hearts.[63] If this is a correct interpretation, then the possibility exists that Christians may receive God's grace to no purpose after conversion and so become backsliders.[64]

FAILURE TO ATTAIN TO THE RESURRECTION

The question of the resurrection appears in a different form in Philippians 3:11. Here we are concerned not with the fact of Christ's resurrection, as in 1 Corinthians 15, but with the question whether the believer can be certain that he will share in the resurrection. For Paul states that his purpose as a Christian is 'that I may know him (sc. Christ) and the power of his resurrection, and may share his sufferings, becoming like him in his death, that if possible I may attain the resurrection from the dead.' The form of words may be thought to suggest that there was some doubt ('if possible') about Paul's attaining to the resurrection.

Certainly the construction used (εἴ πως with the subjunctive) may suggest that there is some doubt about the attaining of the desired result.[65] But elsewhere Paul looks forward with confidence to believers attaining precisely this end. He regards baptism as a kind of foretaste of the final resurrection (Romans 6:5; 2 Corinthians 4:14; Ephesians 2:6; Colossians 2:12), and earlier in this Epistle (Philippians 1:23) he expresses with complete certainty his hope of union with Christ after death.

E. Lohmeyer has suggested that the whole Epistle is an exhortation to martyrdom by one who is on the brink of martyrdom himself, and uses this key to unlock the secrets of nearly every difficult verse in the Epistle. The knowledge of Christ (Philippians 3:10) is then the special knowledge of Him which is vouchsafed to the martyr, and the fellowship of His sufferings is the act of martyrdom itself. The result of martyrdom, which Paul cannot be absolutely certain of attaining, is the special resurrection from the dead before other Christians which is the prerogative of the martyr.[66] In favour of this view are cited the use of the unusual word ἐξανάστασις and the parallels in Revelation 20:4–6 and John 5:21ff.

Although this view is presented with great ingenuity, it cannot be said to be convincing.[67] Yet it does bring out the paradox of the uncertainty expressed here in comparison with Philippians 1:21–23: 'It is characteristic both of faith and equally of martyrdom to be certain and uncertain, sure and unsure; this is its "incompleteness" which dissolves itself only at death.'[68]

The decisive point in interpreting the passage is that Paul speaks with great certainty in Philippians 3:9 of his 'being found in Christ,' an expression which is surely eschatological. It is difficult to believe that he is retracting his words two verses later. The most plausible solution will be that he was uncertain about how his final destiny would be achieved. It is not clear that he regarded his martyrdom as inevitable (Philippians 1:24f.; 2:24), and such evidence as we have suggests that he did not die immediately after writing this Epistle. Life and death were both possibilities. If the former, it was possible that he might not attain to the resurrection by the path of suffering; he might even live to see the parousia (Philippians 3:20f.; 4:5; Colossians 3:4; 4:5). Paul's doubt, then, would not be about his final destiny but about the route to it.[69]

There is, therefore, no uncertainty in this passage about Paul's own perseverance in the faith, and this passage must accordingly be removed from any list of passages which express doubt about final perseverance.[70] For evidence of doubt about attainment of the Christian's goal we must turn to the next set of verses.

FAILURE TO PASS THE TEST

In 1 Corinthians 9:22–7 Paul describes his work as an apostle and evangelist and uses the simile of a race in order to indicate that God's servants must 'run well' if they wish to please God. It is not enough to enter for the race; one must carry on with determination to the end. Similarly, everybody who goes in for athletic sports submits to a strict course of training and self-discipline in order to win a wreath, and by analogy the Christian must be self-disciplined in order to win his incorruptible crown. In his athletics, therefore, Paul runs for the mark, he boxes in order to hit his opponent, and he keeps his body fit by pummelling it; and in all this his aim is to avoid himself being disqualified (i.e. failing to pass the test)[71] after having preached to others.

The crown for which Paul is here striving is that granted for faithful service,[72] but the meaning of 'being disqualified' is not so clear. Does it refer to failure to win this crown for faithful service, in which case the question of loss of salvation does not arise (cf. 1 Corinthians 3:15), or does it refer to Paul's fear lest, having brought others to salvation, he himself should be disqualified from it?[73] In favour of this second possibility we may note that it would give a pointed contrast between 'having preached' (sc. the Gospel) and 'being disqualified.' Moreover, the thought has already begun to move away in verse 25 from the race and its prize to the general concept of the Christian's self-discipline, so that the thought of the prize for service need not be present in verse 27. Finally, this exegesis would give a good connexion of thought with the immediately following section in ch. 10 in which Paul goes on to discuss the fate of those who failed to keep their bodily passions under control and sinned in the same way as the Israelites who perished in the desert. But it must be admitted that the connexion of thought between chs. 9 and 10 may not be very close.[74]

The possibility is, therefore, seriously to be entertained that in 1 Corinthians 9:27 Paul raises the question of his own failure to pass the test and rejection on the day of judgement. Such failure would not be due to poor Christian service, but to failure to withstand the temptations of the body and to keep it under. But although this theoretical possibility is raised, there is little doubt that Paul felt no severe temptation from this quarter (1 Corinthians 7:7), and his overwhelming feeling is one of confidence regarding his own salvation.

What Paul had much more reason to doubt was the perseverance of some of his converts at Corinth. This concern is expressed in 2 Corinthians 13:5–7.[75] Throughout the long section which is here near its conclusion Paul has been dealing with two matters. On the one hand, he has had to defend the fact of his commission from Christ to be an apostle and missionary, and, on the other hand, he has found it necessary to rebuke the very people who questioned his apostolic rights because of their loose living. Although it would appear that the majority of his readers had accepted him and repented of their misdeeds, there was a recalcitrant minority who are addressed by Paul in these verses.

He therefore states that when he visits them he will not spare them if it is confirmed that there have been sinning; his stern demeanour will be a proof to them that Christ is speaking through His apostle. But, he goes on, why should it be his own life for which proof is required? Let his opponents examine themselves to see whether they are in the faith; let them prove themselves. Do they fail to realize that Jesus Christ is also in them, just as He is in Paul, unless perchance they do not pass the test? Paul hopes that they will see that he himself is not rejected by God, but his main thought is that they may not do anything wrong, not in order that (having returned to a state of obedience to him and once again accepted him) they may see that he has passed the test, but simply in order that they may do what is right in God's sight, even if he should appear to them to be a failure. His whole interest lies in their welfare, and it does not matter what they think of him so long as they pass the test.

As regards Paul the test is whether or not Christ speaks through him as an apostle. But as regards the Corinthians the question is whether they are in the faith and Christ is in them; it is their Christian life which is under examination. Paul therefore bids them examine themselves to see whether they are truly Christians, and he expects them to realize that they are — except if[76] they are failures in the test. It is possible that they may not be true believers.

Various arguments have been put forward against this view of the passage. It has been suggested that Paul's suggestion is an ironic one,[77] but this does not necessarily exclude the theoretical possibility of apostasy. Another view is that the question is whether their way of life is consistent with their faith,[78] but this is not what Paul says in the text. More important is the objection that Paul is thinking of men who have never been believers rather than of those who have lapsed from the faith, but this objection is answered by the fact that in 2 Corinthians 12:20f. Paul shows that he has in mind those believers who have fallen into sin and have not yet repented. Such people will be disciplined by Paul if they fail to repent.

6. THE DIVINE AND HUMAN ASPECTS OF PERSEVERANCE

If our argument so far in this chapter has been sound there is evidence that the Pauline doctrine of salvation emphasizes both the believer's assurance of salvation and the possibility of falling into grievous sin and even of loss of salvation.

On the one hand, Paul bases assurance of salvation on the knowledge of God's care for the believer. He teaches in numerous passages the fact of divine calling and election. God's choice has fallen upon those who have become members of His Church, and because of their response to His gracious call they have been numbered among the elect. His purpose for them is conformity to the image of His Son and participation in His glory, and there is no power in the universe which can thwart this purpose. Knowledge of this electing will of God gives strong assurance to the believer that he can and will persevere.

Further, the faithfulness of God to fulfil His promises receives constant stress. It is His declared purpose to bring His people to full salvation, a fact which is expressed in the metaphors of God placing His divine seal upon believers and giving to them the earnest of the Spirit. The promise is made to them that they will appear blameless at the parousia. Consequently God Himself strengthens and establishes those who believe in Him. We may say that from start to finish salvation is regarded as the work of God for and in the believer. In this connexion we should not overlook the tremendous importance of prayer in the writings of Paul; it is a factor of incalculable power as it provides an opening for God to work His sanctifying and preserving purpose in the lives of believers. Although the rationale of prayer is not explained, it is obvious that prayer is a force of great might in strengthening those who are tempted to fall away.[79]

On the other hand, various exhortations are addressed to believers which imply that they also have their part to play in the attainment of their final salvation. The reason for these commands and exhortations is that the believer continually needs to be warned against the dangers which threaten him. Persecution and tribulation may cause believers to fall away. Various heresies threatened certain of Paul's churches, and there was also the possibility of serious sin by Christians; failure to respond to the discipline imposed by the Church in such cases could result in loss of salvation. Even Paul himself seems at times to have been conscious of the demonic threat which overshadows the life of the believer, although his normal mood was one of full assurance regarding his own salvation. The result is that Christians need to be summoned to frequent self-examination lest they fail to persevere.

Paul's teaching thus presents us with the paradox of divine care for the believer alongside the need for the believer to persevere in his faith. This paradox comes to expression in Philippians 2:12f., as the passage is traditionally understood. Having urged the Philippians to live at one with each other and having presented them with the example of Christ's humble service and selflessness (Philippians 2:1–11), Paul makes his appeal: 'Work out your own salvation with fear and trembling; for God is at work in you, both to will and to work for his good pleasure.'

The relevance of this passage for our subject would be lessened if we found it necessary to accept the suggestion of some recent scholars that 'salvation' here refers to the health of the Church as a whole rather than to the salvation of the individual. It is argued that the same word in Philippians 1:28 also refers to the salvation of the Church as a whole, that the context requires a reference to a communal interest, in which an injunction to work at one's own individual salvation would be completely out of place, and that 'your own' need not have an individual sense.[82]

But this exegesis is more than doubtful. It is true that elsewhere in the New Testament σωτηρία may mean 'health' (Acts 27:34), but in Paul the noun is used always of spiritual salvation,[83] and the corresponding verb is also used exclusively in the spiritual sense. It is difficult to see why the word should be given a new sense here when the normal meaning gives a perfectly satisfactory sense to the passage. It may well be true that Paul is thinking of the working out of the consequences of salvation in terms of relationships within the Church, but this does not mean that σωτηρία means the health of the Church.[84] This fact answers implicitly the second argument in favour of the new exegesis; in fact both individual and communal points of view are present in the passage according to the traditional understanding of it. Finally, it is very difficult to take ἑαυτῶν in any other way than as a reference to the salvation of individuals.[85]

These verses, then, must be taken in their traditional sense as an appeal to the Philippians to work out their salvation in terms of love and unity with each other. In doing so, they are to behave with due fear before God. For, says Paul, God is at work in them, i.e. in their hearts.[86] Just as He 'energizes' His servants for their missionary and ministerial labours (1 Corinthians 12:6; Galatians 2:8; 3:5), so His power is at work in the lives of all Christians (Ephesians 3:20; cf. 1:19f.). Its effect is to cause men to will and to act 'for His good pleasure.' The meaning of this last phrase is uncertain, but an attractive rendering is 'for the sake of goodwill,' sc. among the members of the Church.[87] This gives an excellent link with what follows and fits in with Paul's use of εὐδοκία elsewhere (Romans 10:1; Philippians 1:15; 2 Thessalonians 1:11).

Consequently, human action for good in the Church is ultimately ascribed by Paul to the working of God in the hearts of believers. This is in line with his ascription of all good works generally to the work of the Spirit in the believer. It is because of this power that he is able to address exhortations to his readers in the conviction that they will be able to obey them. Yet while he is able to say that the Philippians have always obeyed (Philippians 2:12), he also knows that it might have been possible for him to run and labour in vain (Philippians 2:16), and it remains a fact that the Church had manifested lack of love and a tendency to division. Rather, the need for exhortation shows that there is a possibility of failure to work out salvation. Divine working in a believer does not mean an automatic progress in sanctification, and is compatible with the fact of human weakness, failure, and sin.

Paul, then, did not regard grace as operating in such a mechanical fashion that the believer is inevitably carried on to perfection with no effort on his part. The paradox of grace and freewill is not to be solved by emphasizing the former to the exclusion of the latter. While Paul certainly anticipated the final perseverance of the vast majority of his converts, he never regarded this perseverance as something predetermined and inevitable; always there pressed upon him 'the care of all the churches,' a care which involved him in constant prayer and effort lest any member should fall away and so cause him to have run his course in vain.

While, therefore, the believer who commits himself to the grace of God must rightly beware lest he fall away, he can at the same time rest assured that nothing can separate him from the love of God and can rejoice in the hope of final salvation.

CHAPTER FIVE

The Pastoral Epistles

Whether or not the three Pastoral Epistles are the work of Paul himself,[1] there is every justification for discussing them at this point in our study since their teaching stands closer to that of the undisputed Epistles of Paul than does that of any other New Testament writings. In general it may be said that they show the same understanding of the Christian life as is found in the other Pauline writings. Salvation is the work of Christ through His sacrificial death upon the cross (1 Timothy 2:5f.; Titus 2:14), and the Christian life is the life of God's elect (2 Timothy 2:10; Titus 1:1) who have been washed and justified from their sins through faith and renewed by the Holy Spirit (1 Timothy. 1:14–16; 2 Timothy 1:9f., 14; Titus 3:4–8). It is a life of continuous progress in faith and love (1 Timothy 1:5; 6:11; 2 Timothy 2:15), and it looks forward to final salvation and eternal life at the parousia (1 Timothy 4:8–10; 6:19; 2 Timothy 2:10–13; 4:6–8, 18; Titus 3:7).

There are, however, various new emphases. The idea of individual virtues to be cultivated by the Christian has become more prominent and a great deal of stress is laid on the need for sound doctrine, which is the doctrine handed down from the apostles. This new emphasis is largely explained by the need to meet the danger of false ideas, both antinomian and ascetic, in the realm of conduct. The passage of time inevitably allowed the rise of strange ideas, and with them the possibility of falling away from the true faith. What the Pastoral Epistles fear most is an outward form of Christianity which lacks the moral vitality of a true faith and dabbles in strange ideas to the neglect of the great truths of the Gospel.

1. THE RISE OF EVIL MEN AND IMPOSTERS

In the Pastoral Epistles the rise of apostasy in the Church is seen against a general background of increasing evil in the world associated with the last days (1 Timothy 4:1–3; 2 Timothy 3:1–9, 13). This movement has its roots outside the Church and is the counterpart in Christian thought of the final apostasy which was predicted by the Jews. It was regarded as being directed against the Church, but the dividing line between evil in the world and in the Church is hard to discern since one of the main features of the time was the rise of men who professed religion but denied it by their way of life (2 Timothy 3:5, 8; Titus 1:16). Those who followed this kind of empty religion might be either men who had come into the Church from outside without ever truly accepting the faith or men who were originally Christians but had lapsed from the faith under the influence of outside influences.

In a number of passages we find evidence of the mixed nature of the Church. In 1 Timothy 4:1–3 Paul refers to men who depart from the faith by giving heed to deceitful spirits and doctrines of demons, through the pretensions of liars whose consciences are seared. The liars in this passage are surely non-believers who were exerting an evil influence in the Church, and there is nothing to suggest that they had ever been believers (cf. Titus 1:15).

Similarly, in 1 Timothy 6:5 the men depraved in mind and bereft of the truth who imagined that godliness was a means of gain were probably rich men who professed the faith merely because they hoped to make some financial profit from it. They professed to be Christians, but their profession was a sham. It is true that the following verses contain a warning against the desire for riches which can lead men astray from the faith (1 Timothy 6:10), but this does not prove that true believers are in mind in verse 5.

We may pass the same verdict upon the men who possess the outward form of religion but deny its power in 2 Timothy 3:1–9. So far as faith is concerned, they fail to pass the test, and in reality they are opponents of Christianity.[2]

Finally, in Titus 1:10–16 we are probably to distinguish two groups of people, those who were to be rebuked for their false teaching about circumcision and were regarded as still being Christians, and those who rejected the truth (Titus 1:14) and were heretics of a more advanced degree. These latter are described in scathing language and do not appear to be regarded as ever having been believers.

The dividing lines, however, cannot be drawn rigidly. These passages bear witness to the mixed nature of the Church; it contained men who professed the faith but had never come to belief, and it also contained others who were being tempted by them to apostasy. Thus the Church included men who had no claim to the name of Christian despite their outward profession of faith and were interlopers with no right to be there. We must now ask whether alongside them we must reckon with the possibility of believers who had lapsed from their faith.

2. APOSTASY IN THE CHURCH

1 TIMOTHY 1:3–7

At the very outset of the First Epistle to Timothy we have a glimpse of the beginnings of apostasy. Certain people were being led away into pointless speculations and indulging in new teaching about the law. The novel doctrines mentioned here appear to have been developed on the basis of the Jewish law (cf. 1 Timothy 4:3; Titus 1:10f.), and the pernicious element was that such speculation, despite its stress on ascetic practices and observance of religious ritual (notably circumcision), forgot the need for the conduct which accompanies godliness. It was a stage of danger and temptation which could cause the ruin of those who paid heed to it (cf. 2 Timothy 2:14, 18b; 4:3f.).

1 TIMOTHY 1:19F.

A further stage in downfall is seen in 1 Timothy 1:19f. Various people, including Hymenaeus and Alexander, had given up adhering to the dictates of conscience and are said to have made shipwreck of their faith; as a result they had been delivered up by Paul to Satan. It has been suggested that 'they are said to have given up or to have made shipwreck of that faith which they never possessed except in appearance,'[3] but this is very unlikely. The language suggests a violent rejection of the claims of conscience, and the metaphor of shipwreck implies the loss of a faith once held.

1 TIMOTHY 4:1–3

There is a definite prophecy by the Holy Spirit, presumably through the activity of Christian prophets, in 1 Timothy 4:1–3 that some will depart from the faith by giving heed to deceitful spirits and the doctrines of demons. The verb used (ἀφίσταμαι) implies a departure from a position once held and therefore refers to apostasy from the faith by those who once held it. The fact of apostasy is thus clearly foretold here, although it is to be noted that this is a general prophecy and not a *praedestinatio in malam partem* of particular individuals. But it should be observed that the apostasy described at this point is expressed in ascetical conduct, and it is not necessarily implied that departure from the faith as a whole was included, although it is likely that the asceticism was part of a wider rejection of basic Christian teaching.

1 TIMOTHY 5:3–16

In 1 Timothy 5:8 it is affirmed that anybody who does not provide for his family has disowned the faith and is worse than an unbeliever. The statement is alarmingly strong, even though it is a warning rather than a condemnation of some actual culprit, and is probably to be explained by the fact that such an attitude would betray the presence of the temptation to money-grabbing discussed in 1 Timothy 6 and would also be a basic denial of the Christian law of love. Such *practical* denial of the faith would bring it into severe disrepute in a world in which family responsibilities were taken fairly seriously.

The following verses which deal with the problem of widows, including those who grow wanton against Christ and stray after Satan (1 Timothy 5:11, 15), are difficult to interpret. Many scholars think that two types of widow are in mind.[4] The first type are those who are dependent upon the Church for support. Of these some are self-indulgent,[5] and they should have no claims upon the Church. Although they are 'alive' in the sense that they' belong to the Church, yet spiritually they are 'dead' and so have no claims upon the Church. They are merely nominal believers (1 Timothy 5:3–8).

There appears to be also a second group of widows who performed certain services in the Church. They were to be over sixty years of age, of good moral character, and with a record of Christian service behind them. Younger widows were not to be admitted to this group. For entrance was apparently by taking a pledge to this special service of Christ, and a younger woman might well wish to revoke her vow in order to enter upon a second marriage. In such a case the widow is described as growing wanton against Christ and so standing condemned for violating the pledge which she had made. It would be better not to take such a vow.

But this 'condemnation' about which Paul speaks (1 Timothy 5:12) can scarcely be regarded as the due reward for apostasy. The word should be given the milder translation of 'censure,'[6] and the question of apostasy does not arise. This teaching does not mean that celibacy is specially praised here (cf. 1 Timothy 2:15; 4:3), and in any case it is said to be better for young widows to remarry. If they do not do so, there is some danger that they may stray after Satan, no doubt through temptations to immorality, and this would be a step on the way to apostasy.

1 TIMOTHY 6

The final chapter of 1 Timothy contains warnings against two dangers to faith. It is pointed out that in addition to those who had made their way into the Church for the sake of gain there were also those who had wandered from the faith because of the love of money and become materialists, trusting in wealth instead of in God. The result of such desire is said to be ruin and destruction.

A further danger to faith arose from gnosticism (1 Timothy 6:20f.), and it is important to note that Paul thought it worthwhile to warn Timothy himself against this so-called knowledge. If he were to yield to gnostic teaching — no doubt an unlikely occurrence — he might depart from the faith.

2 TIMOTHY 2:24–6

A number of verses in 2 Timothy refer to opponents of the Gospel and to men who had deserted Paul (2 Timothy 1:15; 4:16), and one of these, Demas who fell in love with this present world (2 Timothy 4:10), may have been a lapsed believer. In dealing with such people Timothy is exhorted to be gentle since 'God may perhaps grant that they will repent and come to know the truth, and they may escape from the snare of the devil, after being captured by him to do his will.' Such people are probably lapsed believers. It is true that the phrase 'repent and come to know the truth' usually refers to conversion to Christianity, but it can also be used of the deepening knowledge of the Christian (Titus 1:1). The parallel in 1 Timothy 3:7 about being ensnared by the devil plainly refers to believers, and the use of 'correction' and 'escape' (ἀνανήφω, literally 'to recover sobriety') also points in this direction. If the opponents may be identified with the false teachers described in

2 Timothy 2:16–18, the case is strengthened. On the whole, therefore, lapsed Christians are probably described here.

From this survey we see that there are clear indications of the possibility and the fact of lapse from the faith in the Pastoral Epistles, and that the causes are especially false doctrine, immoral behaviour and desire for riches. Our next step must be to look at the light shed by the development of Church discipline to meet this situation, and finally we shall consider the theological problem which arises.

3. DISCIPLINE AND EXCOMMUNICATION

The general teaching of the Pastoral Epistles is that Timothy and Titus are to be diligent in refuting false teaching and in silencing false teachers (1 Timothy 1:3; 6:17; 2 Timothy 2:14; 4:2; Titus 1:5, 9, 11; 2:15; 3:8f.). Such rebukes are to be sharp (Titus 1:13), but the Lord's servant must also be gentle towards his opponents (2 Timothy 2:24). The possibility is present that 'God may perhaps give them (sc. the opponents) repentance.'[7] Like faith, repentance is the gift of God and depends upon His will.[8] The suggestion would appear to be that repentance is possible only if God allows it; a person may perhaps have gone so far in apostasy that he cannot be brought back to repentance, although on the whole it seems likely that repentance will be granted by God (cf. 1 Timothy 2:4).

In Titus 3:10f. it is laid down that after a man who is factious or a heretic has been admonished twice he must be 'ignored'; for it is then clear that he is perverted and has become a witting sinner who stands openly condemned. The reference here is probably to excommunication,[9] and the procedure is analogous to that in Matthew 18:15–20.

The difficult passage 1 Timothy 1:20 states that Paul has delivered Hymenaeus and Alexander to Satan, so that they may learn not to blaspheme. Since the purpose of the discipline is remedial (unless the purpose clause is grimly ironical), the view that death as such is meant must be dismissed.[10] We are then left with the same three possibilities as in the case of 1 Corinthians 5:5: excommunication, some physical affliction such as a severe illness, or a combination of the two. The third possibility may well be the right one here, as in 1 Corinthians 5. According to E. F. Scott, 'The Church was regarded as a sanctuary from Satan's power and those expelled from it were thereby given back to Satan, who would now treat them as captured deserters!'[11]

The important point here is that the possibility of restoration and repentance is again present. The purpose of discipline is remedial. One passage has sometimes been thought to refer to the act of restoration of a person who has been under such discipline. In 1 Timothy 5:22 Timothy is urged: 'Do not be hasty in the laying on of hands, nor participate in another man's sins.' There are two possibilities of interpretation here. The text may refer to the ordination of elders, or it may describe an act for the restoration of penitents, and the arguments for the two possibilities are very evenly balanced. The principal argument against the second possibility is that the preceding verses deal specifically with elders, but since the topics treated in this section are very diverse (cf. verse 23!) this point is perhaps not to be pressed.[12] If this second interpretation is correct, then we would have here a further confirmation of the fact that the purpose of discipline was the restoration of the offender to fellowship with the church.

4. THE THEOLOGY OF PERSEVERANCE

From the passages which discuss the possibility and fact of backsliding and apostasy in the Pastoral Epistles we now turn to those passages in which the consequent theological problem of perseverance is raised. We begin with two passages in 2 Timothy 2.

In 2 Timothy 2:8–13 Paul speaks about the power of the gospel and his sufferings for its sake, explaining that he is enduring this for the sake of the elect that they also may obtain salvation.[13] It is this mention of 'endurance' which no doubt leads to the insertion of the 'hymn' which immediately follows and whose purpose is to encourage Timothy to emulate the endurance of Paul:

If we have died with him, we shall also live with him;
if we endure, we shall also reign with him;
if we deny him, he also will deny us;
if we are faithless, he remains faithful —
for he cannot deny himself.

The first two lines of the hymn with their synonymous parallelism speak of the death of the Christian to sin at his conversion and the continual endurance which he must show if he is to share in the heavenly glory of Christ. The third line will then present an antithesis as it echoes the warning of Jesus (Matthew 10:33; Luke 12:9) to His disciples about the danger of denying their Lord under persecution, for He will deny those who deny Him. Since the words are to be spoken by Christians ('If we' is used throughout), the danger is presumably one which they may face.

It is probably best to see in the fourth line a contrast with the previous line. Even if we have periods of unfaithfulness to Christ,[14] nevertheless He remains faithful to us, so that we can turn back to Him and find that He has not changed His attitude to us. The words are thus 'a consolation for a frightened conscience.'[15] ' For Christ's nature is such that He cannot be untrue to it.

We thus have the paradox that Christ must deny those who deny Him, but He remains faithful to His disciples even when they are unfaithful to Him. In other words, the faithfulness of Christ does not preclude the possibility of His disciples being faithless, but it simultaneously indicates His readiness to help those whose faith is weak. The possibility of denial of Christ is admitted, but it is emphasized that Christ continues to care for His disciples and is ready to welcome them back to fellowship if they will respond to His call.

Later in 'the same chapter (2 Timothy 2:19) we find further teaching on this point. Having referred to the way in which Hymenaeus and Philetus were upsetting the faith of some by their empty and heretical notions, Paul goes on to assert that 'God's firm foundation stands, bearing this seal: "The Lord knows those who are his," and, "Let every one who names the name of the Lord depart from iniquity." ' The picture is of an immovable foundation stone (cf. Isaiah' 28:16), which is probably meant to represent the Church (cf. 1 Timothy 3:15) as it still stands firm despite the attacks of heretics.[16] Such a foundation stone could bear an inscription giving the name of the builder and the character of the building.

The first part of the inscription is based on Numbers 16:5 LXX,[17] a text which refers to God's knowledge of those who were His servants over against the rebellious Korah and his company. As Paul uses the text, it expresses the fact that God certainly knows those who belong to Him in the Church. He knows who are true believers and who are not. There is possibly also present the idea that He cares for them and protects them. One must agree with E. F. Scott that 'It is unnecessary to seek a reference to the doctrine of predestination. The meaning is simply that God knows the hearts of men and can discern those who truly believe in Him.'[18] The Church stands firm because God knows His people who are in it.

The idea of a mixed Church is implied here. But there is no

suggestion that the elect are a group predetermined by God with no possibility of addition to or diminution from their number. For the second part of the inscription contains the divine command to those who wish to belong to God: 'Let everyone who names the name of the Lord depart from iniquity.' The thought is probably still based on the story of Korah; judgement fell upon those who were rebellious, but before it fell Moses ordered the rest of the people to depart from the tents of the wicked lest they suffered along with them (Numbers 16:26). The quotation, however, has only one word of contact with Numbers 16:27 ('depart'), and is probably a combination of Isaiah 52:11 and 26:13, already made before its use here. Those who profess to belong to the people of God must withdraw from all manner of evil, thus giving evidence that they do indeed belong to Him. 'God knows . . . His own people, and He knows them to be His when their confession of His name has its outcome in practical goodness.'[19]

This passage, then, emphasizes God's knowledge of those who are truly His in the Church and the responsibility of those who are His people to give evidence of their possession by Him. Such people are not said to be predestinated to a salvation from which they cannot in theory fall away, but are assured of God's gracious care of them as they put their trust in Him.

This is probably the point of 2 Timothy 1:12, where Paul states that he is not ashamed of the gospel and anxious to give up his apostolic calling, for he knows the person in whom he has put his trust and is convinced that He is able to preserve his 'deposit' until the day of judgement.

The older view regarded this deposit as something committed by Paul to God, such as his own salvation (cf. Psalm 31:5; Luke 23:46; Acts 7:59; 1 Peter 4:19),[20] but a more common view in modern times is that the deposit is something which God has committed to Paul, the gospel message or the work of preaching it. This latter is no doubt the meaning of the deposit in 1 Timothy 6:20 and 2 Timothy 1:14, and it would fit the context very suitably. Paul would then be expressing the conviction that, although he himself may suffer and pass on, yet the gospel will continue to be preached and defended against error by the power of God (cf. 2 Timothy 2:9); in this conviction he can then appeal to Timothy to hold fast to the gospel with confidence.[21] Whichever rendering be adopted, the verse as a whole expresses the great confidence of Paul in God to preserve both the gospel and its preachers.

Similarly, he is certain that the Lord who stood by him at his trial and enabled him to preach the word fully will rescue him from every evil and save him for His heavenly kingdom (2 Timothy 4:18; cf. Philippians 1:19; 1 Peter 3:13). Physical deliverance from suffering and martyrdom is hardly indicated; Paul is thinking of being brought safely through the temptations associated with persecution to God's Kingdom. It is notable that he rests his hope entirely upon God at this point; there is no recognition of any virtue in a martyr's death which would guarantee his salvation.

Alongside these passages which indicate the confidence which the Christian should place in God are to be found others which show the need for human perseverance in faith. We may begin by noting 2 Timothy 2:20f., a passage which immediately follows the verse (2 Timothy 2:19) in which the basic relationship of divine knowledge of the Church and human effort to avoid evil was stated. It is now pointed out that any great house contains vessels and utensils of various kinds of material and for various purposes, some noble and others ignoble.[22] The Church, it is implied, contains various kinds of men, and in particular those who are pure and consecrated to God, and those who are contaminated with what is ignoble; the former are ready for any good work, the latter are apparently of no use.[23] It is necessary for men to purify themselves from what is ignoble[24] — youthful passions are singled out for mention — and to aim at righteousness. They must join in with those who call upon the Lord from a pure heart and separate themselves from evil-doers. For the end of evil-doers is dishonour and destruction.

This is but one of several instructions given to Timothy which indicate the steps which must be taken by the man who is anxious to persevere. He must continue faithfully in what he has learned (2 Timothy 3:14), for conformity to the truths of the gospel and the teaching of the Scriptures is essential if men are to be fit for good works and to receive salvation. He must avoid heretical doctrines and myths (1 Timothy 4:7; 6:20f.), train himself in godliness (1 Timothy 4:7f.; 6:11–14), and set his hope upon God (1 Timothy 6:17).

Even Paul himself was not exempt from the need for such effort. He had to fight the good fight and run the race. But he preserved his allegiance to God and therefore could look forward with confidence to receiving his crown (2 Timothy 4:7f.). Similar effort is required from Timothy and his companions (1 Timothy 4:10; 6:12, 19). Christians are to toil and strive because their hope is set on the living God and Saviour. They are to follow the path which will lead them into the full enjoyment of their salvation without being led astray by attachment to other things. It should perhaps be insisted that this is not a matter of salvation by works.[25] For equal stress is laid on the need for sound doctrine (1 Timothy 4:16) as the means of salvation and above all on the need for confidence and hope in God whose grace alone saves men (1 Timothy 1:14–16; 2:5f.; 2 Timothy 1:12–14; 4:18; Titus 2:11–14; 3:4–8).

From all this we may see the great place which is given in the Pastoral Epistles to teaching about perseverance. While God knows those who are His and put their trust in Him, their confidence in God is empty if it is not accompanied by holding fast to the faith and to godly living. Through attachment to false doctrines, to sin and to riches, it is grievously possible for men to fall away from the hope of eternal life and to share in the unbelief of the pagan world. The Church thus becomes a mixed body composed of true believers and false, in which discipline is necessary in order to restrain and restore the sinner as well as to maintain the purity of the Church. Yet despite the fear of apostasy the Church stands firm. Although apostasy is a fearful and real evil in its midst, the man who trusts in God and seeks after godliness will find that God is able and willing to keep him for His heavenly kingdom.

CHAPTER SIX

The Epistle to the Hebrews

The problem with which we are concerned in this study arises especially from a comparison of certain so-called 'warning passages' in the Epistle to the Hebrews (above all Hebrews 6:4–8; 10:26–31; cf. 12:15–17) with other passages in the New Testament, particularly in the writings of Paul and John. The passages in Hebrews appear to teach the possibility of backsliding and apostasy in the Christian life, whilst several passages in Paul and John emphasize more the eternal security of the believer. An investigation of the teaching of Hebrews is consequently of great importance for our study. Historically, also, the Epistle to the Hebrews has played a significant part in the development of the later practice of the Church regarding forgiveness and penitence, and its teaching provided a basis for those who wished to deny the possibility of a second repentance for apostates.[1]

We shall not spend time here in discussing the problem of the destination of Hebrews. On the whole it appears probable that the Epistle was addressed to Jewish Christians and that the danger which threatened them was that of relapse into an apathetic Judaism. The danger was not so much the kind of relapse into legalistic Judaism which Paul feared in Galatia as a drift into an apathy which was content to abide under the shelter of Judaism and thus to lose its grip upon Christ.[2]

A word must, however, be said about the character of salvation and of the Christian life as these are envisaged by the author. The central theme of the Epistle has been variously described as the priesthood of Christ, the nature of Christianity as a world religion and the Christian life as a pilgrimage.[3] There is truth in all these suggestions, but the one which has most to commend it is that the Epistle is concerned with the finality of the gospel.[4] Essentially the Epistle draws a contrast between the old and the new, between the partial and the perfect, and between the earthly and the heavenly. Two ages, two spheres of salvation, two covenants and two ways of atonement are contrasted. Yet the relationship is not purely one of contrast; the same God was acting in both covenants on the same principles and demanding from men the same response of faith. The contrast is not between two opposed entities but between the shadow and the reality or between the type and the antitype. When the perfect has come, it is sin to be content with the imperfect, although the imperfect was a valid way to God before the perfect way was revealed. There can thus be a continuity of pilgrimage, the danger under both covenants being that of failure to adopt the pilgrim way of life through unfaithfulness and lack of perseverance.

The Christian faith is thus presented as God's final revelation of salvation to men. Since the author believes that the Christian faith is the only way of salvation, he elaborates a long argument to show that there can be no question of turning aside from Jesus even to Moses, and he intertwines with it a series of warnings in which he points out, especially by reference to the Old Testament revelation, the dangers facing those who fall back from the faith and obedience which are the conditions of salvation. Only those who hold fast to the end will inherit the promises of God.

For the writer to the Hebrews salvation is primarily, but not exclusively, a future expectation. There is also much stress on the work of Christ in heaven for believers to the almost complete neglect of His work in the believer. Faith, therefore, is more a cable which links believers to heaven than a means by which they are already raised to a heavenly existence (Ephesians 2:6). They live their lives as 'strangers and pilgrims' in this world, looking forward to the coming of Christ to bring them full salvation (Hebrews 9:28). Consequently, the Christian life is more akin to the discipleship of the Synoptic Gospels than to the life in Christ which is the theme of Pauline theology. This does not mean that the Pauline emphasis is completely lacking, but it does imply a different ethos, as a result of which there is more stress than there is in Paul on the need for perseverance and on the danger of apostasy before the goal is attained.

1. THE WARNING PASSAGES

We shall begin our study by discussing the implications of the 'warning passages.' Here it must be borne in mind that these passages are not parentheses in the main run of the argument of the Epistle but form an integral part of a structure in which dogmatic theology and practical exhortations are intricately bound up together.[5] The author himself regarded his Epistle as a 'word of exhortation' (Hebrews 13:22) and the warning passages were indispensable for his purpose. When it is realized that the Epistle is a sermon intended to be read to a congregation,[6] the force of these warning passages becomes even more obvious.

HEBREWS 2:1–4

The first warning passage drives home the lesson of the opening chapter. There it has been shown that Jesus Christ occupies a paramount position, not simply as high priest (Hebrews 1:3b) but above all as the Son of God through whom God's last word to men living in the last days has come. It is of vital importance to pay heed to the Gospel message about Him, and it is fraught with extreme danger to ignore it or to drift away from it, for the result of drifting is worse than the fate of those who disobeyed the law of Moses (cf. Hebrews 10:28).

This warning is addressed to people who have heard the Gospel and responded to it. At no point in the Epistle is it warrantable to assume that the readers originally addressed by the author are not Christians, and in this passage the author distinctly uses the preacher's 'we' and does not exclude himself from his warning. The danger envisaged is neglect of a message which is manifestly true and important. The thought is not so much of the danger which affects a vessel in an unknown sea or river where the rocks and shallows are not signposted, as of the danger of drifting through the culpable negligence of the sailors. The readers know perfectly well that those who disobeyed the old covenant were duly punished, and they have seen that the message of the new covenant has been divinely authenticated by signs and wonders which cannot be gainsaid. The only response that will save them from wilful rebellion and its results is to pay the closest attention to the message and so to avoid slipping away from it.

HEBREWS 3:7–14:13

A second warning passage begins at Hebrews 3:7 after the writer has apparently begun a new section dealing with Christ as high priest. He stresses the faithfulness of Jesus who, like Moses, was set over God's household, but this leads him to the thought that Christians are members of this household only if they display the same faithfulness, and from this there develops a comparison of the Church with Israel and of salvation with the rest promised to the people of God.

Again the writer is addressing Christians — they are 'holy brethren' and 'sharers in Christ' (Hebrews 3:1, 14) — and states that they form the household of God, provided that they hold fast their confidence and pride in their hope (Hebrews 3:6); continuing membership of God's household is conditional upon perseverance. This warning is then developed by an extended quotation from Psalm 95:7–11, in which Israel was warned not to be like its ancestors who tested and provoked God in the wilderness until He swore that they would not enter the promised land. God's people may once again slip away from Him and find that they have exhausted His patience. The particular danger which is in mind is that of having an evil, unbelieving heart which causes men to fall away from God; the deceitfulness or pleasure of sin can harden men's hearts so that although they hear God's word they fail to obey it. They receive the good news, but they become disobedient and distrustful and consequently do not enter into rest (Hebrews 3:12f., 18f.; 4:2, 6, 11). The writer, therefore, appeals to his readers to hold fast to their first faith and not to fall into the backsliding which leads to exclusion from God's promises. Let them hold fast their first confidence to the end. Only so will they enter fully into the 'rest' which is God's destined blessing for His people. Those who are disobedient and faithless will fail to enter into rest. For them, there remains only the possibility of judgement; such is the implication of Hebrews 4:11–13 where it is taught that apparent outward conformity to the faith is useless if it is not accompanied by heart belief.

HEBREWS 5:11–6:20

Already we have seen that the writer envisages the possibility that some of his readers may be slipping from the faith and coming under divine judgement. He believes that unless Christians continue to advance in their faith they are likely to begin to fall back, and therefore he is anxious to press on to the more mature teaching which will strengthen those who are capable of receiving it. The purpose of the present section is accordingly to rouse the readers from intellectual and spiritual lethargy before the doctrine of the high priesthood of Christ is expounded to them. Such teaching will be difficult for them to understand, since they have become sluggish of hearing (Hebrews 5:11), but nevertheless, even if they are really fit only for baby food and not for an adult diet, the writer intends to go on, taking the first principles of Christian doctrine as read (Hebrews 5:12–14).

He therefore states his wish to leave aside the elementary doctrines of Christ and to press on with his readers to maturity (Hebrews 6:1). It should be noted that he does not deny the possibility of further attention to these elementary principles; this would be quite permissible (Hebrews 5:12f.), although it is doubtful whether it would be the best course with this particular audience. In their case further advance is required towards the mature doctrine which is meant to lead those who have received the more elementary doctrine into full maturity of understanding.

The writer now proceeds into a passage that raises many problems. 'This we will do,' he says, 'if God permits' (Hebrews 6:3). Our immediate problem is the nature of what he intended to do, subject to divine permission.[7] The meaning can scarcely be that he intends to return to elementary instruction, and we must therefore look back to verse 1a. This would give as a possible interpretation: 'Let us press on to maturity if God permits. I say "if," for there is a case where it is impossible to go forward, namely when a person completely falls back.'[8] But the weakness of this view is that it makes verses 4ff. refer to the impossibility of going forward whereas in fact they speak of the impossibility of renewal of repentance. It would appear that the writer is rather stating his intention of pressing on to maturity since the only alternative to progress is backsliding and even apostasy. Should a person become apostate, not only is pressing on to maturity out of the question; it is impossible even to relay the foundations. Hence the writer is urging his readers to press on to maturity as the best defence against backsliding, and he does so with the proviso of God's permission, since there may be among his readers those who have in fact slipped so far back that it is impossible for them to profit even by a repetition of elementary doctrine.

In verses 4 to 6 the question of those who cannot be restored to repentance is treated in detail. We must ask first who is thought of as performing the task of restoring backsliders, i.e. what subject is to be understood with the verb 'to restore.' The lapsed themselves can hardly be meant,[9] since otherwise the sentence would surely have been differently worded. There is more to be said for the view that God is meant, since it is He who permits progress (Hebrews 6:3) and acts as judge

(Hebrews 6:7f.). But the lack of an αὐτῷ in the sentence, and the use of 'God's word' rather than 'His word' in verse 5 make this suggestion unlikely. From the context a reference to human teachers, such as the author himself, may be intended, but perhaps it is best to interpret more generally. The point at issue is not the question as to who might be able to restore the lapsed, but the fact that the lapsed cannot be restored. This is important because the passage gives us no right to assert that there may be a special intervention of God to restore those whom men cannot restore.[10]

The second problem that arises is the identity of the people who cannot be restored to repentance. Were they or were they not genuine Christians? The vast majority of scholars accept that they were, but writers of the Calvinistic school such as John Owen have held that they were not members of the elect.[11] A study of the description provided here in a series of four participles suggests conclusively that genuine Christian experience is being described.

The lapsed were 'once enlightened.' The verb no doubt refers to the reception of the light of the gospel in Christian instruction, and it can be used to describe the experience of conversion. The use of 'once' here would be strange if the reference were merely to the reception of a course of instruction and it is probable that the actual acceptance of such teaching, i.e. conversion, is meant.[12]

Second, the lapsed had tasted the heavenly gift. The verb 'to taste' has sometimes the nuance of taking a tiny sip, and is so taken here by Calvin. J. Owen held that there is a difference between tasting and eating and fully digesting.[13] But recent scholars are agreed that the idea emphasized in the verb 'to taste' is that of experiencing the flavour of what is eaten; the amount consumed is not in mind at all.[14] When Christ is said to have tasted death (Hebrews 2:9), there is no suggestion that He got off lightly with a mere taste and no more; rather He experienced its bitter taste to the full. The author's whole point would be nullified here also if he was speaking of 'those who have had a mere glimmer of light and no genuine experience of salvation.'[15] The precise nature of the 'heavenly gift' is uncertain. It is unlikely that the Spirit is meant,[16] in view of the immediately following reference to Him, and it is most probable that salvation is in mind.

We may pause at this point to see what Calvin and Owen make of this phrase. Calvin states that although the context deals with the elect it is the reprobate who are discussed here, and he raises the question whether they can experience partially the gifts of salvation: 'God certainly bestows His Spirit of regeneration only on the elect. . . . But I do not see that this is any reason why He should not touch the reprobate with a taste of His grace, or illumine their minds with some glimmerings of His light, or affect them with some sense of His goodness, or to some extent engrave His Word in their hearts. Otherwise where would be that passing faith which Mark mentions (4:17)? Therefore there is some knowledge in the reprobate, which later vanishes away.'[17] This, however, is surely eisegesis. The contrast between the elect and the reprobate does not occur *expressis verbis* in Hebrews, nor does the idea of regeneration, and it is questionable whether either of them can legitimately be applied to this passage. The reference to Mark 4:17 proves nothing.

John Owen says that the people described here 'had had an experience of the power of the Holy Ghost. . . . Of this state, and of the excellency of it, they had made some trial and had some experience.'[18] He concludes that these people were unbelievers since it is not said that they also ate and digested. But there is nothing here to exclude the possibility that believers are being described, and indeed there is no reason to limit the reference to unbelievers or even to suggest that they are included in the description.

A third characteristic of the lapsed is that they had become sharers in the Holy Spirit.[19] This is surely a mark of the Christian, and there is no place in the New Testament where an experience of the Spirit such as is described here is attributed to people who were not Christians. All that Owen is able to conclude is that 'the Holy Ghost is present with many as unto powerful operations with whom he is not present as to gracious habitations; or, many are made partakers of him in his spiritual gifts who are never made partakers of him in his saving graces, Matthew 7:22, 23.'[20]

Finally, the lapsed had tasted the good Word of God and the powers of the world to come. Here the verb 'to taste' is followed by the accusative case, although in the preceding verse it was followed by the genitive case; C. F. D. Moule holds that the accusative here is 'virtually a substantive clause' giving the meaning 'tasted that the Word of God is good.'[21] The Word of God is the Gospel of salvation, and to taste that it is good means to have a personal experience of its goodness by receiving the benefits which it brings (cf. 1 Peter 2:3). The powers of the world to come are unlikely to be miracles and are rather the blessings of future salvation which are already partially realized (cf. Hebrews 9:11).

This completes the description of the lapsed, and the conclusion is irresistible that real Christians are meant. The most that J. Owen is able to say is 'that the persons here intended are not true and sincere believers in the strict and proper sense of that name, at least they are not described here as such.'[22] He states that there is no mention here of faith. This is surely quite irrelevant, for Christians may well be described and defined from other points of view; for example, in the description there is no mention of faith, in 1 Corinthians 1: 1–10, yet nobody doubts that Christians are there depicted. Owen holds that no characteristic peculiar to believers is described here, but, if our exegesis is sound, what is stated here is characteristic of believers and only of believers. He draws a contrast with the true believers described later in the chapter. But the contrast is surely not so much between two different groups of people as between two possibilities which may affect the same people; thus verses 7f. describe two possibilities which may arise in the same land.

The lapse of these believers is indicated by the verb παραπίπτω which here must mean 'to fall away from the faith.' Although the corresponding noun παράπτωμα means a single lapse or act of sin,[23] and although the passage was later so understood by the Montanists and Novatians, it is difficult to believe that one single act is described here. A total renunciation of Christianity is meant, and the nature of such an act is perhaps intentionally left vague: 'The writer never hints at what his friends might relapse into. Anything that ignored Christ was to him hopeless.'[24]

Two further participles now describe more precisely what is involved in the action of lapsing. To lapse is to crucify Christ to oneself and thus to put Him to ignominy. The verb ἀνασταυρόω probably means 'to crucify *again*,' and implies that the lapsed are metaphorically repeating the act of rejection perpetrated by the Jews at Golgotha.[25] 'Nothing more shameful could be committed than to reject the Saviour.'

It is generally held that these participles are causally related to the main verb 'to renew'; men who fall away cannot be restored because what they are doing is to crucify Christ. The Revised Version margin translates 'the while they crucify . . . ' which would express the fact that repentance is excluded as long as they continue to crucify Christ; on this view the passage would not absolutely exclude the possibility of restoration to repentance, but would simply state that continuance in the state of apostasy will lead to destruction. A. S. Peake, however, asserts that it is a mere commonplace to say that men cannot be renewed while they crucify Christ.[26] The possibility of restoration is, therefore, only doubtfully present in the passage.

We should note, however, that the persons thought of apparently have no desire to repent. The Epistle as a whole is a summons to repentance, and the people indicated here have no desire to be forgiven for their sins; they have rejected the only One who can give them the opportunity of repentance.

Finally, the author uses an analogy to indicate the reasonableness of what he has said. If a field receives rain from heaven and brings forth useful crops it receives a blessing, not merely from men but also from God; but if after receiving rain it produces weeds, it is regarded as reprobate, and is liable to be accursed and will be burned.[27]

Despite this strong language, however, the writer is convinced of better things regarding his readers, and his language now turns to encouragement. They already show signs of things which are connected with salvation, and he longs for them to continue to display such signs. Hence, although he has warned his readers of what their sluggishness may lead to, he is on the whole more confident that they will press on to salvation and he urges them to do so lest through failure to progress they should perhaps fall back into danger.

Having now considered the passage in detail, we may by way of summary glance at the principal views which have been taken of it.

(1) We have seen that the view of J. Calvin and J. Owen that the passage refers to apostasy by unbelievers is untenable.

(2) The view which has commended itself to us is the so-called 'saved and lost' theory. On this view a Christian may be saved and then lost through deliberate apostasy. A number of arguments against this view have recently been suggested by T. Hewitt.[28] He states that there is little support for it elsewhere in the New Testament, but this is a rather sharp begging of the question.[29] He further holds that the theory conflicts with the evidence of other passages which teach the eternal security of those who are in Christ. We shall consider this point in the course of our survey of the New Testament, but for the moment it is enough to note that this argument is not based upon exegesis of the passage itself. Thirdly, Hewitt says that such a possibility of falling away from grace as is suggested in this passage would involve the impossibility of repentance, and this must be for ever. If, however, this is what the passage teaches, then its unacceptability does not prove that the exegesis is false but that the presuppositions of the critic may be questionable. None of these arguments, then, is decisive.

(3) Hewitt himself favours the so-called 'hypothetical' theory. He refers to B. F. Westcott and W. Manson who state, perfectly correctly, that the argument is hypothetical; the writer is describing what would happen if his readers had reached the decisive stage in apostasy, a stage which in reality they had not reached. But Hewitt goes on to argue that the passage means that this is the fate which would overtake a believer if he were to become apostate — a condition which in reality is never fulfilled: 'there is no suggestion in the context that the sin . . . is ever committed by true Christians.'[30] The passage thus describes an imaginary state of affairs; it shows what would happen if the impossibility of a believer turning apostate were to become reality.

This must be pronounced a thoroughly sophistical theory which evades the plain meaning of the passage. There is no evidence whatever that the writer was describing an imaginary danger which could not possibly threaten his readers. What, we may well ask, would be the point of such an empty description? The writer is surely fearful lest this dreadful fate should conceivably overtake his readers, even if he is persuaded of better things concerning them. The element of hypothesis in the passage is not in that the danger is an imaginary one but in that it is only a possibility and not yet a reality in the lives of the readers.

Finally, we must ask whether apostasy is here regarded as unforgivable.[31] It is agreed on all hands that, if the passage does teach the impossibility of repentance, this is only in the case of a definite attitude of apostasy and not in the case of individual sins. C. Spicq has argued that, while with men renewal is impossible, with God it is possible, and cites in favour of this view Mark 10:27 and Romans 8:3.[32] But this view assumes that 'to renew' has a human and not a divine subject (which we have already seen to be doubtful), and it ignores the fact that the supporting texts contain an explicit contrast of the divine and the human which is not even hinted at in this passage. It has often been suggested that repentance is regarded as impossible because the person concerned is unwilling to repent. It is not that God is unwilling to forgive or to provide an opportunity for repentance, but that the apostate himself refuses to repent. 'Ideo impossibile esse dicimus ut tales renoventur quia nolunt renovari. Nam si vellent, esset utique possibile. Quod ergo renovari nequeunt non est excusatio infirmitatis eorum sed culpa voluntatis ipsorum qui malunt veteres perdurare quam re renovare . . . secque fit ut ad poenitentiam redire non valeant.'[33]

No doubt this is true, but we must beware of reading more into the passage in Hebrews than is to be found there.

We seem, indeed, to be compelled to allow that a person may go so far in apostasy that God refuses him the opportunity of repentance.[34] In this passage exegetical honesty demands that this possibility is at least raised. Moreover, it is in conformity with other passages in which we find that there is a limit to the patience of God in urging recalcitrant sinners to return to Him.[35] A stage of 'no return' may be reached by the person who dabbles with apostasy.

HEBREWS 10:19–39

The fourth warning passage applies the lessons which have been taught in the preceding doctrinal section (Hebrews 7:1–10:18) about Jesus Christ as the one true high priest, and consequently the ideas in the previous warning section now reappear in a sharpened form. On the positive side, Christians have every reason to appear before God with confidence, since they have been cleansed in the same way as that in which priests were purified. They must hold fast to their baptismal confession of Christ, and they must encourage each other to good works, especially through their church meetings. All this becomes the more pressing as they see the day approaching, and they must beware lest that day should mean for them judgement instead of salvation (Hebrews 10:19–25; cf. 9:28).

For there is a danger confronting the readers; it is no doubt the same danger as that which has already been described, but now it is described as wilful or deliberate sin, in contrast to the sins which are committed by the 'ignorant and wayward' (Hebrews 5:2; cf. 9:7).[36]

Once again the view has been suggested that the persons who sin in this way are not Christians. T. Hewitt suggests that they are persons who have received Christianity as a formulated system of beliefs but without any personal experience of God in Christ.[37] But, as in chapter 6, the description is clearly of Christian believers. The writer says 'if *we* sin,' and the word 'we' cannot refer to any other group of people than his readers and himself (cf. Hebrews 2:1). Those who are in danger have received the knowledge of the truth (Hebrews 10:26), a phrase which refers to acceptance of the truth at conversion or to renewal of Christian experience after conversion.[38] They are also described as having been enlightened (Hebrews 10:32).

The sin which such people may commit is described as trampling contemptuously upon the Son of God.[39] The sinner regards as common, i.e. unclean, the blood of the covenant by which he was sanctified or cleansed. Covenant blood is mentioned in Hebrews 9:15, and it is often associated with the ideas expressed at the Last Supper (Mark 14:24; l Corinthians 11:25; cf. 1 Peter 1:2). In view of what we know about desecration of the Lord's Supper at Corinth, it is possible that the Supper may be in mind here also.[40] It is more likely, however, that the writer is thinking of some other sin which is so serious that it is equivalent to thinking Christ's blood is unclean, and apostasy under persecution may well be meant.

We note that the blood is described as that by which he has been sanctified, and 'he' in this phrase is undoubtedly the person who commits the sin. T. Hewitt follows J. Owen in supposing that 'sanctification in his case would not be real or internal but merely external, for true sanctification implies separation from sin and dedication to God.'[41] This, however, is to read a subtle meaning into the text which is not there; elsewhere in Hebrews 'sanctified' is a description of true Christians.

The sinner is also said to have insulted God's gracious Spirit. This is a stronger expression than that found in Ephesians 4:30, and implies a wanton insult; it may be right to see here a reference to the blasphemy against the Spirit described in the Gospels.

Such a sin is an act of total rejection of God. The sinner has become an adversary of God (Hebrews 10:27), and he has rejected the very things which were the means of his salvation, the atoning blood of Christ and the Spirit of grace. It is likely that the act being described is recantation of the faith under pressure of persecution. We are told that the readers had previously undergone persecution and suffered public abuse and affliction; they themselves had been plundered of their goods, and some of their friends had suffered bodily ill-treatment and imprisonment. But persecution had apparently not yet led to any cases of martyrdom (Hebrews 10:33f.; 12:4).

In the eyes of the author no punishment can be too severe for such sin. For those who sin deliberately there is no longer a sacrifice for sins, but only the fearful expectation of judgement. Under the Old Testament legislation, no sacrifice was provided for cases of deliberate sin, and this idea is taken over here. Certain sins are so heinous that they come into the category of deliberate sins for which there is no sacrifice. The reason for this is that the sinner is rejecting the one sacrifice which does atone for sin, and there is no alternative means of reconciliation with God. If apostasy to Judaism is in mind, then the author is insisting that the Jewish sacrifices cannot avail for men who reject Christ.

Does this teaching exclude the possibility of such a sinner repenting and being forgiven? Martin Luther held that the writer ignores this point and says nothing for or against it.[42] But the general tenor of the passage, coupled with the teaching of ch. 6, suggests that the impossibility of return may be in the author's mind. In any case, the passage is again a hypothetical one, in the sense that it refers to a danger threatening the readers and not a sin into which they had actually fallen.

HEBREWS 12:12–13:19

The verses with which we are particularly concerned as forming the final warning in Hebrews, 12:15–17, occur in the middle of a passage in which doctrine and exhortation are closely combined. Having stated that what is required of his readers is endurance (Hebrews 10), which is one aspect of faith, the writer is led into a long catalogue of the heroes of faith; with such examples to sustain them, together with that of Jesus Himself, his readers should not grow weary in the face of difficulties and give up the struggle. They should submit to the discipline which they are enduring, and strive after peace with all men and holiness, which is the condition for seeing God (Hebrews 12: 1–14).

Three points are now made, expressive of the dangers which may arise in the Church, and against which precautions must be taken. First, it is possible that somebody may draw back from the grace of God. The reference may be to ceasing to attend the meetings of the Church,[43] and there may be also an allusion to the 'drawing back from the Lord' mentioned in Deuteronomy 29:18, which the author is about to quote. The form of phrase used indicates that an erstwhile believer is meant.[44]

Second, the Church is to see that no malignant member grows up in its midst which will defile the rest of the members. The imagery is drawn from Deuteronomy 29:18 which speaks of the punishment of a man who leads the covenant people of God into idolatry; he is a root bearing bitter and poisonous fruit. Such a person, who imagines himself secure in the stubbornness of his heart and his contempt for God's covenant, will not find pardon; instead, 'the anger of the Lord and his jealousy would smoke against that man, and the curses written in this book would settle upon him, and the Lord would blot out his name from under heaven' (Deuteronomy 29:20). Very probably these thoughts are in the author's mind, although he does not explicitly quote them.

Third, care must be taken lest any immoral or irreligious person arise, like Esau. We note here the close connexion drawn between immorality and idolatry, so that a warning against idolatry can pass over into one against immorality. Probably a literal reference to immorality is meant here, but it is perhaps questionable whether Esau is pictured here as an immoral person and not simply as an irreligious man.[45] In any case, it is his irreligion which is stressed. He refused the birthright which entitled him to the leadership of the family in preference for a meal (Genesis 25:29–34). Later, after he had realized what he had done, and after Jacob had also secured the patriarchal blessing by trickery, he was rejected. His father could not withdraw what he had already given to Jacob. Consequently it is said that 'he found no opportunity to repent.' The phrase is a stereotyped one,[46] and therefore it is unlikely to mean that Esau found no chance of making Isaac change his mind.[47] Rather God did not give Esau the opportunity of changing his mind and gaining what he had forfeited. The author intends his readers to apply this story to themselves and their salvation. Just as Esau was rejected by God, so can they be rejected if they spurn their spiritual birthright.

Finally we are told that all this took place although Esau sought 'it' with tears. Most scholars think that 'it' (αὐτήν) is a reference to the repentance which is the nearer of the two possible antecedents. But it is strange to speak of seeking repentance, and one would have expected the antecedent to be 'opportunity' in this case (which would require the form αὐτόν) It is preferable, therefore, to regard 'the blessing' as the antecedent, and this fits in well with the narrative in Genesis 27:34–38. Esau's tears were of no avail in securing the blessing which he had forfeited.[48] The implication is that it is possible for a man to go so far in sin that he misses the blessing which he might once have received; God may not permit him an opportunity of repentance. Not all sinners go this far; but an apostate may well find that he has stretched the mercy of God to its limit, so that he cannot return.

This warning is reinforced in the following verses. The writer proceeds to compare the fearsome nature of the old covenant and the giving of the law at Sinai with the graciousness of the new covenant associated with the heavenly mountain and city. If men feared to transgress against the old covenant and did not escape punishment under it, how much worse will it be for them to transgress against the new covenant of grace and to ignore the gracious work of God which precedes His judgement; for on that day all that is not from God will pass away, and only the members of God's kingdom will abide. Christians, therefore, should serve and obey God with fear; otherwise they may find that He is a consuming fire to them.

In all this it is not stated at what point a person crosses the limit so that he can no longer find an opportunity of repentance. It is sufficient to know that there *is* a limit which men may cross. The only way to avoid crossing it is by pressing on instead of falling back.

SUMMARY

We may sum up our discussion of these five passages by stating that they warn the readers of the Epistle against the danger of failing to press on towards Christian maturity. Undoubtedly the writer felt that his readers were not making the progress expected of them. He therefore pointed out the danger confronting them. Instead of going forward they were in danger of going back and even of failing to pay attention to the gospel. Such an attitude, if persisted in, could lead to total apostasy from the faith, and this might well be the case if the readers found themselves facing persecution more severe than that which had already been their lot.

In order to counteract this possibility the writer employed various measures. He pointed out the punishments which overtook apostates in the Old Testament. He emphasized that God would not act any differently under the new covenant. In fact it was far worse to commit apostasy under the new covenant, since the message of grace and salvation was so much clearer in it than in the old covenant. Apostasy under the new covenant was an act of witting, deliberate sin, in which Christ was openly put to shame. For a person who persisted in that attitude there could be no forgiveness. Having set his face against Christ, he would find that the opportunity of repentance was taken from him.

The author clearly believed that Christians could fall into this plight. But he never states how it could be determined whether a person had actually gone this far and reached the point of no return. It was enough to warn against a danger sufficiently dreadful for his readers to flee from it without inquiring how near they might come to it and escape unscathed.

2. THE ANTIDOTE TO APOSTASY

The teaching of Hebrews is by no means negative, and we must now consider what the author has to say by way of encouragement to his readers and whether any of his teaching implies their eternal security and freedom from the possibility of apostasy. We should be wrong to think that the danger confronting Christians is the primary theme of the author. His main purpose is to encourage his readers to enter into a mature Christian experience, and having reminded them of the good progress which they have made in the past (Hebrews 6:9–12; 10:32–4) he concentrates on urging them to continue in the same manner. This basic thought is expressed in a number of ways, three of which we now note.

First, the writer recalls his readers to the original message of the gospel which they had heard. In Hebrews 2:1–4 the readers are warned against neglecting the message which was so strongly authenticated to them; the only cure for drifting is to cleave to the message which they heard. Put otherwise, they must hold fast to their confidence and pride in their hope, and hold their first confidence firm to the end (Hebrews 3:6, 14). Let them hold fast to their confession (Hebrews 4:14), and not throw away their confidence, but rather have faith and keep their souls (Hebrews 10:35–9). Such confidence will not be misplaced, since the One who made promises to them is faithful to keep His word (Hebrews 10:23).

This stress on the maintenance of the confession of faith does not mean that faith is regarded simply as an intellectual concept. Even at this stage it should be obvious that ideas of trust and obedience are present. Faith is rather the most inclusive term used in Hebrews to describe the attitude of the Christian to God. It is the firm trust in the unseen God which sustains the pilgrim, and rests on the certainties that Jesus has entered heaven as our forerunner and that God will fulfil His promises to us (Hebrews 6:18–20). It is both the evidence of the reality of the unseen world and the conviction that the blessing of that unseen world will be realized by the Christian. This reflects the apocalyptic outlook of Hebrews which thinks of the coming aeon as a future reality and as a hidden world contemporaneous with and 'above' the present world in which pilgrims live.[49] Hence the idea of faith contains a strong element of hope regarding the future as well as the possibility of access to God's throne of grace in prayer here and now. It finds expression in obedience and the resolute setting aside of sin. It is above all a persistent attitude which is triumphant over the various temptations to disbelief and takes on the character of endurance and zeal.

In addition to adherence to the message of salvation and a living faith, the writer calls his readers to assist each other by mutual exhortation on their pilgrim journey. They are to exhort each other, lest any of them be hardened by the deceitfulness of sin (Hebrews 3:13), and are to stir each other up to love and good works in their assemblings together (Hebrews 10:24f.; cf. 12:12f.). The leaders of the community are to keep watch over the souls of the members, as men who will one day have to give an account of their stewardship. They are to be given obedience, and the pilgrims are to profit by following their good example (Hebrews 13:17).

These may be described as the human requirements for perseverance. In outlining them we have seen that the believer is not striving on his own but has the help of God both directly and also through the work of his fellow Christians. We must now pay closer attention to the divine side in perseverance and see in what ways God enables His people to persevere in their faith.

3. THE WORK OF GOD IN THE BELIEVER

ELECTION AND PREDESTINATION

Predestination does not play any great part in the thought of Hebrews, except in regard to the work of Christ. Hebrews 11:40 speaks of God having Christians in mind even during the period of the old covenant and foreseeing something better for them. But the idea here is not that of the predestination of particular people to salvation, but rather of the fulfilment of God's promises in due time; He wishes all His people together to receive the fulfilment of His promises. The key word in Hebrews is not predestination but promise. Such promises may be pretemporal, but their fulfilment depends in each case upon the faith and obedience of the recipients (Hebrews 4:2; 6:11f.; 10:36).

The idea of election is perhaps to be found in the reference to the assembly of the firstborn who are enrolled in heaven (Hebrews 12:23). The firstborn are not angels; the use of the word is perhaps prompted by the reference to Esau's birthright, and it means men who are numbered as God's sons, just as Israel was (Exodus 4:22).[50] Moreover, men at present on earth are certainly included in the expression; those now dead are presumably spoken of under the name of 'the spirits of just men made perfect' (though this phrase might refer more specifically to believers of pre-Christian days). We have, then, a reference to men whose names are written in the book of life. Does this, however, imply that they are predestined to salvation?[51] It is conceivable that a pre-temporal listing of God's people is meant,[52] but this is not the obvious meaning of this passage, and it may be wiser simply to see an allusion to Psalm 87:5f.: 'And of Zion it shall be said, "This one and that one were born in her"; for the Most High himself will establish her. The Lord records as he registers the peoples, "This one was born there." '[53] On this view the passage speaks of the heavenly burgess roll of the citizens of Zion, and it is not excluded that a man's birthright may be surrendered, just as Esau surrendered his. This passage, then, does not certainly refer to an irrevocable election. Rather, the election of God's people is to be seen in their behaviour as God's children, submitting to His discipline and overcoming the difficulties and temptations which are the lot of pilgrims.

THE FAITHFULNESS OF GOD

If Hebrews is lacking in teaching about election and the grace of God, it is nevertheless full of reference to the divine promises of God's care for His people. We may cite as a characteristic example Hebrews 13:15f. where the promise 'I will never leave you nor forsake you (Deuteronomy 31:6, 8) is offered to Christians to inculcate in them a spirit of contentment with what they possess; there is no need for them to be greedy for earthly possessions because God Himself looks after them. They can therefore say confidently, 'The Lord is my helper, I will not be afraid; what can man do to me?' (Hebrews 13:6, quoting Psalm 118:6, LXX). Human faith is possible only because of divine faithfulness.

Faith, then, is not to be regarded as a human achievement through the exercise of human willpower. According to E. Käsemann, the 'conviction' in Hebrews 11:1 is in some sense an objective datum; faith arises when a man lets himself be convinced by God and so attains to a certainty which is objectively grounded and transcends all human possibilities in its reliability.[54] Similarly, confidence and rejoicing are to be regarded as divine gifts, so that they contain both subjective and objective aspects.[55] It is God who gives men the possibility of making their confession of faith with joy and confidence.

TEMPTATION AND THE WORK OF CHRIST

In Hebrews 2:18 we are told that Jesus, having Himself been tempted, is able to help those who are tempted. What is the nature of this help?[56] According to B. F. Westcott, the one who has wrought propitiation must enter into the experience of the sinner in order that he may support him in his temptation; this Christ does by removing 'the barrier of sin which checks the outflow of God's love to the sinner' and at once bringing 'help to the tempted by restoring in them the full sense of filial dependence.'[57] In other words, the help offered is that of Christ's continual propitiation for sin.

This idea seems rather unlikely, and it is more probable that the thought is of Christ's work of intercession. We may compare Hebrews 4:14–16 where the fact of our having a sympathetic high priest means that we can draw near to God's throne with confidence to receive mercy and grace in time of need. Again, in Hebrews 7:25 it is said that Christ always lives to make intercession to God for those who draw near to God through Him. At the same time, there may well be present the thought of the example of Christ as a means of strengthening those who consider it (cf. Hebrews 12:3).

Through Christ, then, Christians can call upon God for help in time of need and be certain of an answer to their prayer. The thought is summed up in the benediction or doxology which concludes the major part of the Epistle (Hebrews 13:20f.); this may well reflect traditional Christian language, but it admirably sums up what the author has been trying to say. God will equip men to do His will by working in them what pleases Him, and Jesus will care for them as a shepherd tends his sheep. There is divine help to enable Christians to progress in obedience and hence to save them from falling back.

THE PIONEER AND PERFECTER OF FAITH

In Hebrews 12:2 Jesus is described as the pioneer (ἀρχηγός) and perfecter (τελειωτής) of faith. The word 'pioneer' may mean 'originator, founder' (cf. 5:10 where He is the cause of salvation) or one who begins a series and thus supplies an impetus' (cf. 6:20, where He is the forerunner of Christians into heaven).[58] This second meaning is probably the right one in

Hebrews 12:2, where Jesus is the originator of faith in the sense that He Himself displayed it in His steadfast endurance of sufferings (Hebrews 12:3) and thus made open the way of faith to men. Similarly, in Hebrews 2:10 He is said to be the originator of salvation for His people by first entering into heaven whither they also must follow Him. There is no suggestion of His needing to be redeemed first Himself before He could redeem others; rather, by His victorious entrance into heaven He has opened up the way for others to follow Him.

We must digress slightly at this point to note that the idea which we have just rejected is taken up by E. Käsemann in connexion with the idea of perfection.[59] Christ, who in Hebrews 12:2 is said to be the perfecter of faith, is described as being Himself perfected in Hebrews 2:10 (cf. 5:9). For Käsemann this means that the redeemer must first be redeemed himself before he can lead others to heaven. This is an idea familiar to us from the gnostic myth of the redeemer. But its influence here is unquestionably to be rejected. It imports alien ideas into the text, since there has been no hint previously that the author's thought is moving in gnostic circles; it also emphasizes too much the idea of perfection at the expense of the idea of suffering which is clearly the dominant idea in the passage.[60] The passage refers rather to the moral and cultic perfection of Christ as a man who was perfectly obedient to God (cf. 5:10; 7:26–8) and therefore fit to be a high priest. He was perfected through His experiences of suffering and death in which He learned obedience, and the writer draws attention to His descent in order to share the experiences of men without sinning rather than to His ascent.[61]

It is this perfection which Christ gives to believers. By His one sacrifice He has perfected for all time those who are being sanctified (Hebrews 10:14).[62] He bestows upon men His own status as an obedient Son of God, and with Him they receive glory from the God whose purpose is to bring many sons to glory.

This brings us back to Hebrews 12:2 where Christ is the perfecter of faith as well as its originator. This may mean simply that in Him faith is seen to perfection; He is the first and the last, so far as faith is concerned.[63] But in view of the teaching just considered which describes Jesus as perfecting men (Hebrews 10:14; cf. 11:40; 12:23), it may also mean that He is the One who perfects their faith. From start to finish faith is dependent upon Christ and His work. This, however, should not be pressed to mean that faith is created and brought to perfection in men through an inward work of Christ in them.

Christ's work in Hebrews is essentially that of providing a sacrifice and intercession for men.[64]

The conclusion to be drawn is that Jesus is the supreme example of faith who leads His people into a like faith. He has perfected believers by His sacrifice for them, but this does not preclude the possibilities of progress and of retrogression. We have found that great provision has been made by God in Christ for believers in order that they may have a strong faith and attain to perfection; but we have not found evidence of a divine work in the hearts of men which absolutely precludes the possibility of apostasy.

The teaching of Hebrews is thus self-consistent when it warns those who have received the promises of God and put their faith in Him against the possibility of falling from their faith. There is no reason why they must fall from their faith, even under hardship and persecution, for God has provided amply for their salvation, but at the same time they must continually see to it that they progress towards Christian maturity lest through indifference they drift away from the faith and end up in the fearful plight of the apostate. If in Hebrews the possibility of apostasy is depicted more radically than elsewhere in the New Testament, it is equally true that this Epistle is second to none in its emphasis upon the faithfulness of God who will perfect His people as they hold fast their confidence in Him to the end.

CHAPTER SEVEN

The Catholic Epistles

1. THE EPISTLE OF JAMES

For too long the Epistle of James has been regarded as standing on the fringe of the canon and dismissed as unimportant. The recognition that it contains in written form the kind of teaching which the early Church was accustomed to give to catechumens and is one of the earliest specimens of a Christian *didache* which we possess may well lead to a fresh evaluation of it.[1] But while its main interest is in ethics and it is not a theological treatise, we should not make the mistake of M. Dibelius[2] and say that it has no theology. James has in fact a theology of the Christian life and states the need for progress in it with great clarity. He teaches that God gives good gifts to men (James 1:17), the first of which is the new birth through the word of truth by which Christians become the first fruits of God's creatures (James 1:18).[3] In this way the Christian begins a new life which must be sustained by continual reception of the implanted word which is able to save his soul (James 1:21) and of the grace of God which is given abundantly to those who seek it in humility (James 4:5f.).[4] Against this background of doctrine the ethical teaching of James falls into its proper place; it is not an exhortation to good works in the Jewish sense but an injunction to express in daily living the life of God in the soul of the believer. James, therefore, discusses in detail the sins and failings which are incompatible with Christian faith and the heavenly qualities which are its true expression. He emphasizes that the Christian life is lived in a state of tension owing to the continual presence of trials and temptations, but he assures his readers that they may live victoriously by submitting to God and resisting the devil (James 4:7). Temptation indeed is to be regarded as a means of attaining to Christian perfection, since it demands the development of faithfulness and endurance and leads to a crown of life (James 1:2–4, 12). An Epistle which contains such a wealth of teaching is emphatically no 'Epistle of straw.'

It will be apparent that James views the Christian life in an optimistic fashion. Temptation is the pathway to perfection of character and to heavenly glory. He both expects his readers to persevere and exhorts them to do so.[5] At the same time he is fully aware of the dangers of sin, and points out the danger confronting those who become friends of the world: they become enemies of God (James 4:4). The Epistle is a constant challenge to self-examination, a warning against hearing God's word and not doing it.

One passage in particular claims our more detailed attention. What men ought to do when they are suffering, cheerful or ill is indicated in James 5:13–15. The third category interests us. A person who is sick is to call for the elders of the church who will pray over him and anoint him with oil. Their believing prayer will cure the sick man; the Lord will raise him up to health, and, if he has committed any sins, they will be forgiven. The form of words here makes it clear that not all sickness is to be regarded as due to sin and therefore as a divine chastisement (cf. John 9:1–3), but there may be cases where this is so and his healing will then be a token of forgiveness; we may perhaps compare the way in which Jesus both forgave and healed the paralytic (Mark 2:1–12). What happens, however, if the sick man does not call the elders and seek their prayers? May it be that a failure to admit the possibility of sin and to seek healing from the Lord will lead to death? We would then have a situation in some respects similar to that in 1 Corinthians 5.

This suggestion is perhaps confirmed by what follows. In verse 16 the readers are counselled to confess their sins to each other and to pray for each other in order that they may be healed. As it stands, this verse takes up the teaching of the preceding verses and generalizes it. It will then refer to physical healing, and the command to 'confess your sins' will be addressed to the sick, and 'pray for one another' to those who are well.[6]

M. Dibelius has objected to this interpretation on the ground that verse 15 speaks of prayer by the elders leading to a miraculous cure while verse 16 speaks of confession of sin and prayer by any member of the community. He concludes that two originally independent sayings have been brought together and linked by the editorial insertion of 'that you may be healed' in verse 16.[7] Other commentators who have felt this same set of difficulties have suggested that 'heal' must be taken in the broader sense of healing both of body and soul.[8]

It is doubtful whether the editorial theory of Dibelius is necessary. It is questionable whether verse 15 speaks of a miraculous cure, and there is no suggestion that confession of sin is excluded there. Even the generalizing 'one another' in verse 16 need not be regarded as inconsistent with the mention of the elders in particular in verse 15; one would naturally seek them out first of all. Probably verse 16 begins a new section in which the teaching of the previous verses is generalized, and the thought is more of the spiritual health of the church; this is supported by the fact that the following verses take up the question of backsliding. For, although the prayers of the church can bring healing to those who are under chastisement (James 5:16b–18), cases can be imagined in which men sin and do not bother to seek forgiveness by confession of their sin.

It is such people that James has in mind in his closing exhortation (James 5:19f.). A brother may wander from the truth into sin and error.[9] In this case it is the duty of his Christian brother to bring him back. Such an act, if successful, is regarded as 'saving his soul from death and covering a multitude of sins.' The former of these results shows that the backslider was in danger of eternal condemnation at God's judgement; for something more than a physical penalty is surely meant.[10] If a backslider does not confess his sin and repent, he becomes a witting sinner and is in danger of loss of salvation.[11]

The passage as a whole teaches that sickness should lead a person to ask himself whether he is being warned about unconfessed sin, although not all sickness is due to sin. Where a person falls into sin and does not repent of his own accord his Christian brothers have the duty of seeking to save him from condemnation; it is not stated whether or not sickness is present in this case, the emphasis being on the great worth of the act performed by the pastor of souls. Above all, stress is laid on the value of prayer; this means that the scales are definitely weighted in favour of the sinner persevering, although he cannot persevere unless he himself confesses his sin. One may grant that the danger described here is an exceptional one, but even so it is necessary to place alongside the generally optimistic outlook of James his stress on the need to win back believers who are in eternal danger as a result of backsliding.

2. THE FIRST EPISTLE TO PETER

If the optimism of James is of a somewhat sober cast, that of First Peter is clothed in cheerfulness and joy, and the Epistle has been well named 'The Epistle of Hope.' It lays considerable emphasis upon the great power and grace of God in caring for His people even in the midst of persecution. Thus it is addressed to those who are the elect sojourners of the dispersion, elect according to God's foreknowledge (1 Peter 1:lf.) These words imply that God's gracious choice rested upon readers before they were aware of it, His aim being to produce in them obedience and consecration. Consequently, they can be described as an elect nation, called as they were by God out of darkness into light (1 Peter 2:9). Not only did God call them; He also begat them to a new life, not by a corruptible seed, but by an incorruptible seed, the living and abiding word of God(1 Peter 1:23).[12] On the human side, these divine benefits are received by faith, but such faith is 'by' Christ (1 Peter 1:21; cf. Acts 3:16), i.e. it is because of the divine revelation and act of salvation in Christ that the readers have come to belief in God.

God's elect are also kept by Him, guarded by His power through faith for future salvation (1 Peter 1:5). Peter holds together the two thoughts that God succours believers during times of testing and persecution and that testing is a trial for faith in order that its proved excellence may be manifest at the parousia (1 Peter 1:6–9). After the readers have suffered for a little while, God, who called them to eternal glory, will restore, establish, strengthen and settle them, and in view of this hope they should commit themselves to the care of their faithful Creator (1 Peter 5:10; 4:19).

Like the author of Hebrews, Peter sees the Church as God's pilgrim people, subject to the temptations which beset pilgrims. Their salvation is not yet fully realized, and they must live by hope. This means that we must ask whether Peter has any doubts about his readers failing to complete their pilgrimage.

There is evidence to show that Peter was fully conscious of the tension in which Christians live. The number of warnings against the possibility of suffering for wrong-doing probably indicates that this was a real danger for some of the readers (1 Peter 2:20; 3:16f.; 4:3f.; 15).[13] Similarly, persecution was a very real danger, although it is uncertain how far it was imminent for the readers. Such temptations are means of proving the genuineness of faith and serve as a criterion of true and false Christian profession. According to 1 Peter 4:17 the suffering of Christians shows the beginning of divine judgement from the house of God. The allusion is to Ezekiel 9:6 where God's judgement of sinful Jerusalem starts from the temple which was full of sinful practices. Peter's point would appear to be that the purifying and purging work of God will now begin with His people, and what they undergo will be light in comparison with the fate of the ungodly. Through suffering faith is tested.

At the same time, persecution and temptation are the work of the devil who goes about seeking his prey (1 Peter 5:8); 'The danger in mind here is probably that of denying the faith, of being pressed or frightened into ceasing to confess Christ.'[14] Consequently, we are probably justified in agreeing that for Peter election did not necessarily guarantee final salvation.[15] As in the rest of the New Testament Christians are urged to make their election sure; they must stand fast in the grace of God (1 Peter 5:12), resist the devil, be strong in the faith, and be watchful and sober (1 Peter 5:8f.). Let them trust in the promise of the grace which will come to them at the revelation of Christ (1 Peter 1:13) and commit themselves to God's care. The true attitude to suffering is to see that they are sharing in the sufferings of Christ and to know that in their suffering the Spirit is upon them (1 Peter 2:21; 3:17f.; 4:13f.). Seen in this light suffering cannot separate Christians from God, since it really binds them to Him.

First Peter thus gives us one of the most confident approaches to our problem in the New Testament. It does not deny the fact of temptation to give up the faith, but it stresses the possibility of continued perseverance through the recognition that suffering is part of the Christian's lot. Throughout the Epistle there is evidence of a robust faith which takes the realities of sin and salvation with the utmost seriousness and proclaims the possibility of victory through divine grace.

3. THE EPISTLE OF JUDE

The brief letter of Jude was written especially to warn its readers against the danger of false teaching; it points out the fate reserved for the sinful and rebellious and encourages the faithful to continue to build themselves up in the faith in dependence upon the love and power of God. Our task is to discover whether the false teachers whom Jude opposes are to be regarded as lapsed Christians; whether Jude considered it possible for believers to be led into giving up the faith; and what antidotes to apostasy are suggested by him.[16]

THE FALSE TEACHERS

The false teachers attacked by Jude are shown to have been members of the Church, at least outwardly, by their attendance at its love-feasts (Jude 12); they had not yet separated themselves from the Church or formed their own sect. Whether they had lapsed from a faith which they once held is somewhat uncertain. The fact that they are said to have been predestined to judgement (Jude 4) simply means that God's purpose for wicked men is a judgement from which they will not escape[17] and the writer probably has in mind such prophecies of the rise and judgement of false teachers as he refers to in verses 17f. The false teachers are said to have made their way into the Church by stealth; they were not interested in the gospel of the grace of God as a source of power to live holy lives but made it an excuse for licentiousness. Outwardly they may have professed Christ as Lord and Master, but their manner of life denied this profession (Jude 4).[18] They may perhaps have claimed to possess the Spirit, but in fact they were devoid of His presence and were worldly (ψυχικοί) men (Jude 19).

In verses 5–7 and 11 the parallel cases quoted from the Old Testament — the Israelites in the wilderness, the fallen angels, Balaam and Korah — could be regarded as examples of lapse from a righteousness once held, and it could then be suggested that the purpose of the examples is to warn the false teachers about the judgement which faces those who lapse from the faith; this would imply that the false teachers were regarded as lapsed believers. In support of this interpretation we could adduce the fact that the Israelites who fell were those who had been 'saved' out of the land of Egypt; there would then be a close parallel with 1 Corinthians 10:1–13, possibly with a warning against trusting in the efficacy of sacraments for salvation.

According to J. Moffatt, however, 'The direct warning is for the readers; people may *once* be saved and yet fall away *subsequently* into an unbelief which ruins them, as will be the case with you if you listen to these insidious creatures.'[19] The weakness of this attempt to make the primary purpose of the verses a warning to the readers is that it ignores the connexion between verses 5–7 and 8. It is, therefore, preferable to accept the first interpretation.

In verse 12 Jude goes on to describe the teachers as 'fruitless trees in late autumn, twice dead, uprooted.' The expression is strange, and probably Jude thinks of the trees as being doubly dead in that they have borne no fruit and have been uprooted.[20]

Two possibilities arise in applying the metaphor to the false teachers. The first is that there is a reference to the forthcoming judgement or 'second death' (Revelation 21:8, cf. Matthew 3:10; 7:19; 15:13; John 15:6 for the metaphor). This is unlikely, for the contrast in Revelation 21:8 is between physical and spiritual death, whereas there is no thought of physical death here; moreover, the use of aorist participles suggests that the false teachers are already twice dead. We therefore prefer the second possibility, namely that falling back into immorality after conversion is meant. Even so, one must ask whether the conversion was a genuine one. The false teachers may have been dead in sin before they joined the Church and remained dead because they never gave up their sin.[21]

On the basis of this evidence it is impossible to come to a firm conclusion about the false teachers. The view that they may have been lapsed believers cannot be dismissed out of hand, especially as this would appear to be true of the heretics described in 2 Peter, but it is also possible that they were outsiders who had made their way into the Church under false pretences.

THE POSSIBILITY OF APOSTASY

While Jude's stated aim is to urge his readers to defend the faith against its perversions (Jude 3), it is also part of his purpose to warn them against falling into the errors of the false teachers. We have already seen that verses 5–7 may be directed to the readers as well as to the false teachers, and Jude's final appeal to the faithful to build themselves up (Jude 20f.) implies that there is a danger that they may fail to do so, with consequent spiritual disaster.

Particular attention must be paid to verses 22f. which describe the treatment of those who do lapse from the faith. The passage is uncertain textually. The rendering in the *textus receptus*, followed in the AV, has no claims to being original, and there remain two main possibilities. First, there is a long text giving three types of treatment, which reads in the RV as follows: 'And on some have mercy, who are in doubt; and some save, snatching them out of the fire; and on some have mercy with fear; hating even the garment spotted by the flesh!'[22] While this text has the triadic structure which is characteristic of Jude,[23] it is open to the objection that it has the same verb in both the first and the third clauses, a fact which makes it difficult to extract a suitable meaning from it.[24]

Second, there is a short text read by a small number of

witnesses: 'Snatch some out of the fire; but have mercy on those who are in doubt with fear, hating even the garment spotted by the flesh.' This text, which was earlier accepted by C. Bigg, A. Souter, and J. Moffatt, has now been attested by the Bodmer Papyrus of Jude, and its claims to originality have been strongly defended by J. N. Birdsall, who finds it easier to explain the development of the other readings from it than vice-versa.[25] Dr. Birdsall would translate διακρινομένους in this text as 'those who are under judgement' and holds that the misinterpretation of this participle to mean 'those who are in doubt' contributed to the development of the other textual forms.

If we adopt the longer text, we may interpret the three groups of people mentioned as follows. The first group will be the waverers, Christians who have been led into doubt by the false teachers; they are to be treated with pity (or, with the alternative reading, convinced) so that they may continue in the truth without falling away. The second group, those who are to be snatched out of the fire, will be those who have succumbed to the false teaching but may be saved before it is too late. The third group will be the false teachers themselves, those upon whom the Church is 'to have mercy' with fear (lest it be defiled by contact with them) and hatred for their immoral ways (cf. Zechariah 3:4).

If we adopt the shorter text, only two groups are mentioned. The first group will correspond to the second in the longer text, i.e. those who had succumbed to the false teaching and were in dire peril. The identity of the second group will depend on the meaning assigned to ἐλεᾶτε and to διακρινομένους.

Discussions of ἐλεᾶτε have usually been on the basis of the long text. According to J. B. Mayor, the word refers in the third clause to 'trembling compassion, expressing itself no doubt in prayer, but apparently shrinking from personal communication with the terrible infection of evil.'[26] But there is no clear hint of this interpretation in the text, and H. Windisch comments that this idea would have been expressed differently.[27] He himself holds that the idea of showing mercy is psychologically inappropriate and impossible in practice. Since the attestation of ἐλέγχετε is weak, resort has been made to conjectural emendation, the suggestions being either that of G. Wohlenberg, ἐλάσατε (from ἐλαύνω), or ἐκβάλετε, either verb meaning 'to excommunicate.'[28] Neither proposal, however, is very convincing.

Windisch's objection to ἐλεᾶτε is based on the fact that the third clause refers to the worst offenders. This objection would also apply to the second clause in the shorter text if we adopt

Dr. Birdsall's interpretation of διακρινομένους. But if we adopt the shorter text and give διακρινομένους its traditional meaning, then ἐλεᾶτε would give an acceptable meaning. On this view the first clause would refer to those who had succumbed deeply to the false teaching, and the second to those who were in an attitude of doubt and needed to be led gently away from possible danger. The principal objection to this interpretation is that the following words, 'with fear, hating even the garment spotted by the flesh,' would go more fitly with the direction about the severe offenders than with the one about the lesser offenders; but this objection may be overcome if we are allowed to take these words with both of the preceding clauses. The fact that we are thus able to gain an acceptable meaning for the verses in this way is an argument in favour of the shorter text.

Whichever reading be adopted, however, the teaching of Jude includes directions regarding the reclamation of those who needed to be snatched from the fire because they were in grave danger. The force of Jude's direction indicates that here he has in mind those whose spiritual life was in danger because of their acceptance of false doctrine.

THE ANTIDOTES TO APOSTASY

Although Jude envisages the possibility of apostasy as a serious threat to the spiritual life of his readers, he by no means believes that it is a danger into which Christians must necessarily fall, particularly if they take care to continue in the faith with all the help that God gives to them.

(1) He warns the Church against the possibility of false teaching taking them by surprise (Jude 16–19). No doubt it is easier psychologically to resist the enemy whom we know rather than the enemy who works in the dark against us (cf. 1 Peter 4:12). But the fact that Jude appeals to apostolic teaching predicting the rise of apostasy suggests that he attaches more importance to the need to abide by the apostolic tradition than to this psychological consideration. The simplest antidote to false teaching is to abide by the apostolic tradition.

(2) This is reinforced by Jude's encouragement to his readers to build themselves up on their most holy faith (Jude 20). 'Faith' is probably to be taken here as meaning 'object of belief,' although the addition of 'your' indicates that the subjective attitude of accepting this object of belief is also included. It has been suggested that ἑαυτούς should be translated here as a reciprocal pronoun giving the sense: 'build each other up on the

basis of the faith.'[29] This is an attractive suggestion, and it would give a fitting prelude to the advice in the following verses.

(3) The readers are also exhorted to pray in the Holy Spirit (Jude 20b). We are to think here of guidance by the Spirit in prayer so that the person prays in accordance with the will of God. Although the fact of guidance by the Spirit is well attested (e.g. Romans 8:14), this activity is not specifically linked to prayer. He appears as an intercessor for believers in Romans 8:26f. We may, therefore, have to seek the meaning of this passage in the idea of life in the Spirit, so that prayer is regarded as an activity which takes place in the realm of the Spirit (cf. John 4:23). There may be a contrast with the false teachers who do not possess the Spirit (Jude 19).

(4) Through obedience to the two previous precepts, the readers are to keep themselves in the love of God (Jude 21). Although the readers are said to be kept by (or 'for') Jesus Christ (Jude 2), they must also keep themselves in the love of God, i.e. in the love which God shows; those who wander away from the faith can fall away from the sphere of divine love and protection.

(5) As they thus keep themselves in the sphere of divine love the readers will receive the mercy of Jesus Christ which leads to eternal life. Here the vocabulary undoubtedly suggests looking forward to the parousia when Christ will display His mercy and grant eternal life to believers.[30] Once again, therefore, the need for perseverance is inculcated.

(6) Finally, in the concluding ascription of glory (Jude 24f.) all the emphasis is placed upon the keeping power of God. He is able to guard believers so that they do not stumble,[31] and to cause them to stand blameless before His glorious presence on the day when those who have fallen short of His glory will be condemned. Thus the end of the Epistle stresses the fact of God's activity in preserving believers from falling in the same way as the beginning where the readers are addressed as those who are called, loved, and kept by God for Jesus Christ.

Perseverance accordingly is closely linked with the activity of God in believers. Edification takes place by means of faith, which is a gift of God; prayer is made in the Spirit; the readers are to remain in the love of God and await the mercy of Christ; and ultimately it is God who keeps them from falling. At the same time, perseverance depends upon specific *acts* of Christian discipline and devotion; a person who bestirs himself to do these things will not fall. Here is a paradox which does not admit of closer explanation; to speak of synergism is not to elucidate but simply to express the paradox. We have a situation whose limits may be charted, but whose depths cannot be plumbed.

This short book, then, is full of rich teaching on the nature of the Christian life. It is written to the faithful members of the Church and speaks warmly of the love of God which sustains them. By following the author's earnest advice they would be able to withstand the evil propaganda of the false teachers who had come into their midst and to rescue those who were already succumbing to the influence of false doctrine before it was too late.

4. THE SECOND EPISTLE OF PETER

The Second Epistle of Peter bears a close family relationship to Jude. That there is some literary dependence between them cannot be doubted, and it is usually thought that the dependence is on the side of 2 Peter.[32] In any case the writer makes his own whatever teaching he has taken over and applies it to the situation which he was facing. In common with Jude he attacks false teachers who were bringing licentious, antinomian ideas into the Church. But he goes further than Jude as he lays particular stress on the truth of the revelation which, in Jude's words, was 'once for all delivered to the saints' (2 Peter 1:12–20); he refutes the teaching of those who were casting doubts on belief in the parousia (2 Peter 3:1–13), and he calls Christians to a life of holiness (2 Peter 1:1–11) based on the hope of the parousia (2 Peter 3:11–18).

THE FALSE TEACHERS

As in the Epistle of Jude, our first task is to identify the false teachers who are attacked by Peter. The similarity of the description shows that we are concerned with the same kind of heretics as in Jude. Although they are described as belonging to the world of the ungodly, out of which Christians have been rescued like Noah or Lot in earlier days (2 Peter 2:5–8), they belonged to the Church whose love feasts they attended and they may have been lapsed believers. They are described as denying the Master who bought them (2 Peter 2:1). Although the verb 'to buy' is used elsewhere of men who had been actually redeemed by Christ (1 Corinthians 6:20; 7:23; Revelation 5:9; 14:3f.; cf. Galatians 3:13; 4:5), similar words do not always imply this (cf. Mark 10:45; Luke 1:68). Yet the form of the expression would appear to suggest that these men were lapsed believers. Commenting on the parallel passage in Jude, Calvin wrote: 'He means that Christ is denied, when they who have been redeemed by his blood, become again the vassals of the devil, and thus render void as far as they can that incomparable price.'[33]

The error of these men lay in forsaking the right way (2 Peter 2:15) and was evidently closely bound up with immorality. But it also included a rejection of authority in the Church and in heaven (2 Peter 2:10), and an attempt to lead other Christians astray (2 Peter 2:14, 18f.). The false teachers could expect to bear the judgement of God upon their deeds (2 Peter 2:3).

THE POSSIBILITY OF APOSTASY

The false teachers sought to corrupt the members of the Church by an appeal to the pleasures of sin; they enticed them to share their so-called freedom, which was in reality bondage to corruption (2 Peter 2:18f.).

The next verses (2 Peter 2:20–22) present a problem. The general meaning is certainly clear. People who have accepted this false teaching are definitely regarded as erstwhile believers. They are people who have temporarily escaped the defilement of the world through knowledge of Jesus; they have then been entangled and overpowered again by sin and have turned back from the holy commandment delivered to them. This is confirmed by the application of two proverbial sayings. The first speaks of a dog turning back to its own vomit (Proverbs 26:11). The second is very similar to the story of the swine, as found in the Story of Ahikar, 'which went to the bath with people of quality, and when he came out, saw a stinking drain and went and rolled himself in it.'[34]

What is not clear is whether these verses refer to the false teachers themselves or to those who were influenced by them. J. W. C. Wand thinks that the people who were deceived were catechumens — 'men who barely escaped from those who live in error (2 Peter 2:18)' — and that the following verses refer to the false teachers themselves since the description is too mature for young converts.[35] The false teachers will then be regarded as lapsed Christians who had penetrated deeply into Christian knowledge. But the repetition of 'having escaped' in verse 20 from verse 18 suggests that deceived Christians are in mind in that verse. The best solution may be that Peter was not concerned to differentiate clearly between the teachers and their victims at this point.

Lapsed Christians, then, are in view on either interpretation.

Their second state of unbelief is worse than their first, since they no longer have the excuse of sinning unwittingly or in ignorance. Consequently the judgement which faces them is more severe. They have forgotten their cleansing (2 Peter 1:9), and can expect swift destruction (2 Peter 2:1).

The question arises whether forgiveness was possible for such sinners. H. Windisch denies this on the grounds that the cleansing effect of baptism is purely retrospective; after baptism the Christian is pledged to live a blameless life (2 Peter 1:9).[36] But this view is to be rejected. Windisch himself has to admit that a sinless life after baptism is a theoretical rather than a practical possibility, although he is not inclined to credit the New Testament writers with this insight. This of course would be all the more the case in the later New Testament books where any idea (if it ever existed) that Christians might manage to remain sinless in the brief period before the parousia could hardly have been held realistically. In fact the question of renewed forgiveness is not raised by Peter. In favour of the possibility we may cite Jude 22f., but the fact of the absence of corresponding teaching from 2 Peter may perhaps be held to indicate that the thought was not in the author's mind.[37] Our verdict on this point will depend on our understanding of 2 Peter 3:9 (see below).

THE LIFE OF PERSEVERANCE

Finally, we must consider the bearing of Peter's teaching on the doctrine of the Christian life. For Peter a Christian is one who has been called and elected by God; he has been redeemed by Christ, obtained faith, and been granted the power and the promises of God so that he may live a righteous life characterized by the Christian virtues (2 Peter 1:1–11; 2:1). Thus he grows in the knowledge and grace of Christ, and looks forward to being found unspotted at the parousia (2 Peter 3:14, 18). Through divine grace the Christian progresses in holiness.

But this progress is not automatic. The believer must make his calling and election sure so that he may at last enter into the eternal kingdom of Christ (2 Peter 1:10f.). Election does not offer absolute assurance of salvation, for perseverance is also necessary: 'a glorious entry into the eternal kingdom is granted only to Christians who have successfully exerted themselves to live a faultless life.'[38] Lack of perseverance cannot be interpreted to mean that a man was never truly converted, since the description in 2 Peter 1:1–11 is plainly of Christians; nor can it be alleged that Peter teaches salvation by works, since the works are in fact the evidence of divine grace. Through such perseverance a Christian will never stumble, i.e. 'fall into deadly sin.'[39] Yet such stumbling is not impossible, and there is much point in Peter's final warning against being led astray (2 Peter 3:17).

In all this Peter never loses sight of the grace of God which enables men to persevere. He also stresses the love and patience of God, not only towards Christians but also towards all men. The reason for the apparent delay in the parousia is traced to the divine forbearance towards 'you,' since God is not willing that any should perish but that all should reach repentance (2 Peter 3:9). Although this last phrase suggests the conversion of the heathen, the fact that the sentence is addressed directly to the readers suggests that it also applies to them. In that case it may refer to those who are being misled by the false teachers — and possibly even to the false teachers themselves.[40] Thus Peter believes that God is still giving an opportunity of repentance to his readers, although the parousia is set as the limit to divine patience with the world.

CHAPTER EIGHT

The Johannine Literature

The final part of the New Testament to be discussed in our study is the Johannine literature. The five writings which compose it are linked together by common theological concepts to such a degree that, even if the name of John were not associated with each of them by early tradition, they would still be regarded as forming a distinct family of writings within the New Testament. Nevertheless, the differences between them are sufficiently great to warrant our considering the Revelation, Gospel, and Epistles separately.

1. THE REVELATION OF JOHN

While the Gospel of John is most probably an evangelistic book, the Revelation and the Epistles are addressed to believers in order to instruct and encourage them. It is generally agreed that Revelation was written against a background of persecution towards the end of the first century to strengthen and comfort the Church in its period of tribulation. It thus has as its direct aim the encouragement of perseverance among its readers. Against the background of the theology of salvation which John shares with the rest of the early Church,[1] there stands out his call to Christians to be ready to endure to the end, even to the point of martyrdom.[2]

THE SUMMONS TO REPENTANCE

John's theme is developed in his opening chapters by means of his message to the seven churches. It is worth emphasizing that the whole book forms one epistle from the Lord to His church (cf. Revelation 1:4; 22:21) and that, while the seven individual messages addressed to each of the seven churches were no doubt particularly applicable to the church addressed in each case, the whole message was meant for all the churches: 'He who has an ear let him hear what the Spirit says to the *churches*.' Moreover, the messages are addressed not simply to the churches but also to their individual members; both the praise and the blame and the promises of reward and loss apply to the individual members as well as to the groups represented by their 'angels.' Consequently, these chapters are of importance with regard to the perseverance and destiny of individuals as well as of churches.

Backsliding and unfaithfulness were prevalent in most of the seven churches, and John therefore uttered a strong warning to them about divine judgement and urged them to repent. Churches which were lacking in love, tolerated immorality or failed to live up to their reputation were in danger that their lampstands might be removed from their places (Revelation 2:5); the imagery shows that they would be cut off from the Son of man and, so to speak, excommunicated (cf. Revelation 1:12f., 20). Christ will war against the sinful church and spue it out of His mouth; divine judgement will come upon it like a thief in the night (Revelation 2:16; 3:3, 16; cf. 16:15). As a result a church which is on the point of death (Revelation 3:2) will presumably die.

There is no reason to doubt that these warnings were meant to be taken seriously; if necessary, the threats contained in them would be carried out. Yet in every case the possibility of repentance is held out to the erring church. The messages are not predictions of inevitable disaster, and the purpose of John is not to describe a judgement upon the church for unfaithfulness, although the opposition of the demonic powers in persecution is no doubt regarded as a purifying judgement permitted by God. H. Windisch has suggested that John regarded himself as entrusted with a special divine message announcing one last chance of repentance for the church before the parousia,[3] but this is not explicitly stated in the text, although it is plain that a failure to respond would lead to a decisive judgement.

The judgement thus threatened is a judgement upon a church and affects its existence in this world. It does not necessarily affect the earthly fate or salvation of all the individual members; even in the threatened churches there are faithful individuals who will in due time be rewarded (Revelation 3:4), and God's appeal is directed to all who will hear it (Revelation 3:20). We may well presume that individuals who repented would not share in the fate of a church the majority of whose members failed to repent.

VICTORY AND PERSEVERANCE

As far as the individual is concerned, John demands that he should show perseverance in the midst of persecution and trial. The concept which he uses to express this thought is that of victory or of overcoming. Jesus is put forward as an example of victory in His death and triumph over sin and in His future conquests (Revelation 3:21; 5:5; 17:14). Similarly, Christians conquer when they resist sin (Revelation 3:4f.; 21:7f.), persist steadfastly in the works of God (Revelation 2:26; cf. 14:12), hold fast to their faith (Revelation 3:11f.; cf. 14:12) and resist the demonic power (Revelation 12:11; 15:2) even to the point of martyrdom (Revelation 2:10f.). The true Christian is the victorious Christian, and he is promised salvation in the world to come. The Christian life is a constant struggle for victory, and in some cases this struggle may include facing martyrdom. If a person fails to be victorious, his faith must be regarded as of doubtful character.[4]

The various aspects of this attitude may now be listed.

(1) Basically the believer is required to show faithfulness unto death (Revelation 2:10). This is the quality which would be shown by a martyr (Revelation 2:13; cf. 17:14), and its negation is denial of the faith. It would appear that the faith has now become something which must be held by believers (Revelation 2:19; 13:10; 14:12), but such adherence to the faith is not purely formal and intellectual, for it was supremely typified in Jesus Himself who is faithful and true (Revelation 1:5; 3:14; 19:11).

(2) Being faithful entails keeping the commandments of God. Not only persecution but also temptation must be endured. 'Keeping' is a key word of John, and it is applied to keeping God's commandments (Revelation 12:17; 14:12), His works (Revelation 2:26), His word (Revelation 3:8, 10) and hence the words of the Revelation itself (Revelation 1:3; 22:7, 9). Believers are to keep their garments clean from sin (Revelation 3:4; 16:15).

(3) A further aspect of perseverance is patience, i.e. active endurance of trials (Revelation 1:9; 2:2, 3, 19; 3:10; 13:10; 14:12), as well as the chastisement which God employs (Revelation 3:19) to lead those whom He loves to repentance. Those, however, who prove themselves by endurance will be saved from the hour of tribulation (Revelation 3:10).

(4) All of this may be regarded as performing the works of God. The Christian life involves deeds, according to which men will be judged (Revelation 2:2, 5, 19, 23, 26; et al.). This does not mean that John teaches a religion of works, for the deeds are none other than that obedience to God (Revelation 2:26), love (Revelation 2:19) and Christian service (Revelation 2:2) which are the expression of a living faith.

So we arrive at a picture of the Christian life according to Revelation. The emphasis is on faithfulness, witness, and patience through many trials and temptations to the end. It is a life of perseverance, and, if this appears to be a one-sided description which emphasizes the need for human effort, this is because the situation of the Church has led John to emphasize this aspect.

The possibility of failure to endure is mentioned. Christians who fail to persevere will come under judgement (Revelation 2:22f.), and their names will be blotted out of the book of life (Revelation 3:5; 22:19).[5] There is no reason to suppose that these warnings are purely hypothetical, directed against non-existent dangers; the reverse is the case (Revelation 2:22f.). Moreover, the reference to the book of life indicates that John is addressing his warning to believers.

DIVINE ELECTION AND PROTECTION

Alongside this teaching about the need for human faithfulness must now be placed John's references to God's part in preserving His people from evil.

The concept of election does not play a major part in Revelation. In Revelation 17:14 the companions of the Lamb at His conquest of the beast are described as 'called and chosen and faithful,' a description which implies that divine election does not exclude the need for human faithfulness. Those who fall away after the beast do not include those whose names are written in the book of life (Revelation 13:8; 17:8), and yet there is also the warning, mentioned above, that men's names may be blotted out of that book. This is admittedly paradoxical, especially in view of the statement that the names are written before the foundation of the world, but we have no right to resolve the paradox lightly.[6]

In Revelation 7:1–8 there is a pause in the narrative of God's judgements upon the unbelieving world while the servants of God receive His seal upon their foreheads. The purpose of this sealing is evidently to preserve the people of God from the judgements which will fall upon the world, and its effect is seen when the sealed are protected from the locusts associated with the fifth trumpet (Revelation 9:4; cf. Exodus 12:23).

It is both unnecessary and wrong to assume that the sealing has the further purpose of sealing the people of God for martyrdom, as is done by E. Lohmeyer.[7] The description of the sealing is followed by the vision of a great multitude in heaven, men who have come out of the great tribulation and made their robes white (Revelation 7:9–17). In order to substantiate his interpretation Lohmeyer has to assume that the 144,000 who are sealed are not identical with (but form only part of) this great multitude. This differentiation, however, is very unlikely, and it is much more probable that 144,000 is a symbolical number for the countless multitude; the vision of the multitude is a proleptic one at this stage in the book, and is designed to give encouragement to the people of God as they face suffering and possible martyrdom.[8] Here, as often throughout the book, John is thinking of one particular generation, and he does not mention what place is reserved for Christians who have already died, nor does he imply that all who attain to heaven out of the great tribulation will have to tread the path of martyrdom.

If this sealing preserves the people of God from His judgements upon the world, does it preserve them from persecution and from falling away under persecution? This does not appear to be the case. It is true that later the 144,000 who were sealed reappear on Mount Zion, i.e. in heaven, with the Lamb (Revelation 14:1), but since the number is a symbolic one it does not necessarily follow that all who have been sealed will certainly persevere, or that all of them will suffer martyrdom in the persecutions. But, although perseverance is not made a matter of infallible certainty, John does imply that the saints will persevere during the tribulations which they suffer. After the first three chapters the idea of the saints falling away is not mentioned, although the need for perseverance continues to be stressed. Those who respond to the messages to the seven churches with repentance and renewed faith will be capable of endurance. Even if the Church of the latter days appears in the eyes of the world to be a defeated Church (Revelation 13:7), it will be a victorious Church. This victory, however, is dependent not upon the sealing of God's people but upon the endurance of those who conquered by the blood of the Lamb and the word of their testimony and because they loved not their lives even unto death (Revelation 12:11).

The Book of Revelation is, therefore, an appeal to Christians to be conquerors by holding out to the end against the onslaught of the demonic powers arrayed against them. It passes judgement upon Christians who fail to overcome and threatens them with loss of salvation, so that a pure and strong Church may be fitted to face the fury of the devil and antichrist. The final picture is one of perseverance and triumph through the grace of the One who has promised to come soon to lead His people to victory.

2. THE GOSPEL OF JOHN

According to the characteristic teaching of the Fourth Gospel men who are not Christians are in a state which is variously described as sin, condemnation, spiritual death, darkness, and ignorance. To a world thus bound in thrall to the devil came Jesus as the revealer of God and the Saviour. He is Himself both the bringer of salvation and the gift itself; through Him men can enter into fellowship with God the Father and receive eternal life. The manner in which a person passes from the state of sin and death to that of life and salvation is expressed in two ways. On the one hand, a person receives eternal life through an act of faith in Jesus. On the other hand, it is said that belief in Jesus is the result of being drawn to Him by the Father, and there is also mention of a new birth wrought in men by the inscrutable activity of the Holy Spirit. All this suggests that there is a strong predestinarian element in John and we need to ask whether this implies a doctrine of unconditional perseverance. We must also inquire whether the nature of the eternal life which is given to believers is such that it cannot possibly be lost.

DIVINE PREDESTINATION

A number of passages in John suggest that men come to belief only through the drawing of the Father and by virtue of His will concerning them (John 6:37, 44, 65; 8:47; 10:29; 15:16, 19; 17:2, 6; cf. 17:9, 11, 12, 24; 18:9). These statements teach explicitly that those who believe in Jesus are those who have been given to Him and drawn to Him by the Father, and it might well be concluded that they imply the final salvation of those who come to Jesus, since there is no suggestion that there is anything temporary about the purpose of the Father.

Our study of Paul's teaching led to the conclusion that even his most stringent predestinarian language did not exclude the need for human faith; granted that faith is the gift of God, being aroused in men through the divine call which they hear, it is nevertheless a gift which may be refused, so that we are not to think of a secret divine purpose and causation which inevitably makes certain chosen men believe and be saved. But what of John's teaching?

It is expressly stated that those whom the Father gives to Jesus 'come' to Him (John 6:37) and also that Jesus gives eternal life to all whom the Father gives Him (John 17:2). Further, the word 'come' tends to be synonymous with 'believe' (John 6:35; cf. 5:40). These statements suggest that the divine 'drawing' or 'giving' of men to Jesus automatically results in their receiving faith and eternal life. A division of mankind into two classes also appears to be taught, so that men who do not belong to the class of those whom the Father draws and who are not of God (John 8:47) cannot enter the class of sons of God; this would be very like gnostic dualism.[9]

This reasoning and conclusion demand careful examination.

(1) We may begin by mentioning the interpretation of R. Bultmann, who writes: 'The Father's "drawing" does not precede the believer's "coming" to Jesus — in other words, does not take place before the decision of faith — but, as the surrendering of one's own certainty and self-assertion, occurs in that coming, in that decision of faith. . . . If faith is such a surrender of one's own self-assertion, then the believer can understand his faith not as the accomplishment of his own purposeful act, but only as God's working upon him.'[10] We may well accept the second of these two sentences, but the first is open to criticism. It is an attempt to reinterpret the text in terms of Bultmann's own existentialism, in which no place is left for a supernatural, divine influence upon men, and it is open to the simple but conclusive objection that if John had meant what Bultmann takes him to mean he would certainly have expressed himself differently. It is impossible to escape the impression that John is referring to a divine act which precedes faith in Jesus and makes faith a possibility. For John, as for Paul, prevenient grace is a reality.

(2) A more convincing point is that those who base a dualism upon these verses in John neglect the strong universalistic strain which is also to be found in the Gospel. It is stated in a plain and unequivocal manner that Jesus died for the world (John 3:16f.; cf. 1:12, 29; 1 John 2:2).[11] While it is true that no man can come to the Son except the Father draw him, it is also true that 'It is written in the prophets, "And they shall be taught by God." Every one who has heard and learned from the Father comes to me' (John 6:45). When He is lifted up from the earth, Jesus will draw all men to Himself (John 12:32).

(3) We must now observe that the predestinarian language is not rigorously applied in every case. It is possible for men to see

Jesus, and yet not to believe (John 6:36). The whole of the latter part of John 5 criticizes the Jews for not believing in Jesus, and the reason adduced for their unbelief is not that they have not been predestined to believe but that they seek glory from men; there can even be an inversion of the line of thought outlined above when it is said that the reason why they do not have the Father's word abiding in them is because they do not believe in the Son (John 5:38). Again, in John 12:37ff. it is stated that the reason why the people did not believe was that God hardened their hearts in fulfilment of the prophecy of Isaiah, and such hardening is to be understood as a judgement upon a previous failure to believe and not as a hardening *ab initio* which entirely ruled out the possibility of belief. Yet, despite this hardening, some of the people did believe in Jesus, and He continued to offer the gospel of eternal life to the people.[12]

(4) From these considerations we conclude that the purpose of the predestinarian language in John is not to express the exclusion of certain men from salvation because they were not chosen by the Father (although a divine hardening of those who persistently refuse the gospel is taught), but to emphasize that from start to finish eternal life is the gift of God and does not lie under the control of men. A person who tries to gain eternal life on his own terms will find himself unable to come to Jesus because it has not been granted to him by the Father (John 6:65); he has in fact been resisting the leading of the Father. Failure to respond to Jesus is culpable, and judgement takes place as a result of refusal to believe. Human responsibility to accept Jesus as Saviour is clearly taught.

(5) A further step which we may take is that of observing that the sayings about predestination have as their purpose to show the unanimity of the Father and the Son in bestowing salvation upon men. No man can have the Father without the Son nor the Son without the Father, for no man can believe in the Son without being drawn by the Father, and no man can have the Father's word abiding in him without believing in the Son. If the Father draws men to the Son, it is the Son who is the way to the Father (John 14:6; cf. Matthew 11:27).

When we bear in mind that the Gospel of John is addressed primarily to Jews,[13] it seems reasonable to venture the suggestion that John is teaching that Jews who fail to accept the revelation of God which He had already given before the coming of Jesus cannot hope to bypass it and come to Jesus in some other way. Put otherwise, the reason why the Jews failed to believe in Jesus was because they had already failed to believe in the earlier revelations of God to them. The saying that 'He came to his own home, and his own people received him not' (John 1:11) could be applied to the coming of the Word of God to His people before He came in Jesus. The Jews searched the Scriptures, and yet failed to find a witness to Jesus in them (John 5:39f.); they did not have the love of the Father in them, and they had not believed in Moses (John 5:42ff.). So they did not listen to Jesus because they were not of God (John 8:47).

A Jew, then, who had already refused the word of God given to him in the Scriptures would not believe the new revelation given in Jesus (cf. Luke 16:31). Consequently, the same shift takes place as we find in Paul: when the Jews disbelieve, Jesus turns to the Gentiles; He dies for the world, for the children of God who are scattered abroad, and by His death He draws all men unto Himself (John 11:52; 12:31–3; cf. 10:16). He looks forward to the conversion of those who will believe through the witness of the group of disciples originally given to Him by the Father (John 17:20).

When these various points are assembled, it becomes clear that a simple division of men into those who are foreordained to respond to the gospel and those who are foreordained to reject it fails to do justice to the complexity of John's thought. The men whom the Father gives to Jesus are those Jews who have already responded to Him. Certainly a man who does not know the Father, i.e. a Gentile, will be drawn by the Son, but for a Jew to come to Jesus is possible only if he is 'open' to the revelation of the Father which he has already received. The grounds on which the Father draws men are not stated, and His election is known only by the fact of its occurrence. We shall, therefore, be wise not to press the predestinarian language of John too far and draw from it the theory of a logical and inevitable chain of divine causation.

DIVINE PROTECTION

Closely linked with the idea of divine election is the concept of a divine care and protection over those who are given by the Father to the Son. Jesus will lose none of those who have been given to Him by the Father but will raise them up at the last day. He gives to His sheep eternal life; they shall never perish and nobody will be able to snatch them out of the Father's hand. If one of the disciples — the son of perdition — is lost, this is simply the exception which proves the rule that Jesus has kept in the Father's name those who were given to Him (John 6:39f., 44, 54; 10:28f.; 17:12; cf. 17:11, 17, 20f.). Divine preservation of the flock of Jesus is a guaranteed fact; in John 17 Jesus is able to look back over His ministry and say that He has preserved His disciples, and then He prays to the Father to continue to keep them. These words must apply not only to the earthly disciples of Jesus but also to all the other sheep, those who are to believe through the word of the first disciples.

Nowhere else in the New Testament is the fact of divine preservation of the disciples of Jesus so clearly presented as here, and no theology of perseverance and apostasy must fail to give these verses their full value. Yet exegetical honesty compels us to ask whether the will of God can be frustrated by human sin, just as His will for the salvation of all men does not in fact lead to the salvation of all men. Does the power of Jesus prevent men from falling away, or does it preserve only those who continue in belief? Does it enable men to continue believing in such a manner that they cannot possibly fail to continue believing? To answer these questions we must look at John's teaching on the believer's response to God.

TWO LEVELS OF DISCIPLESHIP

We note first of all that John is conscious of the possibility of a superficial and inadequate allegiance to Jesus; men may make a partial response to Jesus (which ultimately is no response), and we shall not be surprised if such men fail to last the pace. Thus in John 6:60ff. a distinction is made within the professing disciples of Jesus in Him between those who believed and those who did not believe. The word 'disciple' can be used for those who are only outwardly disciples of Jesus, since the essential element of faith is lacking.

In this way John is able to account for the attitude of Judas. The mention of him in this context shows that John regarded him as one who did not believe in Jesus.[14] Outward following of Jesus and even membership of the twelve were not necessarily a token of salvation. Already at this point in the narrative Judas is said to be a devil, although it is not until John 13:26 that Satan is said to enter into him.

This raises the baffling question of divine choice in relation to human faith. Judas was one of the twelve, chosen by Jesus, and yet he was not kept by Jesus, since he had given himself up to evil. It remains obscure whether he believed at first and then fell from unbelief, or never believed at all. All that we may say is that one person chosen by Jesus failed to believe, but only this one case is mentioned.[15] We are not entitled to conclude at this point that there is in general the possibility of a divine choice of men which does not lead to lasting faith.

TWO TYPES OF FAITH

From the use of 'disciple' to include a person who is not a true disciple, we must now turn to the use of the word 'faith' in John. A linguistic distinction has often been found in John between the use of the verb πιστεύω with the dative case to express intellectual credence in a person or thing and the use of the verb with εἰς and the accusative case to express trust in a person.[16] Both aspects of faith are recognized to be essential for salvation, and the first, if alone, is inadequate. Mere credence is not an adequate qualification for reception of eternal life; it must be completed by trust and committal. We must disagree with Bultmann's conclusion that 'Practically there is no difference; for one ought to believe Him to be sure that one may trust in Him, and the one is not without the other.'[17] No doubt this is a true sentiment, but it does not mean that cases do not arise where credence is not accompanied by committal.

We must now ask whether there are any cases of disciples falling away from full faith (credence and committal) in Jesus. No conclusion can be drawn from John 6:64–6, although it is likely that Jesus was here addressing those who had never believed in Him at all. In John 2:23 we are told that many believed in His name when they saw His signs, but Jesus did not trust Himself to them because He knew all men. It is implied that this faith was unreal, possibly because it was based simply upon the signs, although elsewhere 'belief in His name' is regarded as true faith which leads to salvation.[18] It is possible that there can be a trust in Jesus which is inadequately based on miracles and needs to be deepened before it can be said to be the condition of receiving eternal life. Superficial trust may be indicated also at John 7:31 where the people who trust in Jesus ask, 'When the Christ appears, will he do more signs than this man has done?'[19] The same is probably true at John 12:42 where many of the authorities trust in Jesus but fear to confess Him openly lest they be put out of the synagogue; such men are better than complete unbelievers, but they are in grave danger because they fall under the condemnation of John 5:44.

These examples suggest that John knows of a weak and inadequate trust in Jesus as well as a belief which is no more than intellectual credence, but it is not absolutely clear whether he regards it as leading to eternal life or not. It may, however, be significant that he never speaks of men giving up their faith and so forfeiting eternal life.

ABIDING IN THE SON

The element of trust and commitment in faith is particularly emphasized and expressed in John by the use of the verb 'to abide' (μένω) which might almost be said to be the Johannine equivalent for 'to persevere.' From its plain secular meaning of remaining in one place this verb has come to have the developed theological sense of remaining in a life-giving relationship with God.

On the one hand, the relationship between Jesus and the believer can be described in terms of the abiding of Jesus in him, although this is at once qualified by the addition of the inverted form, that the believer abides in Jesus; this double expression indicates that the relationship between the believer and Jesus is analogous to that which exists between the Father and the Son (John 15:4f.; 14:10; 15:10b). Similarly the Spirit is said to abide in the disciples (John 14:17).

On the other hand, the verb is used to express the need for believers to abide in Jesus. In John 15:4 the abiding of the disciples in Jesus is probably to be taken as the condition for His abiding in them, and it is in any case the condition for them to bear fruit and to receive answers to their prayers (John 15:4–7). They are to let the words of Jesus abide in them (John 8:31; 15:7; cf. 5:38), and abiding is the result of being fed with His flesh and blood (John 6:56).

John thus uses the verb 'abide' to express the need for disciples to continue in their personal commitment to Jesus; the abiding of Jesus in them is not an automatic process which is independent of their attitude to Him, but is the reverse side of their abiding in Him. Just as men are summoned to believe in Jesus, so they are summoned to abide in Jesus, i.e. to continue believing.

If a man does not abide in Jesus, the true vine, he is cast forth as a branch and is destroyed by fire (John 15:2, 6). For a branch is useless if it does not bear fruit, and branches can bear fruit only if they abide in the vine. Fruit-bearing is not simply another way of expressing 'abiding' as R. Bultmann contends;[20] it expresses the outward result of abiding, and, although this is not expressly indicated, it may be understood as referring to manifesting the love which is described in the following verses and bringing other men to belief in Jesus (cf. John 4:36; 12:24; 17:20).

In John 15:16 Jesus says that He has chosen His disciples to bear fruit which will abide. Who, then, are represented by the branches which are broken off, or rather which may be broken off? Those broken off are described as branches of the vine and hence as believers. The passage will then teach that believers who fail to continue in their belief will be cast away. Such people may be those who never passed the stage of intellectual credence and were therefore never true participants in eternal life, but this is not explicitly stated, and the passage must be regarded as one warning believers in general and placed alongside those other passages which affirm the keeping power of God.[21] Here we have a case where men are in Christ and yet may fail to bear fruit.

Consequently, it is not surprising to find in John 16:1 an explicit statement that the purpose of Jesus' teaching is to prevent the disciples from stumbling or falling away.[22] Even if they should be excommunicated from Judaism because of their allegiance to Jesus, they must not give up their faith. Similarly, Jesus found it necessary to pray that the Father would keep the disciples (John 17:11, 15, 24), even as He had kept them (John 17:12). All this indicates that the disciples stand under the threat of being lost, for otherwise they would not need to be guarded. Their safety depends upon God.

SUMMARY

We have seen that the weight of emphasis in the Gospel of John falls upon the fact of divine preservation of those who are given by the Father to the Son and believe in the Son. Having been drawn by the Father, believers become members of the flock of Jesus, and He will raise them up at the last day. Those who are Christ's sheep know that He will preserve them to the end. Where lapse from the faith occurs, this may be explained by the suggestion that those who lapse never passed beyond the stage of superficial discipleship or superficial belief.

But we have also found that there is a universal offer of salvation in John. In a variety of ways Jesus summons men to belief, and He validates His call by signs, witness, and teaching. All of this is surely to be taken seriously; it is not a piece of play-acting, a kind of foreordained drama, or an outward disguise to cover up secret inward movements preordained by God. Moreover, it is important that the predestinarian teaching is not taken to its logical conclusion in double predestination. Although there is a divine hardening of those who refuse to believe, it is not suggested that those who do not believe were ordained not to believe, since lack of belief is culpable.[23] There is no indication that a man may wish to believe in Jesus and find the way barred to him, except perhaps if he has been persistent in unbelief.

Further, despite the promises of preservation Jesus continually exhorts His disciples to abide in Him and warns them about the danger of falling away. It is impossible to believe that these warnings are spoken merely to professing disciples. For the command of Jesus is not that men should test themselves to see whether they were ever truly converted and born of the Spirit, but that they should abide in Jesus, i.e. continue in the faith which they already have. This point should be stressed. No doubt it is often appropriate for disciples to examine themselves to see whether they have been truly converted. But there comes a stage when a person must be certain of the fact of his conversion; this is a point which is developed in 1 John, which is written that men may know that they have eternal life (1 John 5:13). If a man is continually unsure about the fact of his salvation, the Christian life becomes a mirage; Christian experience is never free from doubt, and the whole of what a man has known of God in personal communion stands under a gigantic question mark. It is impossible to think that the New Testament commands to self-examination are meant to produce this effect. They do not say, 'Did you truly believe?' or 'Were you truly converted?' but 'Are you continuing in the faith?' This is surely what is meant by John's use of 'abiding.' 'Abiding' is not something extra to be added to faith but describes the nature of faith as something that continues. John's way of exhorting his readers to persevere as Christians is to tell them to 'abide' in Christ.

It is through this continual abiding that a person remains one of Christ's sheep. While he remains in this relationship he knows that he is preserved by the Father and the Son and looks forward to the life of heaven. He believes the word of Jesus, that no one shall snatch him out of His hand. But he also knows that this promise is true only for those who hear the voice of Jesus and follow Him, and that therefore he must continue to trust in Jesus.

Can the believer lose his confidence and cease to persevere? Or can the Good Shepherd allow His sheep to fall away into unbelief? John names no case except that of Judas, whose conversion and belief must remain at least doubtful. But the warnings given by John are pointless if there is no danger. In the end we are confronted by the sharpest expression of the paradox of divine protection and demonic temptation in the

New Testament. Here logic breaks down, and the believer can only take refuge in the promises of Jesus. He knows that he is safe in the care of Jesus, but at the same time he knows that the obligation is laid upon him to abide continually in Jesus lest he be cast away as a branch.

3. THE EPISTLES OF JOHN

The Epistles of John, of which the First Epistle concerns us particularly, were written to Christians in order to confirm them in their possession of eternal life (1 John 5:13), and much of the author's space is used in showing what are the marks of possession of eternal life or the criteria of 'eschatological existence.'[24] Although these various criteria are individually stated in absolute terms, this does not mean that they are to be thought of in isolation from each other. It is not enough to have a true faith in Jesus as the Son of God (1 John 2:22–5) or a love for God and one's fellow Christians (1 John 2:5f.; 3:10, 23), unless the faith is accompanied by love and the love by faith. Further, love must express itself in keeping the commandments of God, so that the believer lives a life in which through the power of his faith in God he is victorious over sin, the world and the devil (1 John 2:12–14; 5:4). If he does stumble into sin, he is quick to confess his sin and seek cleansing (1 John 2:1f.), for his chief aim is to be sinless (1 John 3:4–10). Such a person is born of God (1 John 3:1, 9) and possesses the Spirit of God (1 John 3:24; 4:13). He has confidence for the day of judgement (1 John 4:17) and will not shrink away in shame at the parousia of Jesus but will be made like Him (1 John 2:28–3:2).

As might be expected, John affirms strongly here also the doctrine of perseverance. A man born of God and kept by Him cannot sin (1 John 3:9, 5:18)[25] and can overcome the world. At the same time, his progress to final salvation is not automatic. For example, although John teaches that all believers through their possession of the Spirit have knowledge (1 John 2:20), it is still necessary for him to give them plentiful admonition and teaching. He has to urge them to keep the commandments of God (1 John 2:7) and to abide in Jesus (1 John 2:28; cf. also 1 John 2:15, 24, 27; 3:3, 18; 5:21; 2 John 7–11). He knows that they can and do fall into sin.

A MIXED CHURCH

The particular danger which faced John's readers arose from the presence in the Church of false teachers who held erroneous ideas about the person and work of Jesus. John regards these teachers as manifestations of antichrist, inspired by his spirit (1 John 2:18; 4:3). They cannot be regarded as believers who have eternal life, for they do not show the marks of believers: they do not hold the true doctrine about Jesus (1 John 2:22f.), nor do they keep God's commandments (1 John 2:4), nor do they love their brethren (1 John 4:20). Although they profess to know God, they do not possess His Spirit (cf. 1 John 4:1–3). Nevertheless, they had at one time been members of the Church, from which they had now departed, possibly to set up a sect of their own (1 John 2:19). Had they been true believers they would have continued in the Church; their departure was a clear sign that none of them really belonged to the Church. While they were still in the Church, therefore, it was a mixed Church.[26]

It is not absolutely clear whether the false teachers are regarded as men who had never really possessed eternal life (but had made a profession of faith and become members of the Church) or as men who had fallen from the faith. The former view is adopted by E. Schweizer,[27] but there is some evidence which might be held to favour the latter view. In 1 John 2:24 the readers are admonished to abide in the truth. Although the author feels fairly confident that they will do so, he warns his readers against being led astray by the false teachers; they are to look to themselves lest they lose what they have worked for, i.e. eternal life.[28] Anybody who presses on to advanced doctrine and does not remain in the doctrine of Christ does not have God (2 John 7–11). These verses express the possibility that John's readers may go astray and lose their salvation — and we note that this warning is addressed to people described as 'elect' (2 John 1). Hence we must allow the possibility that believers might lapse from the true faith through following the false teachers, whether or not the group of teachers were themselves regarded as lapsed believers.

SIN AND PERSEVERANCE

The teaching of 1 John about sin in the believer is expressed in sharp paradox. The experience of being born of God and thus receiving the divine nature is said to make the believer sinless; he does not and cannot sin. The person who sins does not know Christ (1 John 3:6–10; 5:18). But other statements maintain that a person who claims sinlessness is a liar and that there is a divine provision for those who do sin; John's purpose in writing is that his readers may not sin — a strange purpose if in fact there was no likelihood of their sinning (1 John 1:8–2:2). We note further that he can speak about seeing one's (Christian) brother sin in the context of his statement about the sinlessness of Christians (1 John 5:16f.).

This paradox is hardly to be resolved by theories of interpolation or use of discrepant sources; the way in which the apparently contradictory statements are placed alongside each other in ch. 5 rules this out. Nor can the references to sin be taken as referring purely to pre-baptismal sin.[29] Rather John is opposing the gnostic claim to a sinlessness which was held to be compatible with lawlessness according to the peculiar definition of sin in gnostic theology. He is insisting on the ideal of the Christian life, that the Christian does not commit persistent sin, over against the moral indifference of the false teachers, and at the same time he may well be remonstrating with Christians who had not yet overcome sin.[30] A person who continues in sin has no claim to be regarded as one who has been born of God.

This may be interpreted in two ways. It may be taken to mean that, while a man born of God may be 'overtaken' by a sin for which he can be forgiven, he cannot be led to commit a severe sin, and therefore the only people who commit such sins are people who were not born of God. This is difficult to square with the undoubted fact that Christians may experience severe lapses into sin. Alternatively, the teaching of John may mean that a person who falls into severe sin can lose his title to be called born of God unless he confesses his sin and seeks forgiveness. A man may fall into sin through failure to abide in God, and therefore must continually abide in God.

This second view seems preferable, provided that it is not understood in such a way that the power of God to keep those who abide in Him from sinning is denied. For, as we have seen, John speaks of an advocate for Christians who sin. Moreover, to the work of Christ he adds the task of the Christian brother to intercede for his brethren when they commit sins which are not mortal.[31] Sin is presumably not mortal when it is unwitting; it may cause death if the sinner is unrepentant when he learns of it, but John teaches that in answer to prayer God will give life to the sinner.

THE PROBLEM OF MORTAL SIN

There are, however, mortal sins, and the duty of prayer is not laid upon Christians in this case. By mortal sin John must mean a sin which may be committed by a believer, for the reference is still to brethren. The allusion is to certain sins which, according to the teaching of the Old Testament and of Judaism, could be expiated only by the death of the sinner.[32] These were sins committed wittingly, with a high hand. But to what is John referring? It is unlikely that he is thinking of sins which are rewarded with capital punishment in the secular world. He may mean sins which God punishes with the physical death of the sinner, but it is more likely that spiritual death and exclusion from eternal life are meant, a fact which presumably implies the prior possession of eternal life by the sinner. What kind of sin is meant is uncertain; most probably it is the sin of apostasy in the form of denying the divinity of Jesus, i.e. the sin of the false teachers, the sin of antichrist. At the same time the sin of hating the brethren may also be included.[33] We have already seen that believers may conceivably fall into these sins.

Many scholars regard this sin as unforgivable, and adduce the parallels of the unforgivable sin in the Synoptic Gospels and the apostasy described in Hebrews. Yet this is not absolutely certain. It is not said whether or not the sinner can find forgiveness and eternal life. Although prayer for him is apparently not commanded,[34] the promise of 1 John 2:1f. is not explicitly revoked. The reason may be perhaps that in 1 John 5:16a the prayers of the church will secure forgiveness for a believer's unwitting sin, but in 1 John 5:16b the sinner himself must seek forgiveness by confession of his witting sin. Even so it is difficult to see why prayer should not be made for him. It must be remembered that the New Testament does know the possibility of a sin which is unforgivable because the sinner refuses to repent, and it also knows the fearful danger of a man reaching a point where God withdraws His mercy from him. This point is surely known to God alone, and A. E. Brooke suggests that in such a case the man must be left to God alone; for men cannot know what God's will is, and where the man's own will is directed against God prayer may be useless.[35] Thus, while the possibility of sin leading to death is to be recognized, the possibility of forgiveness is equally present, even if in extreme cases there is a limit to the divine mercy.

According to 1 John, then, sin is a possibility among believers, even to the point of denial of Christ, and the teaching of the Epistle is not fully accounted for if sin is regarded as a possibility only among those who have never been truly converted. At the same time it must be most strongly emphasized that such serious sin is spoken of only as a possibility and indeed as a rare possibility. It is not the normal issue of the

Christian life. That life is essentially one in which the believer abides in Christ and does not, yea cannot, sin as a result of the power for victory which God gives to those who are born of Him. The teaching of 1 John is thus very close to that of the Fourth Gospel.

CHAPTER NINE

Conclusion

Throughout the exegetical study which has occupied our attention in this book our interest has been focused on the basic question whether a person who has received salvation through faith in Jesus Christ can lose the divine gift and in the end fail to enter the heavenly kingdom of God. It is time now to draw together the general conclusions which have emerged from this study, to provide an answer, if possible, to the theological problem of the perseverance of the saints, and to ascertain what practical lessons may be learned for the life of the Church today.

1. THE BIBLICAL TEACHING

THE BACKGROUND

We began our study by considering the antecedents of New Testament doctrine in the Old Testament and related literature. In the Old Testament salvation was conceived as a this-worldly enjoyment of the promised land in which the people of God enjoyed His blessing and had communion with Him, both corporately in the worship of the temple and individually in the type of piety reflected in the Psalms. This, however, was an ideal picture. The prophets saw the history of Israel as a continual record of sin and faithlessness. The people rebelled against God, they were backsliders and apostates, and they frequently transgressed against the covenant which God had made with them. All this took place despite the various promises of God to care for His people, contingent upon their obedience and faithfulness. Consequently, they were judged by Him times without number; their country was overrun by its enemies, and they themselves were transported to foreign lands or put to death. They ceased to enjoy the benefits of salvation.

Thus the fact is certainly established that many of the people of God failed to enjoy God's blessing as a result of their falling away from Him. At the same time, however, the people as a whole never entirely fell away from God; there were godly individuals who formed a 'remnant,' and they were able by God's grace to make a new start. While there was a limit to God's patience, He also showed His mercy in making a new start with the remnant of His people, and the prophets looked forward to a 'golden age' in the future when the people of Israel would all know and serve God faithfully.

Within this general framework of God's dealings with the nation as a whole we examined the legal teaching enshrined in the sacrificial system and found the same general pattern. By his deliberate sin a man could cut himself off from the people of God and cease to enjoy the divine blessing. Since the punishment was death, there was no possibility of the man regaining salvation; this did not mean, however, that the judgement upon him was exclusively retributive, for it was also intended to be a warning to other men not to sin in the same way but to return to God in repentance.

While, therefore, the Old Testament knows of no inevitable perseverance of the people of God, and contains many examples of His judgement upon backsliders and apostates, it also contains the promise that God would heal the backsliding of His people and establish them in the future.

These basic ideas from the Old Testament were taken up and applied to the contemporary situation by the Qumran sect. The men of Qumran saw themselves as living in an age of apostasy by Israel generally, but they regarded themselves as composing the pious remnant who would shortly inherit the promised bliss as a result of God's final intervention in history. They had withdrawn from the faithless nation round about them and entered into a new covenant with God. Their literature, particularly their hymns, expressed a profound trust in God and His power to prevent the faithful from going astray, but this did not exclude the possibility of members of the sect going astray and falling into sin and apostasy. While it was possible for members of apostate Israel to repent and find admission to the sect, it was also necessary for members of the sect to be disciplined because of their sins, and, in extreme cases, to suffer the punishment of final and irrevocable expulsion from the sect and possibly even of death.

Orthodox Judaism, as represented by the Rabbinic literature, also recognized the possibility of apostasy among God's people, the Maccabean period being the most conspicuous historical example. Although the Rabbis anticipated a general increase in godlessness and wickedness in the heathen world before the coming of the Messiah at the end of history, they do not appear to have envisaged a general development of apostasy among the people of God.[1] We may relate this to a shift of interest in their thinking to the thought of the messianic age and the world to come and the conditions under which individual Israelites would participate in future blessings. The idea of resurrection had developed, and it was held that all Israel would be raised up to share in the life of the world to come. But this general statement was subject to certain restrictions. Since the Rabbis taught a doctrine of universal sinfulness, they had to stress the need for forgiveness as the means of entrance to the heavenly world. The one supreme qualification for forgiveness was the repentance of the sinner; in theory, repentance could atone for any sin, but it was recognized that there were cases where a man might prove unrepentant or where God might refuse to accept his repentance, and in such cases a man might forfeit his hope of salvation. Normally a system of discipline would intervene before a man reached such a state of hardness of heart in order to lead him to repentance. Thus there was hope that every Israelite would enter the world to come if only he would repent of his sin, but it was recognized that this was by no means inevitable and that certain men would not enter the world to come.

It is difficult to say how far ideas of predestination and determinism affected these doctrines. That such ideas are found here and there is not to be denied. But the evidence hardly favours the view that the men who finally enter the messianic kingdom or the world to come have been predestined to do so by God who efficaciously causes them to repent and remain faithful to Him.

THE NEW TESTAMENT CONCEPT OF SALVATION

Although the idea of falling away from God and ceasing to be a member of His people was fairly commonplace in Jewish thought, it would be quite wrong to assume that this same idea was necessarily characteristic of the thought of Jesus and the early Church. There is a difference in thought which is based on a different concept of salvation. First, the New Testament definitely thinks of the era of salvation as being already present.

We saw that in the Gospels Jesus taught the imminent coming of the kingdom of God; although the consummation of the kingdom was still future, we found that the present time was regarded as one in which the blessings of the kingdom were already partly realized and in which men were summoned to live as disciples of Jesus in a manner worthy of entrance into the coming kingdom.

After Pentecost, however, the early Church thought more and more of the era of salvation as having come. The gift of the Holy Spirit had been poured out, and forgiveness was offered to men. The idea of the coming kingdom of God receded somewhat into the background, and increasing emphasis was placed upon the Church as the company of people who already receive God's blessings. Paul teaches that the believer has already been justified by a decisive anticipation of the verdict at the last judgement and now lives a life of union with Christ as a member of His body. John in particular thinks of the two aeons, and teaches that believers already belong to the new aeon of salvation and partake of that eternal life which will be fully realized in the world to come at the parousia.

A second point may be added. K. Lake and H. J. Cadbury drew a distinction between two ways of salvation: there is the Hebraic idea of the universal efficacy of repentance and there is also the Hellenistic idea of a miraculous change of nature, sacramentally received.[2] This distinction between salvation by means of a human attitude of repentance and by means of a divine act of regeneration may be rather loosely expressed but it serves to remind us that in several parts of the New Testament the idea of salvation as a result of a new birth is expressed. A definite change takes place in the nature of the believer through the work of the Spirit, and the question may be raised whether such a change is irreversible.

This New Testament teaching that the era of salvation is now come and that men may be born into a new life may be thought to rule out the possibility of falling away altogether; the promised era of fulfilment has now come, it may be said, and the time in which backsliding and apostasy were a sad feature of the life of the people of God is now past. But this conclusion would be unjustified. There is no doubt that the New Testament as a whole regards the present era as a *Zwischenzeit* between the first and second advents of Jesus and looks forward to the full revelation of the kingdom of God and the glory which is to come. At the present time the Church is weak and oppressed by temptation; it suffers in hope of the coming glory. Its aim is sinlessness, but it knows that it is still far from perfection. The

Epistle to the Hebrews develops the idea of pilgrimage as the form of life of God's people under both covenants, and Revelation emphasizes the need for renewed repentance by a sinful Church. Moreover, there is never any suggestion that baptism, the outward sign of new birth, cannot be undone — although it is equally true that it is never said to be repeatable — and it is not unlikely that the possibility of the new birth itself being annulled is also to be found. In short, it would be false to assume that the conception of salvation in the New Testament excludes the possibility of the believer falling away.

THE ARGUMENT FROM PREDESTINATION

We must now ask whether the biblical doctrine of predestination rules out the possibility of apostasy and guarantees the perseverance of the elect people of God.

According to the Calvinist interpretation of the New Testament, God chooses beforehand the men who are to believe in Jesus Christ, receive the Spirit, and so obtain salvation. He puts His plan into effect by calling them through the gospel and they respond with faith. But it is inconceivable that God's purpose of salvation for the elect should be thwarted, and therefore, it is held, the elect will certainly persevere to the end; election means election to final salvation. On this view, although men's faith appears outwardly to be their own act and although they are not necessarily conscious of any compulsion but act of their own accord, their faith is due to the irresistible influence of God upon them. Indeed, faith is not possible apart from this, since all men naturally are in a state of sin and death from which they cannot rise by their own efforts. They must be awakened by God, and He awakens only those whom He intends to save.

Although this view claims to be based entirely upon the Bible and to represent biblical teaching faithfully, it is difficult to believe that it does so. It teaches that divine grace is given only to a limited, specified group of mankind — the elect — and it carries the corollary that God passes over or, to put it bluntly, rejects the rest of mankind. According to B. B. Warfield, 'Their (sc. the biblical writers) doctrine of election, they are free to tell us, for example, does certainly involve a corresponding doctrine of preterition,' and Warfield's insistence that the lost would be a 'relatively insignificant body' in size[3] by no means removes the difficulty which is felt. While it is to be granted freely that there is no compulsion upon God to show mercy to any of a disobedient, sinful race and that He has absolute freedom to grant or withhold mercy as He pleases, it is impossible to avoid the impression that the picture of God thus presented is of One who is unjust; the concept of divine grace has not been properly understood in terms of divine justice. W. B. Pope was abundantly justified in writing, 'There is no necessity in the system more hard, no dogma more intolerable than that which requires us to believe in a large and most affecting expenditure of the grace of God intentionally insufficient for salvation.'[4]

Above all, this view completely fails to do justice to the teaching of the Bible in which God's will for the salvation of all mankind is expressed. It is true that the upholders of a rigid theory of predestination do not shrink from declaring that the death of Christ was for the benefit only of the elect and attempt to show that the 'all' for whom He died are merely 'all the elect.' To discuss the relevant passages would necessitate too great a digression at this point, and we must be content simply to register our feeling of certainty that this is a false interpretation of the New Testament. And to suggest that the offer of the Gospel which is couched in universalistic terms in the New Testament is directed merely to a hidden and limited group among its hearers is to impose a meaning upon the text which can claim nothing in its support.

Accordingly, the view that God has predestinated a limited number of men to salvation, with the result that the remainder have no opportunity of responding to the Gospel, is not to be deduced from the biblical teaching. What in fact we have discovered from our survey of the New Testament is that God has chosen the Christian Church to be His people, and that in certain individual cases He has chosen men for His work. Whenever men are saved from their sins it is because God has taken the initiative. Salvation is *entirely* by His grace; it comes to men *only* through the call of God in the Gospel and their consequent response. But this call does not always rouse faith in the hearer, for many who hear reject the message. This, however, does not justify us in postulating two kinds of divine call, one which has no result because God has not willed it to have a result, and another 'effectual' call which irresistibly converts the hearer. The New Testament leaves the impression that rejection of the divine call is due to human sin, and is content to leave the matter there as part of the mystery of iniquity.[5] Nor does it discuss why the call comes to some men and nations and not to others.

We must rule out the view that God foreordains a certain number of elect to salvation with its logical consequence that they are bound to persevere to the end and attain final salvation.[6] May it not be the case, however, that when a man responds to God with faith and commits his life to Him a divine plan comes into action which includes his perseverance? This can be determined only by a consideration of the actual circumstances of the Christian life, both the dangers which threaten the believer and the divine grace which sustains him.

TEMPTATION AND CONFLICT

The New Testament knows of many dangers in the life of the Christian and each of its authors would have echoed Paul's words that only through many tribulations shall we enter the kingdom of God (Acts 14:22).

The reaction of the outside world to believers is to persecute them, with the aim either of forcing them to give up their faith by denying God or of liquidating them; in both cases, so far as the world is concerned, the believer is defeated. Believers, therefore, are frequently tempted to give up their faith because of the difficulties of maintaining it amid fierce opposition.

A more subtle form of temptation is to accept false doctrine. In whatever form this presents itself, Judaism and various forms of incipient gnosticism being the principal varieties in the New Testament, the temptation is to blunt the edge of faith in Jesus Christ and ultimately to destroy it altogether.

A third form of temptation is to various forms of sin and immorality. The significance of this form of temptation is that it causes the believer to deny the power of God to preserve him from sinning, to return to the very things from which he was saved by belief in Christ (and which by their nature exclude a man from the kingdom of God), and to perform those acts which are expressly forbidden by the Lord whom he professes to serve. In other words, sin is an act and attitude which is incompatible with the obedience of faith, and hence constitutes a denial of faith.

To these three types of threat should possibly be added a fourth one, the development of weariness in the faith, in which the believer gradually drifts away from his faith and passes into the state of apostasy.

The question now arises as to how far these temptations and tribulations put the believer in jeopardy. We may note first that the New Testament does not regard the Christian as a person who must be entirely free from sin if he is to be a Christian at all. While sin is obviously inconsistent with faith, it does not immediately and automatically extinguish it. There is full provision for the sinful Christian to turn to God and claim renewed forgiveness. This is a truth which is enshrined in so sacred and central a place in the teaching of Jesus as the Lord's Prayer. For the person who is overtaken by sin and cries for forgiveness there is the assurance of a welcome from the Father. Nor is such forgiveness merely for what may be called unwitting sins. The distinction between unwitting and witting sins is an important one, but it would be entirely wrong to conclude that the Christian who sins wittingly is thereby excluded from forgiveness. Such a conclusion would be absolutely contrary to Christian experience, especially to the experience of the Christian who is all too conscious of the existence of the kind of inward struggle portrayed in Romans 7. It would be wrong to press the New Testament passages which speak about forgiveness for sins done in ignorance to the point where forgiveness for witting sins is excluded.[7]

Yet, having said this, we must also state that the witting sinner is in a dangerous situation. The New Testament contains too many warnings about the danger of sin and apostasy for us to be complacent about these possibilities. Jesus summone His disciples to endure to the end. The Acts gave a warning about the rise of false teachers in the Church. Paul earnestly warned his readers against flagrant sin and the danger of heresy, and had resort to the most severe discipline in order that they might ultimately be saved. Hebrews insisted strongly on the danger of believers drifting away from the faith. John spoke of the possibility of branches being severed from the vine. These are but a few representative statements and indicate the drift of New Testament teaching. Moreover, as we saw in our discussion of Hebrews, these dangers are real and not 'hypothetical.'

A final point is that the New Testament refers in an admittedly small number of cases to Christians falling into apostasy. There are passages which speak prophetically of the love of many growing cold and of men departing from the faith, and there are other passages where men who once believed are said to have fallen into sin and apostasy. These cases have been discussed in detail above, and we have seen that the possibility of genuine Christians falling into apostasy is not to be explained away.[8]

THE FAITHFULNESS OF GOD

These threats to faith are not the only or the main thing taught in the New Testament. There is also much evidence that God cares for believers and preserves them from falling away. The care of God for the 'little flock' is a very important part of the teaching of Jesus; it is presented as an antidote to fear for the future, but it is also regarded as a means of enabling the disciples to withstand persecution. What Jesus taught is taken up by the rest of the New Testament. Acts shows us Paul commending the believers to the grace of God and praying for them. In his Epistles Paul prays for his converts with a view to their being sustained to the parousia. He lays great stress on the faithfulness of God who is able to preserve Christians amid persecution and temptation, and he boldly asserts that nothing can separate the Christian from the love of God. Believers already have the assurance that they belong to God and can call Him Father, and they possess the earnest and seal of the Spirit. The Pastoral Epistles show us Paul at the end of a faithful ministry, confident of obtaining his own crown.

Such ideas are presented equally strongly in John. There we find that the group of disciples have been given to Jesus by the Father; during His ministry He preserves them from falling away, except for the son of perdition, and He will raise them up at the last day. They are His sheep and nobody can pluck them out of His hand. Before His passion He prays to the Father to continue to keep them, so that in the end they may be with Him and share His glory. Similarly, Peter can speak of believers as being kept by God for a salvation to be revealed at the parousia, and the Revelation shows us a Church of Christians who conquer in the midst of persecution and tribulation.

From this brief survey it is apparent that believers may be confident of persevering through the power of God, and the majority of believers do persevere. To state anything less would make an utter mockery of the New Testament doctrine of salvation. Nevertheless, we cannot forget the threats to perseverance which have been mentioned, and the possibility or even the fact of men who fail to persevere. The student of the New Testament and the Christian believer are thus faced with a distinctive problem, and it is now time to examine the various solutions which have been propounded to it.[9]

2. THE THEOLOGICAL PROBLEM OF PERSEVERANCE

THE MIXED CHURCH

One obvious solution to our problem is that those who fall away from the Christian Church were never truly converted to the faith. In the course of our study we have gathered abundant evidence that the New Testament writers are aware that the Church is a body of mixed composition. The visible Church, i.e. the company of people who profess to believe in Jesus Christ and have submitted to the rite of baptism, contains men whose belief is superficial and unreal. Many such people may appear for a time to be genuine in their belief, but in a time of testing it becomes apparent that they do not truly own Jesus Christ as their Lord. We found this point of view put forward with great clarity in Matthew; it is possible, for example, to call Jesus 'Lord' without a true surrender of one's life to Him. There is no good reason for doubting that this teaching, although especially found in Matthew, goes back to Jesus Himself. The same view is to be found in Paul, and, although he does not give very much prominence to it in his undoubtedly genuine Epistles, it is stated clearly in the Pastoral Epistles. It is also to be found in the Johannine literature, where it is taught that membership of the group of disciples is no guarantee of salvation: only abiding trust in Jesus leads to eternal life.

In numerous places the existence of this distinction is sufficient to explain why some Christians fall away into apostasy. When a time of testing comes, the real nature of their profession is exposed, and it becomes clear that they never truly believed in Jesus.

We may accept this explanation of many cases of apostasy without any further ado. It is no doubt true that the suggestion of a distinction between the visible and invisible Church is not always favourably accepted in contemporary theology, but we would submit that the New Testament evidence compels us to accept the distinction. It may be submitted that the reason for this uneasiness with the notion of an invisible Church lies in the fact that there are two fairly distinct ways of defining the Church. On the one hand, the Church may be regarded as an institution created by God whose existence is to be seen in the traditional 'marks' of the preaching of the Word, the administration of the sacraments and the exercise of discipline. In this case the validity of the visible/invisible distinction is not clearly apparent, since the Church is present wherever the marks are to be seen. But, on the other hand, the Church may also be regarded as the company of believers or of the elect, and in this case a visible/invisible distinction is right and proper in order to indicate who are and who are not members of the Church in God's eyes. Whatever terminology be used, a distinction can properly be drawn between outward profession and inward acceptance of the Christian faith. It was certainly the view of those who had to deal with the intrusion of heresy into the New Testament Church that the false teachers were often people who were masquerading as members of the Church under false pretences.

For the Calvinist this 'mixed Church' theory is the complete explanation of the cases of apostasy recorded in the New Testament; those who fall away are in every case the non-elect who never truly believed in Jesus and were attached in a purely outward manner to the Church. But we cannot be happy that this theory is adequate to explain the whole of the evidence.

First, we must remind ourselves of those cases where it is impossible to conclude with certainty that the apostates had never been true believers; although the instances are admittedly few, it would be unwise to conclude that they can and must be forced into the 'category of cases of apostasy by merely professing believers.

Second, we have to reckon with the warnings addressed to believers against falling away. As we noted earlier, these warnings exhort believers not to lose the salvation which they have already received or to surrender the faith which they already profess; they cannot be regarded as commands to believers to test themselves to see if they were truly converted in the beginning. If the Calvinist theory were true, the warnings would necessarily take such forms as: 'Make sure that you really were converted,' 'Beware lest what you think is an experience of salvation by faith is really nothing of the kind,' and 'Examine yourself to see whether you really are what you profess to be.' Naturally some commands of this form are to be found. But the main type of warning is to beware lest one gives up the faith which one already holds or loses the salvation which one already enjoys. Put otherwise, the positive command is not to begin to be a genuine believer but to continue and persevere in the faith which one already has; the believer is not to add some new ingredient to faith, without which it was not true faith, but to maintain the faith. In Johannine terminology, 'abiding' is not a fresh quality to be added to faith but the maintenance of a faith already held, and in Hebrews the ideas of perseverance and zeal make the same point. The command is not to go back to the beginning and start afresh with genuine conversion, but to hold fast the faith to the end. The New Testament takes for granted a present experience of salvation of which the believer is conscious. Here and now he may know the experience of Christian joy and certainty. He is not called to question the reality of this experience on the grounds that it may be illusory because he was never truly converted; rather, he is urged to continue to enjoy salvation through abiding in Christ and persevering in faith.

The 'mixed Church' theory is accordingly not adequate to explain the whole of the New Testament evidence.

THE SOLUTION OF R. BULTMANN

Alongside the Calvinist solution to the problem, we may place that of Arminianism. This simply states that the divine protection of the believer does not necessarily rule out the possibility of his falling away, although, as we noted earlier, this possibility is regarded as a very slight one.

It is difficult to find modern evangelical statements of this point of view, but it may be useful to see it presented in extreme form by a non-evangelical writer, R. Bultmann. It is by no means easy to sum up Bultmann's understanding of the New Testament, but it is hoped that the following brief outline will not be too unjust to the complexities of his position. For Bultmann, Christian faith is centered solely upon Christ, and through such faith the believer enters upon eschatological existence. Such existence can be described in terms of love, joy, and peace, although Bultmann appears to have the gravest difficulty in providing any objective description of what these words mean; they are apparently to be understood only by the person who takes the step of faith. Bultmann finds it difficult to give any reasons why anybody should take the step of faith. The believer must simply accept Jesus as the revealer of God, although it cannot be proved that He is the revealer, and it cannot be stated what He reveals except just this one thing, that He is the revealer. There are no objective grounds in the ordinary sense for accepting Him, and certainty comes only through taking the leap of faith. Only through taking the existential decision is the believer confirmed in doing so.[10]

The consequence is that faith itself has no ground of certainty about its own continuation.[11] Salvation does not depend so much upon an initial conversion as upon a continuous attitude of faith. To speak of divine care and protection of the believer is simply to bring out the real nature of faith, i.e. that it is a deliberate renunciation of one's own self and earthly security and a complete openness to God, to other men, and to the future.[12] Faith is the surrender of all one's own claims. In such a system there is no place for any kind of supernatural power. There is, therefore, no certainty of any kind that the believer will persevere; nor is it certain that there is a future life to which one would wish to attain[13] — one can only persevere. Faith 'is never possessed as a secure possession or as a quieting insight, but rather constantly has to make its way against all the temptations that continually emerge out of existence and give man the illusion that he can still dispose of himself.'[14]

This explanation is no more satisfactory than the Calvinist position. There is a certain attractiveness about it with its attempt to bring out the state of jeopardy in which the believer stands every hour, but there is little of that consciousness of the power and succour of Christ which characterizes the authentic Christian experience.[15] There are so many weak points about the view of Bultmann that it cannot possibly be accepted as a faithful rendering of New Testament doctrine, although its author would presumably wish it to be regarded as such. Its basic weakness is a complete dehistoricizing of the Christian faith, so that faith becomes an attitude entirely divorced from any relation to historical circumstances and events.[16] Again, we may criticize Bultmann for the way in which he deprives the Christian life of content. It is extremely difficult to see why anybody should adopt the Christian way if it can be described only in the purely formal categories employed by Bultmann. It is significant that Bultmann can discuss the theology of Paul without ever mentioning prayer, and his discussion of prayer in the theology of John is extremely formal. The communion with God, of which A. R. George has written, is totally neglected. Christian assurance of salvation is minimized. It is true that Bultmann notes the assurances given to faith in Paul and John, but they are deprived of all value. Linked with this is the fact that the Holy Spirit is regarded not as the power of God working in the hearts of men but as 'the new possibility of genuine, human life.'[17] There is, in short, no comfort available for the believer to assure him that he will persevere.

Although Bultmann emphasizes that faith must rest solely upon God through the Revealer, it is impossible to escape the impression that in the end faith is a purely human phenomenon and its preservation depends upon human effort. Although he does justice to the fragility of Christian existence in this world, we must ask whether proper regard is paid to the strong assurances of perseverance which are given to believers in the New Testament. Arminianism of this kind is not a true development from New Testament teaching.

THE SOLUTION OF G. C. BERKOUWER

The most considerable attempt in recent years to arrive at a solution of our problem is that of G. C. Berkouwer in the volume of his 'Studies in Dogmatics' entitled *Faith and Perseverance.*[18] Berkouwer stands avowedly in the strict Calvinist tradition, but he is keenly aware of the criticisms which may be made of that tradition and of modern trends in theological study. He is anxious, therefore, to avoid the impression of constructing a closed, logical system, and denies explicitly that perseverance is simply to be understood as the logical consequence of election. Moreover, he recognizes the point which we found taken to its extreme form in Bultmann, that the Christian life is to be conceived dynamically rather than statically; salvation is not simply a gift received once for all at conversion but is an experience which continues and which must therefore be continually appropriated. Where he differs decisively from Bultmann is in his greater stress on the biblical teaching about the protection of God as a supernatural power which must be taken realistically and seriously.

For Berkouwer perseverance is to be understood in terms of the divine preservation of the believer. This preservation becomes a reality as the believer commits himself to God in faith. To persevere means to cease to trust oneself — for there is no security in oneself but only the possibility of lapse — and to cast oneself upon the preserving grace of God. Yet this casting of oneself upon God is not a human act in the sense that man can perform it of his own volition or by his own power; it is itself the result of divine grace. For example, the various warnings against failure to persevere are the means which God in His grace uses to lead believers to trust in Him as their preserver. No grounds of confidence of perseverance can be found in the believer himself as a *man*, but there is a basis for final perseverance in the fact that faith consists in our being grasped in *God's* hand. The admonitions and warnings thus turn out to be one of the ways in which perseverance is attained. Because perseverance thus rests upon the faithfulness of God to care for and to warn His people, the believer who trusts in Him can be completely assured of perseverance to the end. Hence Berkouwer finds that the New Testament teaches the final perseverance of the saints, and the possibility of apostasy does not arise. There is a continuity in faith which is safely led past the dangers of disbelief.

This exposition of Berkouwer is most refreshing and is a genuine attempt to do justice to the insights of Calvinism in the light of a fresh appraisal of the biblical material. He has rightly grasped the essential point that perseverance depends upon the believer resting in the keeping power of God. Again, Berkouwer rightly holds that the believer can give expression to his confidence in the keeping power of God who has begun the work of salvation in him and will continue it to the end. He correctly sees also that this expression is one which is to be made only by faith, in the language of prayer and trust.

But certain difficulties remain. It is difficult to feel that Berkouwer has done justice to the force of the warnings against falling away in the New Testament. He does not face up to the fact that the danger against which they warn is a real and not a hypothetical danger. Although his exposition of Hebrews 6 is not very luminous, he would appear to adopt as a general principle of biblical interpretation the view of T. Hewitt that the dangers against which the believer is warned are not real dangers because the believer never in fact disobeys the warnings.

This view of the exhortations and warnings is common in Calvinist writers. The use of them does not prove that any of the elect is in danger of apostasy; nevertheless they are necessary to prevent them from falling into apostasy.[19] The elect cannot apostatize because by God's secret counsel they are the elect and because He keeps them from apostasy by giving them exhortations and warnings to which they will infallibly respond, just as they once responded to His initial effectual calling to salvation. Thus Berkouwer explicitly holds to a doctrine of irresistible grace:[20] 'God's grace does not stop short at the limits of human freedom of choice,' and faith and grace cannot be set over against each other since this would produce a synergistic doctrine of grace. The stress is thus on the utter sovereignty of grace. It is sure to triumph in the end, and it does so through the faith in God which His grace itself arouses in the believer.

There are a number of problems here. Since the irresistibility of grace is not such that the believer is infallibly preserved from the possibility of sinning, we must be pardoned for wondering whether it automatically preserves him from the possibility of falling away. It is not a question of whether grace is stronger than temptation, but of whether grace inevitably overcomes temptation. Berkouwer would presumably object that if we do not accept his view then synergism creeps in. But at the back of this objection there would appear to lie a misapprehension of the relation of human response to the offer of divine grace. The Calvinist insists very rightly that man is not able to contribute anything whatsoever to his salvation; he cannot do anything to merit grace, and he cannot add anything to it. Grace alone is sufficient to save him. Hence it is concluded that the faith which accepts grace must itself be regarded as the work of grace and not as the work of man himself. The decision to accept grace is taken out of the hands of man and ascribed to the working of grace. But this conclusion makes the mistake of ignoring the fact that a distinction is to be drawn between the meritorious work of earning grace and the entirely neutral act of receiving grace. To receive a gift is not a meritorious act, and there seem to be no *a priori* grounds for denying the ability of man to receive grace. Of himself he is unable to make any response to God, and his response is entirely due to the fact that God first calls him, but it is unnecessary to take the further step of arguing that his response is also given to him by God.[21] The result of God's gracious act is that man is free to accept or to resist the gospel, not that he is made free to respond by a process whose effect is analogous to the results of post-hypnotic suggestion in that the agent carries out by 'free choice' at one level of his consciousness what has been commanded at another level of consciousness.

A second difficulty may be seen by a comparison between this view of the warnings addressed to the elect and the view taken of the threats of eternal punishment by upholders of universalism. Writing as a universalist, J. A. T. Robinson claims that on the subjective level the warnings of divine judgement must be taken with all seriousness by men: 'To the man in decision — and that means to all men, always, right up to the last hour — hell is in every way as real a destiny as heaven. Only the man who has been genuinely confronted by both alternatives can be saved.' It is the existence of this choice which leads a man to decision. For a long time he may refuse heaven. But at some point on the road every man will find himself confronted by Christ and overwhelmed by divine love, and he will surrender to

Him. So in the end only heaven is objectively real; all men will ultimately find themselves there.

The difficulties in this attempt to reinterpret the biblical teaching about Hell so that it is only subjectively true are obvious enough. What may not be so obvious is that if we substitute 'all the elect' for 'all men' in Robinson's argument we obtain the Calvinist view of the warnings. Put otherwise, Robinson has extended the scope of 'the elect' to include all men, and in effect applied the Calvinist understanding of the warnings to the elect to the threats of judgement for all men. This means that the Calvinist is treating the warnings against falling away with as little seriousness as Robinson treats the threats of eternal punishment; in both cases the warnings are deprived of objective content.

Moreover, while Robinson at least attempts to preserve the 'subjective' truth of the threats for the unbeliever, the Calvinist may not even do this. The whole point of the Calvinist stress is that even on the subjective level the elect know that they cannot come under judgement for apostasy. What happens now? If a professed believer falls into grievous sin and remains impenitent, the Calvinist is forced to say, 'You are not one of the elect,' despite whatever assurances of his election the believer may earlier have produced and on which he may be tempted to rely. But this means, first that there is no infallible certainty about one's election, for one can never be sure that he will not fall into such grievous sin as may call his election in question, and, second, that once again justice is not done to the character of the biblical warnings which do not say, 'Beware lest you have never truly been converted,' but rather 'Make your calling and election sure: hold fast the confession of your faith without wavering, for he who promised is faithful' (2 Peter 1:10; Hebrews 10:23).

Such commands can be disobeyed by the 'elect,' but at the same time there remain the elements in biblical teaching which indicate that God can and does work by His Spirit to influence men for good. There is the mysterious working of prayer, and the fact that Christians are ready to confess that their good impulses are due to the work of God and not to themselves. The Christian life cannot be understood in terms of natural causation. But the alternative is not necessarily a divine determinism, so that whatever happens in the life of the believer is the result of a secret divine causation. We must be content to recognize that the processes of divine and human causation cannot be fully integrated by our human understanding. To do so is to press beyond the limits of what has been revealed to us.

K. Barth has well written: 'No doubt human love of God, the ordination of men to Sonship, and their calling to be witnesses of the Resurrection, are genuine occurrences, consequent upon God's knowledge of men and taking place in the knowledge of the true and only God. But this must not be taken to mean that His love has brought into being a particular temporal human being and having and doing, which is the result of a divine causation which took place concretely as the first of a series of temporal occurrences. Predestination means the recognition that love towards God is an occurrence, a being and having and doing of men, which takes place in no moment of time, which is beyond time, which has its origin at every moment in God Himself, and which must therefore be sought and found only in Him.'[22] We must be content to admit that as finite creatures we cannot fully understand the ways of God in relation to the world, and therefore we must beware of pushing beyond the evidence of Scripture to philosophical and dogmatic schemes which may distort that evidence.

TOWARDS A SOLUTION

We have now seen that the positions of both Arminians and Calvinists have their weaknesses. The Arminian view ascribes altogether too much to the will of man, despite the guarded nature of its affirmations, and the Calvinist view ascribes everything ultimately to the irresistible grace of God. Is there a third possibility?

In our study we have found repeatedly that the way to persevere is simply — by persevering. The believer is not told that he is one of the elect and therefore cannot fall away, nor is there any particular character of his faith which indicates that he is the kind of person who cannot fall away. He is simply told to continue in obedience and faith and to trust in the God who will keep him from falling. He perseveres by persevering. Perseverance is not some particular quality of faith or something to be added to faith, but the fact that faith continues. To speak of the need to develop endurance, as the New Testament does, is the same thing as saying that one must continue to believe despite every temptation to disbelieve.

Such persevering faith is faith in God through Jesus Christ and is at all times a response to His grace. It is faith in the God who keeps, establishes, and strengthens believers, committal of oneself to His Lordship and His care. But such committal does not mean that the believer no longer needs to watch lest he stumble and fall. He must still beware of temptation. The fact that he can still fall into sin shows that he is not preserved miraculously by God from falling, although God is able to keep those who trust in Him from falling and never refuses His grace to those who seek it. God's power enables men to battle against temptation, but does not relieve them from temptation or from the necessity to fight against it. The way to victory is by constant submission to God.

Therefore, when a believer raises the question, 'Am I sure to persevere?' the answer which he receives is not a statement but an imperative, 'Carry on persevering!' We remember that when Jesus was asked, 'Are they few that be saved?' He replied, 'Strive to enter in!' One is commanded not to speculate but to believe!

Nevertheless, we ask whether we have any assurance that we shall persevere to the end. The New Testament answers our question with its promises that nothing can separate us from the love of God, and that nobody can steal away the sheep of the Good Shepherd. Alongside the imperatives stand the promises. We do not need to fear in the midst of temptation, for we know that if we trust in God, His power will preserve us. And such trust is not presumption but is a confidence grounded in our experience of divine grace. Thus Paul could face the test of martyrdom knowing that he would be victorious through the power of God. When the believer puts his trust in God, he is entitled to be confident.

But, we go on, how can we be confident that we shall continue to trust in God? If no outside power can separate those who love God from Him, can we separate ourselves from that love? Can we be confident that our faith, strong at the moment, will not grow weak? The point of the Epistle to the Hebrews is that this possibility cannot be ruled out, but it is meant to drive us to renewed faith in God, because the danger is a real one.[23] But at the same time the New Testament most certainly teaches that God strengthens the faith of the believer so that he may withstand temptation; He does not forget those who trust in Him. Hence, while the New Testament knows the possibility of failure to persevere, it also knows the fact of growth in grace and the knowledge of Jesus Christ so that the Christian can attain to a confidence which lifts him above the fear of falling away. It is perhaps in this idea of growth and development in faith that the key to the problem is to be found. Faith is something which grows and becomes stronger and consequently more removed from the fear of falling. And yet this does not mean that the assurance of perseverance is for a spiritual élite; it is for the weakest believer who is prepared to cry, 'Lord, I believe; help my unbelief.'

In short, we cannot go beyond the teaching of the New Testament which places side by side the possibility of failure to persevere and the greater possibility of a confidence in God and a continuing faith which, as it is sustained by God, is preserved from the fear of falling away. We must rest content with this twofold emphasis and not try to deny either side of it.

It may be objected that this conclusion deprives the Christian of an absolute confidence in perseverance. But it must be remembered that the Calvinist does not have an absolute confidence either; it is always possible that he may not be one of the elect, and he must constantly strive to make his calling and election sure. This does not mean that the Calvinist lives in an attitude of uncertainty or even of despair, for he may claim the 'whosoever' promises, but at the same time there is not the certainty of irresistible logic, since it is admitted that a man may taste deeply of the grace of God and yet fall away.[24] There is a similar element of logical uncertainty in the conclusion which is suggesting itself to us in this study, and one must be prepared to admit the necessity of this in order to drive believers to a closer trust in their faithful God. At the same time, there is a confidence which can grow and deepen, and hence the possibility of the faith that God will preserve us for His heavenly kingdom.

It is possible, therefore, to maintain the confidence of the believer without committing ourselves to a watertight logical system of irresistible grace and unconditional election to final salvation, and at the same time to give a realistic meaning to the warnings of the New Testament. We have found it necessary to admit the possibility of falling away: John Bunyan, it will be remembered, saw that there was a way to hell even from the gates of heaven.[25] We have been unable to state that attainment of final salvation logically follows on from true conversion. We have been unable to give a rationale of why some Christians persevere and others do not, because in our opinion the Bible does not provide this, and it is dangerous to impose a dogmatic system, whether that of Calvin or Arminius, upon the Bible. But we can say firmly that, while it is possible for a Christian to fail to persevere after a genuine experience of salvation, yet, with all the promises of a faithful God to sustain those who trust in Him, the main emphasis of the New Testament is on confidence and assurance of final salvation.

It will be seen that the position at which we have arrived is not so very far from that of G. C. Berkouwer, in that we agree that it is possible for the believer, even though he knows of the possibility of apostasy, to be confident of persevering because he puts his trust in God. This may not be true for every believer — the Hebrews needed to be warned that they were in danger — but it is what the New Testament regards as the norm. There can thus be a place in the Christian life for the hymns both of Toplady and of Wesley which we cited at the beginning; exultant confidence and anxious fear must be held together of the Christian in a paradox, although the normal progress should be towards an increasing confidence which removes the fear of apostasy. Such a paradox arises because the New Testament knows neither the rigid logic of Calvinism nor the 'casualness' of Arminianism but teaches us to put our trust in God.

Our answer, therefore, to the theological problem which gave rise to this study, is a refusal to press the New Testament to give a logically rigid solution. The New Testament is content to hold together the facts of perseverance and apostasy in paradox, and to rest the confidence of the believer not on a logical argument but on the faithfulness of the God in whom he must continually trust. As he thus trusts, he finds that God is indeed faithful and that only his own wilfulness and failure to trust can cause him to fall; as he grows in trust, he is able to proclaim with the voice of faith that nothing can separate him from the love of God. Not even the last enemy, death, and the physical and mental weakness which may precede it can break the relationship with God enjoyed by His people during their earthly lives; He remains faithful, so that they are kept by the power of God.[26]

3. THE PRACTICAL IMPLICATIONS

THE LIFE OF PERSEVERANCE

Since the emphasis in the New Testament has proved to be on the fact of perseverance, it comes as no surprise that it teaches clearly the way of perseverance. It recognizes that the faith of believers continually needs to be strengthened by the grace of God, and it offers practical methods of strengthening. Undoubtedly, the main thrust of these is to convince the believer of the faithfulness, love, and power of God. Much of the New Testament material is plain teaching about the promises of God.

Faith must be nourished on this theology of God's care for the believer. Hence there are frequent commands addressed to the members of the Church to examine themselves. Those who have an inadequate or merely nominal faith must be led to a true faith in Christ, and those who already believe must be urged to maintain the faith which they already have. Such exhortation is given through preaching and teaching. In this connexion we have noted a frequent injunction to believers not to neglect meeting together. No doubt this is in order that they may have the benefit of exhortation and the sense of unity and encouragement which arises through Christian fellowship. But it may also be presumed that there is a more theological basis for this injunction in the fact that in the meeting of believers the presence of God is especially felt. In the meeting the Church becomes in reality the body of Christ in which the Spirit operates as believers aid each other. This emphatically does not deny the presence of God with the solitary Christian, but it does stress the paramount importance of the Christian meeting as one of the essential aids to perseverance.

DISCIPLINE AND RESTORATION

In the New Testament the efforts of the Church to help its members went beyond admonitions and warnings. When a member showed signs of falling away and did not respond to admonition and encouragement, the Church had recourse to more serious methods of discipline in order to bring home to him where he stood.

Such discipline is not something which the Church may or may not employ according to its own whim and fancy. It is a prescribed course of action of which we have found evidence in all the main strata of the New Testament. There is no need to repeat here the details of the system; all we need to remember is that the system of repeated warning, followed ultimately, if necessary, by excommunication, was applied in a manner suitable to the circumstances and not as a rigid formula. What we now stress is that discipline had two functions.

First, the undoubted purpose of the act was to make plain to the offender the grim reality of his position. By his sin he was cutting himself off from God and the hope of salvation — whether he was regarded as a true believer who was falling away or as a merely nominal believer whose lack of faith was now becoming apparent — and the effect of excommunication was to give plain expression to the fact that as an unrepentant sinner he was rejected by God. It has been pointed out that the sacraments of baptism and the Lord's Supper have an element of judgement in them,[27] and the giving of the sop to Judas by Jesus was described as *eine Art satanisches Sakrament* by W. Wrede.[28] One may perhaps think of excommunication as a sacramental severing of the sinner from the grace which he has already rejected for himself. The Church thus makes plain to the sinner what he is doing: he is cutting himself off from the hope of salvation.

Second, the purpose of excommunication is also redemptive. From the teaching of Paul it seems certain that the sinner could be received back into the Church if he repented of his sin. Similarly, James taught the duty of believers to confess their sins to each other, and knew the possibility of forgiveness in cases of sickness which appeared to be due to sin.[29] At the same time Paul knew the possibility of a discipline which failed in its saving purpose because the sinner failed to repent. Hebrews taught that there were cases where a man might reach the point of no return; since, however, Hebrews does not refer explicitly to excommunication in this connexion, it is uncertain whether excommunication itself is there regarded as a final, decisive act of rejection which cannot be rescinded. Our study has suggested that there is a limit to the patience of God — Jesus spoke of sin which can never be forgiven — and even that a person may be unable to find the divine blessing though he seeks it with tears; but at the same time we have seen the reality of divine forgiveness for those who do repent. The sayings about a limit are not to be taken lightly or explained away, and they stand as a warning to the apostate or the intending apostate, but the same New Testament book which most clearly utters this warning also knows of One who is able for all time to save those who draw near to God through Him, since He always lives to make intercession for them.

4. THE MODERN SITUATION

Although our aim throughout this book has been confined to making an objective survey of the biblical material, we may conclude by noting briefly the relevance of our conclusions to the pastoral problems of the Church today.

It has become obvious that the New Testament recognizes that the Church on earth is inevitably a mixed Church, composed of true believers and nominal adherents. This is not said to be an ideal state in which the Church ought to acquiesce.

The New Testament says nothing to support the idea of a *Volkskirche*, for its picture is indubitably of a 'gathered' community of those who profess faith in God through Jesus Christ. At the same time it is content to make faith the basis of membership. Faith will be accompanied by a certain manner of life — clearly a man who is flagrantly immoral and refuses to repent can scarcely by recognized as a believer — but it is not the manner of life in itself or conformity to some special code of belief which is the basis of membership.

The practical point which emerges is that the Church must labour to see that all its members have a living faith in Christ. The great majority of those who slip away from the Church are those who became its members without a real and living faith. It is a mistake to assume that a desire to join the Church is synonymous with a real faith in God through Jesus Christ. There would appear to be a need for a much greater stress on confession of faith as the one and only basis for Church membership, and care should be exercised that those who join the Church realize the significance of what they are doing and honestly believe from their hearts.

It will no doubt be pointed out that there are dangers if the Church or its ministers attempt to gauge the faith of its would-be members and act as arbiters over the hidden motives of men's hearts, but the recognition of such dangers does not absolve the Church from the need to face up to the far greater spiritual dangers of allowing men and women to fail to realize that faith in Jesus Christ is the indispensable qualification for membership of the Church. Evidence of a genuine conversion and experience of salvation, reflected in a changing way of life, is surely essential if the Church is to protect its members and would-be members from misapprehension of the true nature of Church membership.

Within the Church there is need for much more stress on a doctrine which we have seen to form an integral part of the New Testament teaching about the Christian life. At the same time there is need for considerable pastoral care of those whose faith is growing cold. The art of loving admonition between the members of the Church is something that has largely been lost in the contemporary Church, and yet faithfulness to the New Testament pattern suggests that this is something which needs restoration today. Christians must be encouraged to examine themselves to see whether they are in the faith and to grow in faith and steadfast endurance. Sometimes in the past such self-examination has been associated with the 'fencing of the table' at the Lord's Supper and, although we may have reservations about the way in which this has been practised, some such act perhaps needs a new emphasis today as a means of leading Christians to examine themselves and to put their trust afresh in Christ for forgiveness and salvation.

With regard to those members of the Church who appear to have lost all faith in Christ there would appear to be a clamant need for some kind of discipline to be practised. The suggestion is one that may receive cool reception in this day and age, but it is difficult to believe that the Reformers were wrong when they included in the 'marks' of the Church the maintenance of godly discipline. Recognition of the abuses to which systems of discipline have been open in the past should not lead us to condemn the principle itself but to seek to temper justice with mercy and to practise a loving but firm care of the members of the Church.

Above all, however, there needs to be an emphasis on that positive growth in Christian faith and trust which is the key to perseverance and to assurance of perseverance. This must be part of the message of the preacher as he feeds the flock with the Word of God week by week, for a doctrine which occupies so central a place in the message of the New Testament cannot be overlooked in a well-balanced biblical and expository ministry. But in these days when the ordinary services of the Church often fail to attract the very people who are in the greatest need of hearing the Word of God other means than the pulpit must also be tried. It is therefore fitting to remember that in the New Testament one of the chief antidotes to falling away was the meeting of Christians for mutual edification. Whatever name it may pass under, the fellowship group has a vital part to play in the nourishment of Christian faith and its potentialities need to be explored far more than they are at present. The Church which is concerned about the spiritual life of its members will see in the form of fellowship the heaven-sent house group or some such answer to its need. It has been often said that the Methodist Church was strong when its class meetings were strong; today in all branches of the Church we need a rediscovery of the power of Christian fellowship to impart a new vigour to Christian living.

The New Testament is rich in its teaching about Christian perseverance. Through the exposition of its message in the spoken word, both from the pulpit and in the fellowship meeting, the grace of God will win in its hearers the response of an ever deepening trust in His keeping power so that they go on from strength to strength until they arrive in Zion:

Omnipotent Lord, my Saviour and King,
Thy succour afford, Thy righteousness bring:
Thy promises bind Thee compassion to have;
Now, now let me find Thee almighty to save.

Rejoicing in hope, and patient in grief,
To Thee I look up for certain relief;
I fear no denial, no danger I fear,
Nor start from the trial, while Jesus is near.

I every hour in jeopardy stand;
But Thou art my power, and holdest my hand:
While yet I am calling, Thy succour I feel;
It saves me from falling, or plucks me from hell.

O who can explain this struggle for life,
This travail and pain, this trembling and strife:
Plague, earthquake, and famine, and tumult, and war,
The wonderful coming of Jesus declare.

Yet God is above men, devils, and sin,
My Jesus's love the battle shall win;
So terribly glorious His coming shall be,
His love all-victorious shall conquer for me.

He all shall break through; His truth and His grace
Shall bring me into the plentiful place,
Through much tribulation, through water and fire,
Through floods of temptation and flames of desire.

On Jesus, my power, till then I rely,
All evil before His presence shall fly;
When I have my Saviour, my sin shall depart,
And Jesus for ever shall reign in my heart.[30]

Notes

NOTES TO THE INTRODUCTION

1. V. Taylor, *Forgiveness and Reconciliation*, pp. 159–65.

2. See the criticisms of R. N. Flew, *The Idea of Perfection in Christian Theology*, Oxford, 1934, pp. 53ff., and B. B. Warfield, *Perfectionism*, New York, 1931, I, pp. 239–82.

3. 'Perseverance,' translating προσκαρτέρησις, is found with reference to steadfast prayer in Ephesians 6:18. The NT word for perseverance is ὑπομονή, inadequately translated as 'patience' in AV: it means steadfast endurance under temptation. The verb ὑπομένω also occurs frequently.

4. Cf. πίπτω 'to fall' (Romans 11:11, 22; 14:4; 1 Corinthians 10:12; 13:8; Hebrews 4:11; Revelation 2:5); παραπίπτω 'to fall away, transgress' (Hebrews 6:6), παραρρέω, 'to drift away' (Hebrews 2:1); the root σκανδαλ-, 'to stumble, offend' is also important. See H. Schlier, TDNT, I. pp. 512–514.

5. The word 'apostasy' does not occur in AV. The verb ἀφίστημι is used of giving up the faith in Luke 8:13; 1 Timothy 4:1 and Hebrews 3:12, and is used of departure from God in the LXX (ἀποστασία [Acts 21:21; 2 Thessalonians 2:3] is not used of apostasy by Christians).

A distinction must be drawn between the possibilities of a general increase of wickedness and godlessness in the unbelieving world (often called 'the final apostasy' in dependence on 2 Thessalonians 2:3 and 1 Timothy 4:1) and of the denial of the faith by erstwhile believers. Our interest is purely in the latter possibility; for the former, see W. Bousset, *Der Antichrist*, Göttingen, 1895; B. Rigaux, *Lés Epîtres aux Thessaloniciens* (EB), Paris, 1956.

6. This has been fully discussed by R. Bohren, *Das Problem der Kirchenzucht im Neuen Testament*, Zollikon-Zürich, 1952.

7. The word 'backslider' (not found in NT) may be conveniently used to designate Christians who draw back from a true faith in Christ to a merely outward profession of faith or to no profession at all.

8. W. E. Sangster, *Let Me Commend*, 1949, pp. 101–24. Cf. J. Highet, *The Scottish Churches*, 1960.

9. *Minutes of the Methodist Conference*, 1967, pp. 104f.

10. See F. Greeves, *Theology and the Cure of Souls*, 1960.

11. For the history of the doctrine in general see the admirable sketch by W. Telfer, *The Forgiveness of Sins*, 1959; for the early Church see H. Windisch, *Der Hebräerbrief* (HNT), Tübingen, 1931, pp. 52–6; J. N. D. Kelly, *Early Christian Doctrines*, 1960, pp. 216–19.

12. Augustine, *De Dono Perseverantiae, De Correptione et Gratia*; J. N. D. Kelly, op. cit., pp. 366–9, 484f.

13. J. Calvin, *Institutes*, 11, 3:11–14; III, 21:7; 22:7; 24:6f; W. Niesel, *The Theology of Calvin*, 1956, pp. 168f.; R. S. Wallace, *Calvin's Doctrine of the Christian Life*, Edinburgh, 1959, pp. 333–8 (especially p. 336, n. 2). For the influence of Augustine on Calvin, see J. Calvin, *Concerning the Eternal Predestination of God* (translated with an introduction by J. K. S. Reid), 1961, pp. 62–8, 187f., and (for Calvin's own teaching) pp. 21f., 130f.

14. M. Luther, *Lectures on Romans* (translated by W. Pauck), 1962, pp. 246–55.

15. D. S. Adam, 'Perseverance,' in ERE, IX, pp. 769–71; A. A. Hodge, *Outlines of Theology*, 1896, p. 547.

16. E. D. Starbuck, 'Backsliding,' in ERE, II, pp. 319–21; A. Harrison, *Arminianism*, 1937; G. C. Berkouwer, *Faith and Perseverance*, Grand Rapids, 1958.

17. *The Westminster Confession*, 3:6; 11:5; 12; 13:3; 14:3; 17; 18.

18. John Goodwin wrote *Redemption Redeemed* in 1651. John Owen replied in *The Doctrine of the Saints' Perseverance Explained and Confirmed*, 1654 (*The Works of John Owen*, edited by W. H. Goold, 1850–55, Vol. XI), and Goodwin made a rejoinder in *Triumviri*, 1658. On Goodwin see A. W. Harrison, op. cit., pp. 151–5; W. J. Strickland, 'John Goodwin as seen through his controversies of 1640–1660,' unpublished Vanderbilt thesis, 1967 (I owe this reference to *Dissertation Abstracts*, April 1968, 4260 A).

19. A. A. Hodge, op. cit., pp. 111, 542–7; J. Murray, *Redemption, Accomplished and Applied*, Grand Rapids, 1955; G. C. Berkouwer, op. cit.

20. J. Wesley, *Predestination calmly considered* (*Works*, 1831, pp. 204–59); *The Perseverance of the Saints* (*Works*, X, pp. 282–98); see also *A Call to Backsliders* (*Works*, VI, pp. 514–27). It is to be noted that Wesley, like other Arminians, did not deny the reality of perseverance as a normal Christian experience; he taught that in addition to assurance of present salvation a believer might also have assurance of final perseverance as a kind of extra; see A. S. Yates, *The Doctrine of Assurance*, 1952.

21. W. B. Pope, *A Compendium of Christian Theology*, 1880,[2] III, pp. 132–147; H. M. Hughes, *Christian Foundations*, 1927, p. 200.

22. Quoted from *The Church Hymnary*, No. 703.

23. Quoted from *The Methodist Hymnbook*, No. 480. It is interesting that neither hymnbook contains both hymns.

24. L. Boettner, *The Reformed Doctrine of Predestination*, Grand Rapids, 1932, p. 182.

25. It should perhaps be stressed that Arminian authors do not regard the possibility of loss of salvation as a very likely one (W. B. Pope, op. cit., III, p. 132). The point contested is rather the whole determinist system of Calvinism which *logically* excludes the possibility of falling away.

NOTES TO CHAPTER 1

1. The vocabulary includes: *'āzabh* 'to forsake'; *shûbh* and *sûgh*, both meaning 'to backslide'; *sārar* and *mārah*, 'to rebel, be stubborn'; *zûdh*, 'to sin presumptuously'; *bāghadh*, 'to be treacherous, deceitful, rebellious'; *nā'as*, 'to despise. spurn'; and *sûr*, (*śûr)*, 'to turn aside.'

2. W. L. Holladay, *The root sûbh in the OT*, Leiden, 1958; cf. E. Jacob, *Theology of the Old Testament*, 1958, pp. 289f.

3. The significance of the last sentence quoted is that all these provocations took place in the midst of God's saving activities. Cf. also Nehemiah 9:16–31.

4. The same thought may be present in Hosea 11:5–9 (so RSV), but a different exegesis of the passage, transforming it into a threat, is given by T. H. Robinson (with F. Horst), *Die Zwölf kleinen Propheten*, Tübingen, 1954^2, pp. 44f.; cf. P. R. Ackroyd in PC, 536f., 537a. See also Psalms 106:40–46; 107:10–16.

5. N. H. Snaith, *The Distinctive Ideas of the Old Testament,* 1944, pp. 121f. Cf. Jeremiah 31:31–34; 32:37–41.

6. Cf. Psalm 80:3, 7, 19; Lamentations 5:21.

7. It should be remembered that the doctrine of a future life with post mortem rewards and punishments plays a negligible part in the thought of the Old Testament as a whole, although individual piety did begin to grasp the idea that communion with God could not be broken by death. Thus in general death itself had the character of a final judgement upon the sinner. There was no thought of the godly Israelites of past generations being raised up to share in the future kingdom of God envisaged by the prophets (except in such isolated and marginal passages as Isaiah 24–27 and Daniel 12:1–3).

8. Although our exposition has been based largely upon the teaching of one individual prophet, Jeremiah, and no attempt has been made to trace a developing idea throughout the Old Testament literature, it should be clear that the ideas discussed above form an integral part of the Old Testament doctrine of sin. The basic philosophy of history may be traced in both the D and the P strands of the Pentateuch (according to the generally accepted literary analysis), if not earlier, as well as in the associated historical documents; it is also found in Hosea, Ezekiel, and Isaiah 56–66, as well as in the Psalms.

9. Note also that care was taken by the provision of cities of refuge to ensure that a man who committed 'unintentional murder' (i.e. manslaughter) would not be dealt with summarily by the avenger of blood without a trial.

10. N. H. Snaith, in PC, 204i.

11. Cf. S. R. Driver and H. A. White, *The Book of Leviticus*, 1898, p. 68.

12. *b^e^yadh rāmāh*, Numbers 15:30; Psalm 19:13 (MT 14); cf. Deuteronomy 17:12 (*b^e^zādhôn*).

13. Exodus 12:15; Leviticus 7:20f. and frequently. It is disputed whether the phrase originally meant 'to excommunicate' or 'to put to death'; the latter is probably the usual meaning (cf. Leviticus 20:2–5).

14. H. Schultz, *Old Testament Theology*, Edinburgh, 1895, II pp. 87f.

15. N. H. Snaith, *The Distinctive Ideas of the Old Testament*, p. 66.

16. A. R. S. Kennedy, *Leviticus and Numbers* (Century Bible), Edinburgh, no date, p. 65.

17. C. R. Smith, *The Bible Doctrine of Salvation*, 1941, p. 89.

18. C. R. Smith, op. cit., pp. 88f, 93.

19. Cf. H. H. Rowley, 'The Meaning of Sacrifice,' BJRL, XXXIII, 1950, pp. 74–110 (especially pp. 96–8); S. Herner, *Sühne and Vergebung in Israel*, Lund, 1942, pp. 77–92.

20. N. H. Snaith, op. cit., pp. 60f.

21. The question whether such a person will be accepted by God in the next world is not raised in the Old Testament.

22. H. H. Rowley, op. cit., p. 97, states that 'it is clear that in the thought of the Old Testament sacrifice is not the only organ of atonement,' quoting in support 2 Samuel 12:13.

23. It is uncertain whether some Psalms written in the first person singular may not have had a communal reference, but, even if this is the case, individual application was surely permissible.

24. This of course does not mean repudiation of the need for sacrificial worship.

25. L. Köhler, *Old Testament Theology*, 1957, pp. 215f.

26. Confession of sin, which is an expression of repentance, was required as an act of sacrifice (Leviticus 5:5f.). Cf. E. Lohse, *Märtyrer und Gottesknecht*, Göttingen, 1955, p. 46.

27. The discussion of these extra-biblical sources does not imply that their teaching is in any way on a level with that contained in Scripture. Our purpose is simply to discover the Jewish attitudes current in New Testament times with a view to shedding light, by way of similarity and difference, on the teaching of the New Testament.

28. The Sadducees also claimed to represent traditional views, but, although they had a great influence on the government of Palestine in the first century A.D., they do not appear to have had any decisive influence on religious thought. A special section has not been devoted to the Pseudepigrapha as such, since these writings are only of marginal interest for our theme. Note, however, how the language of apostasy continues to be used in Testament of Dan. 5:6f.

29. We follow the general consensus of scholarly opinion which identifies the Qumran sect with the Essenes or an Essene group and dates the composition of their writings within the broad limits 150 B.C. to A.D. 68.

30. Cited (as CD) from C. Rabin, *The Zadokite Documents*, Oxford, 1954, 1:2–5; cf. 2:14–3:19. See also the Oration of Moses (1 Q22) 1:6:11. (For this and other documents see A. Dupont-Sommer, *The Essene Writings from Qumran*, Oxford, 1961). The vocabulary used to describe the apostasy of Israel is the same as in the Old Testament.

31. F. F. Bruce, *Biblical Exegesis in the Qumran Texts*, 1960. See, for example, CD 1:13–18.

32. Habakkuk Commentary (1 QpHab), 7:7f.

33. Thanksgiving Hymns (1 QH), 1:21f., 25–27; 4:29ff.; 6:6, 19; 9:14–16; 17:23–25; cf. CD 20:28–30.

34. Manual of Discipline (1 QS), 1–2.

35. According to F. F. Bruce (op. cit., pp. 57–63; *Second Thoughts on the Dead Sea Scrolls*, 1961[2], p. 114), only the rebellious leaders of the people would perish; the work of the sect would make propitiation for the rank and file. This seems doubtful because the phrase used, 'to make propitiation for the land,' is used in parallel with the phrase, 'to make propitiation for all who volunteer for holiness,' and is thus limited in meaning (cf. 1 QS 5:6f.; 8:2f., 6; 9:3–5; 1 Q28a (The Rule of the Congregation) 1:3; 1 QM (The War Scroll) 2:5).

36. Josephus attributed a doctrine of fatalism to the Essenes (Bellum Judaicum 2:8:14), and they appear to have been much more rigid than the Pharisees in this belief.

37. Cf. 1 QS 3:15; 1QH 1:7ff.; 5:3f.; 13:8–10; 15:13–17; and 1 Enoch 9:11; 39:11.

38. J. van der Ploeg, *The Excavations at Qumran*, 1958, pp. 112–18; cf. M. Mansoor, *The Thanksgiving Hymns*, Leiden, 1961, pp. 55–7, 62–5.

39. The use of capital punishment is mentioned in CD 9:1, but no details are given. According to Josephus (Bel. 2: 8:8), the sentence of expulsion was tantamount to death among the Essenes, since they dare not partake of ordinary food. He states that men on the point of death through such starvation were often received back into the community out of compassion and regarded as having endured sufficient punishment. But no doubt the really apostate man would have had few scruples about returning to ordinary food. For a detailed discussion see G. Forkman, *The Limits of the Religious Community*, Lund, 1972, pp. 39–86. Forkman analyses carefully the differing pictures of discipline found in the Manual of Discipline, the Damascus Document and Josephus, and he draws special attention to the element of loving reproof which had to precede disciplinary measures (1 QS 5:24–26; CD 20:17ff.).

40. S. Holm-Nielsen, *Hodayot*, Aarhus, 1960, p. 284. A. Marx ('Y a-t-il une prédestination à Qumran?' in *Revue de Qumran*, VI, 1967, pp. 163–81) holds that the term 'predestination' is inappropriate: it would be better to speak simply of 'grace.'

41. For this section I have used principally the collection of texts in H. L. Strack and P. Billerbeck, *Kommentar zum Neuen Testament aus Talmud und Midrasch*, München, 1956[2], giving my own translation

from Billerbeck's German. H. Danby, *The Mishnah*, Oxford, 1933, has been used for quotations from the Mishnah. For Rabbinic theology, G. F. Moore, *Judaism in the First Centuries of the Christian Era*, Cambridge, USA, 127–30, is indispensable.

42. SB, IV, pp. 816ff.; Moore II, pp. 344f.

43. R. A. Stewart, *Rabbinic Theology*, Edinburgh, 1961, p. 12.

44. SB, III, pp. 119–21; O. Michel, *Der Brief an die Römer* (KEK), Göttingen, 1957[11], p. 76.

45. Pesahim 54a (Baraita), in SB, I, p. 974; cf. SB, I, pp. 162–72.

46. Yoma 8:8; cf. Moore, I, pp. 498, 500f. Even before the destruction of the Temple the principle had been established that it is basically the moral attitude of the repentant sinner which gives value to his sacrifice; this insight enabled the Jews to adapt themselves to a situation in which sacrifice was no longer possible. The opinion of Rabbi Judah the Prince that repentance was not always necessary (Yoma 85b, in SB, I, p. 637) appears to have been completely isolated and to have rested on his own modification of the teaching found in Pirqe Aboth 3:12; cf. E. Lohse, *Märtyrer und Gottesknecht*, pp. 22f., 27f.; Moore, III, pp. 151f.

47. SB, I, pp. 170–72.

48. Yoma 8:9. Cf. Yoma 86b (Baraita); Aboth of Rabbi Nathan, 39, 40 (SB, I, p. 171). Sir. 5:4–7; 7:8.

49. Purely ritual offences were assigned to the category of unwitting sins, Shebuoth 1–2.

50. Rabbi Ishmael (ob. *c.* A.D. 134) said: 'There are four kinds of atonement. If a man commits a sin of omission and repents, he does not leave the place (where he offered his prayer of repentance) without being forgiven (by God), as it says in Jeremiah 3:22 . . . If a man commits a sin of commission and repents, the punishment is suspended until the Day of Atonement, as it says in Leviticus 16:30 . . . If a man has committed sins punishable by extirpation (by the hand of God) or judicial execution and repents, the punishment is suspended by his repentance and the Day of Atonement, and only his sufferings effect (full) atonement, as it says in Psalm 89:33 . . . But if a man has desecrated the name of God and then repented, his repentance cannot suspend the punishment and the Day of Atonement cannot effect atonement; repentance and the Day of Atonement effect atonement for a third, suffering on the remaining days of the year effects atonement for a third, and the day of his death completes the atonement, cf. Isaiah 22:14 . . . Sin offering, guilt offering, death and the Day of Atonement only effect atonement in conjunction with repentance.' (Tos. Yoma 5:6ff. (190), in SB, I, p. 169).

51. Sanhedrin 107b (SB, I, pp. 84f.). The essence of the story is found in several texts. It is related more briefly in P. Hagigah 2, 77d (30) with no mention of Jesus and with the replacement of Rabbi Joshua ben Perahyah by Rabbi Judah ben Tabai. For the principle see also Tos. Yoma 5:11 (191) (SB, III, p. 690), and the converse in Aboth of Rabbi Nathan 40 (SB, II, p. 618).

52. SB, I, p. 172; cf. the rest of the text in SB, III, pp. 689f., 269, and Midrash on Psalms 1, 22 (12b) (SB, III, p. 690).

53. SB, III pp. 743f.; cf. Hullin 13b (SB, IV, p. 333) and Leviticus Rabbah 2 (134b) (SB, III, p. 744).

54. Tos Kiddushin 1:14f. (337) (Moore, I, p. 521; cf. SB, I, p. 166).

55. P. Hagigah 14b (Moore, I, p. 413); P. Hagigah 2, 77b (60) (SB, IV, p. 835).

56. P. Hagigah 2, 77b (49) (SB, III, p. 689).

57. Moore, I, p. 522, quoting P. Hagigah 2, 77c.

58. P. Hagigah 2, 77c (5) (SB, I, p. 809). Another tradition relates that Elisha suffered in Gehenna (SB IV, p. 1,046).

59. Moore, I, pp. 525f.

60. Rosh ha-Shanah 17b–18a (SB, III, p. 80; Moore, I, pp. 522f.). The reference is apparently to retribution in this life rather than to eternal destiny (Moore, III, p. 160), but the general principle is unaffected, especially in view of the passages quoted earlier.

61. SB, IV, pp. 293–333; cf. R. Bohren, *Das Problem der Kirchenzucht im Neuen Testament.*

62. For criticism of Billerbeck's presentation and a reinterpretation of the evidence see C.-H. Hunzinger, *Die jüdische Bannpraxis im neutestamentlichen Zeitalter* (unpublished dissertation, as summarized in TL, LXXX, 1955, cols. 114–115); 'Spuren pharisäischer Institutionen in der frühen rabbinischen Überlieferung', in G. Jeremias (et al.) (ed.), *Tradition und Glaube* (Festgabe für K. G. Kuhn), Göttingen, 1971, pp. 147–156; D. R. A. Hare, *The Theme of Jewish Persecution of Christians in the Gospel according to St. Matthew*, Cambridge, 1967, pp. 48–56; G. Forkman, *op. cit.*, pp. 87–114.

63. The difficulty is accentuated by the fact that considerable changes took place in Judaism after A.D. 70; the Pharisees gained the upper hand in the community and began to apply the rules of their own group to the people at large.

64. A complicating factor is introduced by the development of a doctrine of purgatory among the Rabbis. In a dispute between the schools of Shammai and Hillel in the first century A.D. regarding the fate of those who were neither fully righteous nor fully wicked the school of Shammai suggested that they underwent a temporary period in Gehenna (Tos. Sanhedrin 13:3; Rosh ha-Shanah 16b–17a; see Moore, II, p. 318; SB, IV, pp. 1033f.). This view was developed in the second century. The periods of purgatorial suffering for various classes of sinners were casuistically determined. Before this, apostates had been regarded as suffering eternal punishment (SB, IV, p. 1052), but now purgatorial punishment came to be regarded as expiatory in effect, and the older doctrine that repentance after death was impossible was modified (SB, IV, pp. 1047–9); nevertheless this privilege was not extended to all classes of sinners (SB, IV, pp. 1049–59; cf. Moore, II, p. 387).

The development of the doctrine of purgatory does not affect our general conclusions. Despite its first century origins, it was really too late to influence New Testament thought (most of the quotations in support of it come from *c.* A.D. 250 at the earliest); it was by no means universally accepted (SB, IV, pp. 1057–9), and during the first century and still later the possibility of repentance after death was denied (2 Esdras 7:82; 9:12; 2 Baruch 85:12f.; 2 Enoch 62:2; SB, IV, pp. 1040, 1048f.). The doctrine that even apostates might be saved for the World to Come through purgatorial discipline has comparatively late attestation. It is doubtful whether the beginning of this teaching should be set as early as Billerbeck thought. The whole problem is worthy of thorough examination.

65. Cf. Genesis Rabbah 3:8 (quoted by R. A. Stewart, *Rabbinic Theology*, p. 24).

66. R. A. Stewart, ibid.

67. SB, IV, p. 7; cf. Berakhoth 33b (SB, I, p. 583); Moore, I, pp. 453–6.

68. Moore, I, p. 456. An exception will, however, be found in the fourth-century teaching in Midrash Esther 1:1 (82a) (SB, I, p. 982).

69. SB, IV, pp. 7f.; other references in Moore, I, pp. 455f. 70. Josephus, Bellum Judaicum 2:8:14; Antiquities 13:5:9; 18:1:3, quoted in SB, IV, p. 344. The meaning of 'fate' is uncertain; see Moore, I, pp. 456–8.

NOTES TO CHAPTER 2

1. One may compare, for example, the articles by J. W. Bowman on 'The Life and Teaching of Jesus' and J. Marsh on 'The Theology of the New Testament' in PC (639a–52b, 659a–72c) to see how little difference there is in essentials between the teaching of Jesus and the theology of the synoptic evangelists.

It will be clear that the approach adopted here is an essentially 'conservative' one, ascribing a high degree of historical accuracy to the Gospels, in contrast to the 'radical' approach of R. Bultmann and his followers who believe that many reported sayings of Jesus are in fact *Gemeinde-Bildungen*. It is impossible to give a detailed justification of this position here. It must suffice to remark that English scholarship as represented by V. Taylor, *The Formation of the Gospel Tradition*, 1935², and C. H. Dodd, *History and the Gospel*, Cambridge, 1938, has indicated that another approach to the Gospels than that of radical scepticism is possible, and indeed there are indications that there is a growing dissatisfaction even in Germany with arbitrary theories which deny the possibility of reliable knowledge of the historical Jesus. Such studies as H. Riesenfeld, *The Gospel Tradition and its Beginnings*, 1957, and C.F.D. Moule, 'The Intention of the Evangelists' in A.J.B. Higgins (ed.), *New Testament Essays in Memory of T. W. Manson*, Manchester, 1959, pp. 165–79, are indicative of the growth of a more cautious point of view.

A detailed study of the subject would require an examination of the differing points of view that may be found among the three Evangelists in their presentation of the teaching of Jesus. In the case of Mark the question of perseverance and apostasy does not seem to have attracted especial attention from the Evangelist. Matthew, as will be clear from the discussion in the text, brings out particularly the fact that the group of disciples includes some whose adherence to Jesus was nominal, and stresses the fact that the day of judgement will reveal those who have persevered in faith and obedience to the will of God. The distinctive outlook of Luke has been studied in detail by S. Brown, *Apostasy and Perseverance in the Theology of Luke*, Rome, 1969. He argues that Luke deliberately replaced the typical New Testament understanding by his own distinctive view in which faith is 'ecclesialized': 'the bearer of the faith is not the individual Christian but the community . . . the Christian perseveres not by proving his faith but by remaining in *the* faith . . . The Christian life is characterized not by the testing of this faith but by the call to moral action' (op. cit., p. 146). Brown's work contains many interesting suggestions, but it suffers from an over-subtlety in discovering theological nuances in Luke's editorial activity. Its conclusions do not affect the general validity of the thesis advanced in this work.

2. See H. Ridderbos, *The Coming of the Kingdom*, Philadelphia, 1962; G. Lundström, *The Kingdom of God in the Teaching of Jesus*, Edinburgh, 1963, N. Perrin; *The Kingdom of God in the Teaching of Jesus*, 1963; R. Schnackenburg, *God's Rule and Kingdom*, 1963; G. E. Ladd, *Jesus and the Kingdom*, 1966; G. Klein, 'The Biblical Understanding of "The Kingdom of God," ' *Interpretation*, 26, 1972, pp. 387–418. See also my article, 'Kingdom of God, of Heaven,' in the *Zondervan Pictorial Bible Encyclopaedia*, Grand Rapids, 1975, III, pp. 801–9.

3. SB, I, pp. 180f. See C. H. Dodd, *The Parables of the Kingdom*, 1961 , pp. 60f.

4. The fact that 'kingdom' must mean both 'God's eschatological act and the new order created by His act' is emphasized by G. E. Ladd, 'Kingdom of God — Reign or Realm' in JBL, LXXXI, 1962, pp. 230–8; cf. S. Aalen, ' "Reign" and "House" in the Kingdom of God,' in NTS, VIII, 1962, pp. 215–40.

5. Matthew 20:21 is a correct interpretation of Mark 10:37; Luke 14:15 and 17:20 may be editorial compositions, though not necessarily so.

6. Matthew 13:43 is generally regarded as editorial. Matthew 20:1–16 refers to the eschatological judgement, and Matthew 22:2 to the messianic banquet. Luke 19:11 and 21:31 are editorial.

7. In Mark 9:47 the future reference is guaranteed by the parallelism with 'be cast into hell'; cf. 9:43–5. Mark 10:24–7 is timeless, but cf. 10:23, 30b. Similarly Mark 12:34 and Matthew 21:31 are timeless. Matthew 23:13 may refer to preventing men from qualifying for entry to the kingdom. G. E. Ladd, *Jesus and the Kingdom*, holds that some of these sayings apply to present experience of the blessings of the kingdom.

8. In Luke 18:29 the reference is editorial.

9. All but two of the Beatitudes in Matthew 5:1–12 are in the future tense. A future meaning is required in Matthew 5:10 by the parallelism

with 5:11, and in 5:3 the analogy of the remaining Beatitudes, the analogy of the Woes in Luke 6:24f., and the fact that ἐστίν can represent an Aramaic timeless expression all combine to make the future reference both possible and likely.

10. The linguistic problem of ἤγγικεν in Mark 1:15 is not yet solved. But the more common meaning of the verb is 'has drawn near' rather than 'has arrived' (W. G. Kümmel, *Promise and Fulfilment*, 1957, pp. 19–25), and the fact that Matthew attributes the same teaching to John the Baptist (Matthew 3:2) indicates either that he thought that the kingdom had come at the time of John's baptism (which is unlikely) or that he regarded the kingdom as imminent both then and in the ministry of Jesus. The solution to the problem may be that in the ministry of Jesus and the mission of His disciples the saving power of God draws near to those who hear the message so that they have the opportunity to respond to it with faith. The saving power of God is thus near both temporally (it is here now, but it was not before; Mark 1:15) and spatially (it is near to those who are reached by the mission; Luke 10:9).

11. Matthew 4:14–16 shows that the evangelist regarded the ministry of Jesus as a period of fulfilment. Although Matthew 11:12f. is obscure in meaning, it certainly appears to indicate the present activity of the kingdom. Despite the attempt of R. H. Fuller, *The Mission and Achievement of Jesus*, 1954, to extract a future meaning from it, Matthew 12:28 must undoubtedly be taken in a present sense. Luke 17:21 probably means that the saving power of God is among the disciples; see W. G. Kümmel, op. cit., pp. 32–36; C. F. D. Moule, *An Idiom Book of New Testament Greek*, Cambridge, 1953, pp. 83f.

Many scholars adduce certain of the parables as evidence for a doctrine of 'realized eschatology' in regard to the kingdom (C. H. Dodd, op. cit.). This interpretation is very unlikely. See (on Mark 4:3–9) C. E. B. Cranfield, *Mark* (CGTC), Cambridge, 1963[2], pp. 148–51; (on Mark 4:26–9; 4:30–34; Matthew 13:33, 24–30, 47–50), W. G. Kümmel, op. cit., pp. 128–38; and (on Mark 13:28f.), G. R. Beasley-Murray, *A Commentary on Mark Thirteen*, 1957, pp. 94–8. I have discussed certain aspects of the problem in *Eschatology and the Parables*, 1963.

12. A present sense is found in Romans 14:17; cf. 1 Corinthians 4:20. For the Kingdom of God as a future concept in Paul, see J. Weiss, *Der erste Korintherbrief* (KEK), Göttingen, 1910, pp. 361f.; H. Lietzmann and W. G. Kümmel, *An die Korinther I, II* (HNT), Tübingen, 1949[4], p. 173. For Luke-Acts, see E. Haenchen, *Die Apostelgeschichte* (KEK), Göttingen, 1959[12], p. 109, n. 5. For Matthew, see C. H. Dodd, *Matthew and Paul*, Exp. T, LVIII, 1946–47, pp. 293–8 (reprinted in *New Testament Studies*, Manchester, 1953, pp. 53–66). In Revelation, believers are already a kingdom (1:6, 9), but their period of reign is still future (5:10; cf. 12: 10).

For the kingdom of Christ see 1 Corinthians 15:24; Colossians 1:13; and in the Gospels Luke 22:30f.; 23:42; Matthew 13:41; 16:28;

20:21. See O. Cullmann, *The Early Church*, 1956, pp. 105–37, especially pp. 109f.

13. 'Membership of this eschatological community founded by Jesus does not in itself guarantee acceptance into the future kingdom' (R. Schnackenburg, op. cit., p. 231).

14. J. Jeremias, *New Testament Theology*, 1971, I, pp. 113–118.

15. Quoted by M. Black, *An Aramaic Approach to the Gospels and Acts*, Oxford, 1967[3], p. 126. See also J. Jeremias, *The Parables of Jesus*, 1963[2], p. 190.

16. This is its undoubted meaning in John 12:40, where it is a translation variant for the more common ἐπιστρέφω. See J. Dupont, 'Matthieu 18, 3: ἐὰν μὴ στραφῆτε καὶ γένησθε ὡς τὰ παιδία,' in E. E. Ellis and M. Wilcox (ed.), *Neotestamentica et Semitica* (Studies in Honour of M. Black), Edinburgh, 1969, pp. 50–60.

17. J. Jeremias, ibid.

18. The point of the saying is to be found in the insignificance of children in the ancient world; the modern idea of 'the child in the midst' had not been developed. See also R.V.G.Tasker, *Matthew* (TNTC), 1961, p. 175.

19. This key saying is frequently said to be a formulation of the message of Jesus in the later vocabulary of the Christian Church (E. Lohmeyer, *Das Evangelium des Markus* (KEK), Göttingen, 1959[15], pp. 29–31). The evidence is not compelling: the use of καιρός and μετανοέω is amply attested in the authentic teaching of Jesus, and the Semitic form of πιστεύετε ἐν implies a Palestinian background for the saying (though not necessarily, of course, a dominical origin). There is, accordingly, no good linguistic reason for denying that Jesus may have spoken in this way and that the later vocabulary of the Church was developed from His words. See the detailed evidence provided in the comments of V. Taylor, *Mark* (Macmillan), 1953, pp. 165–7.

20. The words 'in me' in Matthew 18:6 are editorial (as is shown by a comparison with Matthew's source, Mark 9:42), but may rest on a true understanding of the trend of Jesus' teaching. Mark 15:32; Matthew 9:28f. and Luke 22:67 do not refer to faith *in* Jesus. See A. M. Hunter, *The Work and Words of Jesus*, 1950, p. 88. See also J. Jeremias, *New Testament Theology*, I, pp. 159–166.

21. Note that the idea of faithfulness (Matthew 24:45; 25:21–3; Luke 16:10–12) indicates that faith must be a continuing attitude (cf. Mark 13:13).

22. μαθητής occurs 43 times in Mark, 73 in Matthew, 37 in Luke, 78 in John, and 28 in Acts. In general see K. H. Rengstorf in TDNT, IV, pp. 415–60; G.E. Ladd, *Jesus and the Kingdom*, pp. 248–54.

23. TDNT, IV, pp. 434f.

24. It is assumed above that μαθητής in the Gospels is the equivalent of *talmîdhā'*. It has, however, been argued by T. W. Manson (*The Teaching of Jesus*, Cambridge, 1935[2], pp. 237–40), that Jesus used the Aramaic word *sh[e]wilyā'* instead of *talmîdhā'* to indicate his opposition to the scribal system; on this, see the comment of W. D. Davies, *Paul and Rabbinic Judaism*, 1955[2], p. 361.

25. R. Bultmann, *Das Evangelium des Johannes* (KEK), Göttingen, 1959^{16}, p. 128, n. 7.

26. F. F. Bruce, *Second Thoughts on the Dead Sea Scrolls*, 1961^{2}, p. 127.

27. T. W. Manson, ibid., notes that Jesus Himself rarely used the word 'disciple.' But the use of the word in all four Gospels to describe His followers, their manner of addressing Him as a rabbi or teacher, and His summons to men to 'follow' Him all show clearly that the idea of discipleship was a basic one in His ministry.

28. K. H. Rengstorf, *Das Evangelium nach Lukas* (NTD), Göttingen, 1949^{5}, pp. 205f., notes that Zacchaeus, possibly a man with family responsibilities, was not called to join Levi in the travelling band of disciples.

29. It is possible that the word 'disciple' is used in different senses in the various Gospels. Thus R. P. Meye, *Jesus and the Twelve*, Grand Rapids, 1968, has argued that in the Gospel of Mark the Evangelist has identified the disciples of Jesus as consisting solely of the Twelve. Clearly this raises the question whether some of the teaching addressed by Jesus to the disciples is understood by Mark to be addressed only to those called to be apostles and missionaries. Similarly, it can be argued that the same restriction in terminology is to be found in Matthew; however, U. Luz, who defends this view, argues that this group of twelve disciples is meant to be typical of Christians as a whole ('Die Jünger in Matthäus-evangelium,' *Zeitschrift für die NT Wissenschaft*, LXII, 1971, pp. 141–171). H.-J. Degenhardt, *Lukas — Evangelist der Armen*, Stuttgart, 1965, pp. 27–41, has tried to show that the instruction given to the disciples in Luke is meant only for the leaders of the church, but he is demonstrably wrong on this point (I. H. Marshall, *Luke: Historian and Theologian*, Grand Rapids, 1971, p. 207, n. 1; H. Schürmann, *Das Lukasevangelium*, Freiburg, 1969, I, p. 321).

Any such differences in terminology as may be discerned at this point are concerned basically with the narrative style of the Evangelists. It is noteworthy that Jesus Himself made little use of the term 'disciple'; see Mark 14:14; Matthew 10:24, 25, 42; Luke 14:26, 27, 33; John 8:31; 13:35; 15:8.

30. The use of the appellative, Κύριε presents problems which cannot be discussed here. In the Gospels it is a title of respect (equivalent to Aramaic *marî*) such as was used by pupils in addressing a teacher. But there are indications that there was an element of obedience in the usage, so that greater significance could be attached to the title; see the undoubtedly genuine saying, Matthew 7:21, and also John 13:13. Cf. O. Cullmann, *The Christology of the New Testament*, 1959, pp. 203–6, especially p. 205.

31. V. Taylor, *Mark*, p. 205, quoting from TWB, IV, p. 459 (= TDNT, IV, p. 455).

32. This context of teaching is presumably the *Sitz im Leben* of Luke 6:40; Matthew 13:52 may also be relevant.

33. On ἀκολουθέω see E. Schweizer, *Lordship and Discipleship*, pp. 11–21. R. Bultmann's denial (*Theology of the New Testament*,

1952, 1955, I, p. 9) that personal allegiance to Jesus was required fails to do justice to the sayings which go beyond requiring men merely to take Him as an example or as a prophet with no significance or personality of His own, and rests on an inadequate treatment of Christology in the Gospels (effectively refuted in O. Cullmann, op. cit.).

34. This interpretation belongs to the earliest Christian preaching; see R. H. Mounce, *The Essential Nature of New Testament Preaching*, Grand Rapids, 1960, pp. 60–128.

35. G. R. Beasley-Murray, *Baptism in the New Testament*, 1962, pp. 67–72.

36. J. D. G. Dunn, *Baptism in the Holy Spirit*, 1970, p. 52, argues that the disciples did not believe in Jesus and become 'Christians' until Pentecost (Acts 11:15, 17). But while full certainty that Jesus was Messiah and Lord did not come until after the resurrection, it is nevertheless true that discipleship before Easter was based on allegiance to Jesus.

37. Regeneration is not mentioned in the Synoptic Gospels, but the thought of Matthew 18:3 is not so very far removed from it, and in any case regeneration is much rarer in the rest of the New Testament than is sometimes thought.

38. Cf. H. K. McArthur, *Understanding the Sermon on the Mount*, 1961, pp. 122f., 137f. J. Jeremias, *The Sermon on the Mount*, 1961, pp. 13–15.

39. The fact that the Sermon on the Mount is preserved in the Gospel of Matthew, one of the later books of the New Testament, is a clear indication that its teaching was regarded as being binding on the contemporary Church.

40. It will be seen that in accordance with the conclusions reached earlier about the coming of the kingdom we regard the ethic of Jesus as meant for the period before the consummation of the kingdom rather than as a 'Design for Life in the Kingdom of God' (A. M. Hunter). This latter designation is of course correct in so far as the kingdom is already realized, but it tends to obscure the fact that acceptance of the ethic is an indispensable requirement for entry into the consummated kingdom. It goes without saying that, while the principles of the ethic are eternally valid, the teaching is cast in terms of life in this world (to be precise, in the first century A.D.) before the parousia.

41. R. Bultmann, op. cit., I, p. 20.

42. J. Jeremias, op. cit., pp. 24–34.

43. R. N. Flew, *Jesus and His Church*, 1943[2], pp. 17–98; R. Schnackenburg, op. cit., pp. 215–34; J. Jeremias, *New Testament Theology*, I, pp. 167–178. The basic fact that Jesus founded a new community is not in my opinion to be rejected in the light of the studies of G. Johnson, *The Doctrine of the Church in the New Testament*, Cambridge, 1943, pp. 46–58, and E. Schweizer, *Church Order in the New Testament*, 1961, ch. 2. See also C. K. Barrett, *Jesus and the Gospel Tradition*, 1967, ch. 3.

44. *Pace* W. G. Kümmel, *Promise and Fulfilment*, pp. 138–40.

Kümmel (p. 87) has to admit that Jesus expected His disciples to continue to meet for table fellowship after His death.

45. C. E. B. Cranfield, *Mark*, pp. 150f.; cf. my *Eschatology and the Parables*, pp. 30f.

46. See the cautious defence offered by C. E. B. Cranfield, op. cit., pp. 158–161, and C. F. D. Moule, *The Birth of the New Testament*, 1962, 149–52.

47. Although 'understanding' (συνίημι) is a favourite concept in Matthew, it is already found in Mark, and would appear to be a valid interpretation of the teaching of Jesus at this point; cf. Mark 4:12 (from LXX).

48. The verb σκανδαλίζομαι is used elsewhere of professing disciples; see below.

49. For ἀφίστημι 'to fall away,' see p.217, n. 5; cf. also Jeremiah 3:14; Daniel 9:9; 1 Enoch 5:4; Wisdom 3:10.

50. Matthew's version links together two passages which appear separately in Luke, and probably also includes material from another source; T. W. Manson, *The Sayings of Jesus*, 1949, pp. 176f.

51. The parallel in Luke 13:26f. indicates that to be in contact with Jesus is not enough in itself to save a man; he must respond to His message and depart from iniquity. Note that Matthew's emphasis on 'doing the will of God' is not merely 'moralistic' (T. W. Manson, ibid.), but stresses the need for the complete surrender of faith which is expressed in a new way of life.

52. E. Schweizer, *Church Order in the New Testament*, 4e (p. 56).

53. On the problem of authenticity see *Eschatology and the Parables*, pp. 12, 31–4. Even if the form of the interpretation be Matthaean, it nevertheless correctly represents the intention of Jesus.

54. T. W. Manson, op. cit., p. 195. C. H. Dodd, 'Matthew and Paul' (*New Testament Studies*, pp. 55f.) thinks that the reference is to the kingdom of Christ (a wider concept than the Church) which begins at the resurrection.

55. The kingdom is likened to the parabolic image as a whole and not to any one part of it; J. Jeremias, *The Parables of Jesus*, pp. 100–3.

56. The phrase resembles the Rabbinic 'son of the Age to Come,' i.e. one who belongs to or (as here) is destined for the future kingdom; cf. Matthew 8:12 where the phrase is used of Jews who would not in fact receive the Kingdom. The 'sons of the evil one' are those who show his character in their lives.

57. So A. H. M'Neile, *Matthew* (Macmillan), 1915, p. 202; W. O. Walker, Jr., 'The Kingdom of the Son of Man and the Kingdom of the Father in Matthew,' *Catholic Biblical Quarterly* 30, 1968, pp. 573–579. The future kingdom is regarded as an earthly one (cf. W. O. E. Oesterley, *The Gospel Parables in the Light of their Jewish Background*, 1938[2], pp. 23ff.).

58. J. Jeremias, op. cit., p. 227, n. 90.

59. It is almost universally accepted that we have here two originally independent parables, or fragments of parables (verses 1–10, 11–14), which have been fused together; J. Jeremias regards both as

authentic parts of the teaching of Jesus, op. cit., pp. 63–6, 187–9. The fusion of the two parables is, however, not inapt.

60. J. Jeremias, op. cit., pp. 187–9.

61. There is no suggestion of predestination here since, according to the imagery of the parable, the man himself was at fault for not having provided himself with a wedding garment.

62. For the interpretation of the parable offered here see *Eschatology and the Parables*, pp. 40–3.

63. J. Jeremias, op. cit., p. 53, thinks that Luke 13:22–30 suggests that the parable was originally spoken to the crowds and interprets it accordingly. In this case, however, the application to the mixed group of disciples would not be an unfair extension of the words of Jesus.

64. R. V. G. Tasker, *Matthew*, p. 233.

65. J. Jeremias, op. cit., pp. 58–63.

66. In the parable of the pounds (Luke 19:11–27) the third servant is simply mulcted of his pound; in view of the fact that it is the rebellious citizens who suffer the extreme penalty, this may have meant for Luke that he was merely deprived of his responsibilities within the kingdom. In this particular case it is difficult to be sure what was the original teaching of Jesus, and it would be unwise to press the details too far in either version of the story.

67. E.g. J. Schniewind, *Das Evangelium nach Matthäus* (NTD), Göttingen, 1950[5], p. 254.

68. For the Jewish teaching see SB, IV, pp. 977–86, and for the New Testament teaching see 2 Thessalonians 2:3–12; 1 Corinthians 7:26; 1 Timothy 4:1; 2 Timothy 3:1; 1 Peter 5:10; Revelation 3:10; et al.; also E. Stauffer, *New Testament Theology*, 1955, ch. 53.

69. Cf. Isaiah 66:7f. It is doubtful whether these sufferings are to be thought of as the 'birth pangs of the Messiah'; the point of the metaphor seems to lie rather in the greatness of the suffering (cf. SB, I, p. 950).

70. E. E. Ellis, *The Gospel of Luke* (New Century Bible), 1967, p. 257.

71. Hatred: Mark 13:13; Luke 6:22; 21:17; reproach: Matthew 5: 11; Luke 6:28; slander: Matthew 5:11; excommunication: Luke 6:22; betrayal: Mark 13:9, 11f.; killing: Matthew 10:28; 23:34; 24:9.

72. A. Schweitzer, cited by J. Schniewind, *Matthäus*, p. 88; J. Jeremias, 'The Lord's Prayer in Modern Research' in Exp. T. LXXI, 1959–60, pp. 141–6; cf. *The Prayers of Jesus*, 1967, pp. 105f.; E. Lohmeyer, *The Lord's Prayer*, 1965, pp. 191–208.

73. H. Seesemann (TWB, VI, pp. 23–37) holds that each and every kind of temptation is meant, including eschatological tribulations.

74. J. Jeremias, *The Parables of Jesus*, pp. 44, 55; *Unknown Sayings of Jesus*, 1958, pp. 58, 64; V. Taylor, Mark, p. 555. For the view that Mark 14:34, 38 refer to the parousia, see C. K. Barrett in Exp. T, LXVII, 1955–56, p. 144; *Jesus and the Gospel Tradition*, p. 47.

On the other side see K. G. Kuhn, 'New Light on Temptation, Sin and Flesh in the New Testament' in K. Stendahl, *The Scrolls and the*

New Testament, 1958, pp. 94–113; W. G. Kümmel, op. cit., p. 125, n. 75; H. Seesemann, ibid.

75. The references are discussed by W. G. Kümmel, op. cit., pp. 54–9.

76. W. G. Kümmel, op. cit., pp. 65ff.

77. Luke 22:31f., adduced by J. Jeremias, *The Parables of Jesus*, p. 216, surely refers to Peter's imminent denial of Jesus.

78. J. Jeremias, *New Testament Theology*, I, p. 202.

79. C. E. B. Cranfield, *Mark*, p. 196.

80. The phrase has been added by Matthew, but may represent authentic tradition.

81. C. E. B. Cranfield, op. cit., p. 313.

82. Mark 9:43ff. is, however, probably attached to 9:42 on the catch-word principle. See also Romans 14:15, 21; 1 Corinthians 8:9, 11.

83. We must ask, however, whether this will can be frustrated. See below, p. 83.

84. For the value of Mark 13 as a reliable source for the teaching of Jesus, see G. R. Beasley-Murray, *Jesus and the Future*, 1954.

85. H. H. Rowley, *The Biblical Doctrine of Election*, 1950, pp. 166, 173.

86. J. B. Lightfoot, *Colossians and Philemon* (Macmillan), 1886[8], p. 218. Note how the terms 'called,' 'chosen' and 'faithful' are synonyms in Revelation 17:14.

87. K. L. Schmidt in TDNT, III, pp. 494f.

88. G. Schrenk in TDNT, IV, pp. 186f.; K. Stendahl in PC, p. 791. See also J. Jeremias in TDNT, VI, p. 542, who argues that 'many' is tantamount to 'all' (cf. 2 Esdras 8:3); the first clause emphasizes the wideness of the invitation.

89. For the authenticity of these verses see especially J. Jeremias, *The Parables of Jesus*, pp. 154–6; W. L. Knox, *The Sources of the Synoptic Gospels*, Cambridge, 1957, II, pp. 113f.

90. G. Schrenk in TDNT, IV, p. 188.

91. See AG, *s.v.* III, 3a; MH, III, p. 144.

92. The parallel in Matthew 24:24 has ὥστε with the infinitive, and here also the construction expresses no more than a contemplated result; cf. Matthew 27:1; see BD, 391[3].

93. In Mark 14:35 (cf. Matthew 26:39 with ἐστίν added) a real condition is expressed. Similarly in Romans 12:18. But Galatians 4:15 expresses an unfulfilled condition. In Acts 20:16 (with the optative for the indicative of direct speech) a real condition (which was in fact fulfilled) is expressed (cf. BD, 385[1]; but a different understanding of the sentence with εἰ meaning 'whether' is also possible).

94. Thus Matthew 24:24 adds καί, 'even.'

95. It may be worth asking whether the saying does not imply a shortening of the period before the parousia similar to that implied in Mark 13:20.

96. G. R. Beasley-Murray, *Jesus and the Future*, pp. 227–30, is almost alone in supporting this possibility. While the vocabulary is

similar to that of Mark 13, giving the impression that this section may be based upon it, the evidence for Matthaean style is not very strong — certainly not as strong, for example, as in the interpretation of the parable of the tares. The teaching of the section is clearly alluded to in Didache 16:7f.

97. In this connexion His teaching on trust in God should not be overlooked: Matthew 6:25–34; 10:26–33 emphasize the Father's care for those who trust in Him.

98. Luke 21:14f. expresses a similar thought without reference to the Spirit. The version in Matthew and Mark is defended by G. R. Beasley-Murray, *A Commentary on Mark Thirteen*, p. 46, against the arguments of C. K. Barrett, *The Holy Spirit and the Gospel Tradition*, 1947, pp. 131f.

99. In Mark 3:4; 5:23, 28, 34; 6:56; 10:52; 15:30, 31 *bis*, the reference is clearly to preservation of life. In 13:20 deliverance from death is probably meant. (Because of the presence of the elect among those suffering tribulation (the Jews are no doubt meant), the Lord mitigated the fury of the tribulation (cf. Genesis 18:32), lest all men should have perished). In 8:35 *bis* the meaning is evidently to preserve one's life or real existence. The verb clearly means the same as 'to enter the Kingdom' in 10:26, and this verse gives the nearest parallel to 13:13.

100. W. Foerster in TDNT, VII, p. 991, states that the reference is to deliverance out of the Messianic woes and into the Messianic kingdom.

101. G. R. Beasley-Murray, *A Commentary on Mark Thirteen*, pp. 51–3.

102. The view that an independent tradition is preserved here by Luke (so T. W. Manson, *The Sayings of Jesus*, p. 323; G. R. Beasley-Murray, *Jesus and the Future*, pp. 226f.) is preferable to the view that Luke has simply rewritten his Marcan source (H. Conzelmann, *The Theology of St. Luke*, 1960, p. 125).

103. The saying may mean: 'Even persecution is under God's control: you cannot be harmed unless He allows it' (G. R. Beasley-Murray, *A Commentary on Mark Thirteen*, p. 52) or: 'You cannot really be harmed, whatever you suffer' (A. Plummer, *Luke* (ICC), Edinburgh, 1901[4], p. 480).

104. The question whether sodium chloride can in fact lose its flavour is irrelevant; the reference is obviously to some salty substance whose salt content might be lost.

105. J. Schniewind, *Matthäus*, p. 51. Cf. Mark 9:50 and Luke 14:34f.

106. Cf. also Matthew 24:43–51. Although the original meaning of διχοτομέω in v. 46 is still uncertain, it is clear that the punishment of exclusion from the Kingdom is in mind (the unfaithful have no share in the Kingdom); O. Betz, 'The Dichotomized Servant and the End of Judas Iscariot,' *Revue de Qumran* VI, 1964, pp. 43–58, adduces 1QS 2:16f. to elucidate the saying.

107. J. Jeremias, *The Parables of Jesus*, pp. 53–8.

108. On the interpretation of the saying see O. E. Evans, 'The Unforgivable Sin,' in Exp. T, LXVIII, 1956–57, pp. 240–4; on its form and authenticity see A. J. B. Higgins, *Jesus and the Son of Man*, 1964, pp. 127–32; H. E. Tödt, *The Son of Man in the Synoptic Tradition*, 1965, pp. 118–20, 312–18; F. Borsch, *The Son of Man in Myth and History*, 1967, pp. 328–9; C. Colpe in TDNT, VIII, pp. 442f.; E. Schweizer in TDNT, VI, pp. 397f., 405, 407.

109. Matthew 12:31a is parallel to Mark 3:28; Matthew 12:31b to Luke 12:10b; Matthew 12:32a to Luke 12:10a; and Matthew 12:32b to Mark 3:29 (cf. W. C. Allen, *Matthew* (ICC), Edinburgh, 1912[3], p. 136). In addition to differences from Luke which may be due to assimilation to Mark there is one variant (Matthew: εἴπῃ λόγον κατά; Luke:ἐρεῖ λόγον εἰς) which may be a translation variant from Aramaic (cf. M. Black, op. cit., pp. 194–5) and, if so, may indicate that the Q form existed in two recensions.

110. J. Wellhausen, *Das Evangelium Matthaei*, Berlin, 1904, pp. 62–3.

111. C. Colpe in TDNT, VIII, pp. 439, 442f., 452f., 457.

112. Exorcism was associated with the Messiah, but there is no Rabbinic evidence for associating the Holy Spirit with exorcisms; E. Schweizer in TDNT, VI, p. 398.

113. The Q form of the saying is found at this point in Matthew as a result of his policy of conflating his sources. Luke 12:8–12, however, gives the impression of being a unity; it contains a number of Aramaisms and was assigned by W. Bussmann to his Aramaic source 'R' (see T. W. Manson, *The Sayings of Jesus*, pp. 20, 106).

114. Luke 12:9 and 10 can hardly have been originally linked together (T. W. Manson, op. cit., p. 110).

115. O. Cullmann, *The Christology of the New Testament*, pp. 152–5, allows the possibility in this saying. The examples offered by C. Colpe, TDNT, VIII, pp. 430–433, are not convincing.

116. For this possibility see H. von Baer, *Der heilige Geist in den Lukasschriften*, Stuttgart, 1926, p. 75 n. 3.

117. J. Jeremias, *Abba*, Göttingen, 1966, pp. 145–52, especially 150–1.

118. Mark 1:10; Matthew 12:28. The power of the Spirit was associated both with the Messiah and with the Servant of Yahweh.

119. A. H. M'Neile's view (*Matthew* (Macmillan), 1915, p. 178) that 'all' includes blasphemy against God (cf. Gospel of Thomas 44) is unlikely.

120. B. F. Westcott, cited by A. Plummer, *Matthew*, 1909, p. 180. E. Lohmeyer, *Markus*, p. 80.

121. A. H. M'Neile, op. cit., p. 179.

122. H. W. Beyer in TDNT, I, p. 624; C. Colpe in TDNT, VIII, pp. 442f.

123. K. H. Rengstorf, *Lukas*, p. 155.

124. A. Fridrichsen, 'Le Péché contre le Saint-Esprit,' in *Revue d'Histoire et de Philosophie religieuse*, III, 1923, pp. 367–72.

125. G. Bornkamm, *Jesus of Nazareth*, 1960, p. 212. Similarly, E.

Schweizer in TDNT, VI, p. 397f.; H. E. Tödt, op. cit., p. 119; A. J. B. Higgins, op. cit., pp. 130–1; C. Colpe in TDNT, VIII, p. 452f.

126. In Luke 12:10 both 'speaks' and 'blasphemes' are probably future actions; the former is certainly so. Cf. F. H. Borsch, op. cit., p. 329.

127. C. K. Barrett, *The Holy Spirit and the Gospel Tradition*, pp. 105–7.

128. See the fuller discussion (on which this present section of the chapter is based) in I. H. Marshall, 'Hard Sayings — VII. Luke 12:10' in *Theology*, LXVII, Feb., 1964, pp. 65–7.

129. Quoted by A. H. M'Neile, op. cit., p. 178.

130. Summarized by V. Taylor, *Mark*, p. 242.

131. E. Stauffer, *New Testament Theology*, p. 108.

132. For a date soon after 40 B.C. see J. Jeremias in TDNT, V, p. 687, n. 245; similarly C. Colpe in TDNT, VIII, p. 423, n. 180. A much later date in the second century A.D. is proposed by J. C. Hindley, 'Towards a Date for the Similitudes of Enoch: An Historical Approach,' in NTS XIV, 1967–68, pp. 551–565. A similar view, based on the absence of fragments of the Similitudes from the Qumran finds is upheld by J. T. Milik, 'Problèmes de la Littérature Hénochique à la Lumière des Fragments Araméens de Qumran,' in *Harvard Theological Review*, LXIV, 1971, pp. 333–378.'

133. SB, I, pp. 485–7, 956–9.

134. Cf. O. Cullmann, *The Christology of the New Testament*, p. 163. On the Son of man problem see I. H. Marshall, 'The Synoptic Son of Man Sayings in Recent Discussion' in NTS, XII, 1965–6, pp. 327–51; 'The Son of Man in Contemporary Debate' in EQ, XLII, 1970, pp. 67–87.

135. E. Schweizer, in TDNT, VI, p. 407, n. 483.

136. The form of the saying in Matthew 12:31f. adds nothing of moment to the teaching given in Mark and Luke, and we have therefore not discussed it separately.

137. Matthew has used Mark 9:33–37 (with the insertion of Mark 10:15), 42–8, as his framework. For the use of Q, cf. Luke 17:1–4; ? 15:3–7. According to G. D. Kilpatrick, *The Origins of the Gospel according to St. Matthew*, Oxford, 1950^2, vs. 10, 18, 19f., 23–24 are from M. They are said not to form a coherent section, but in view of the form of such a sayings collection as the Gospel of Thomas this is not an insuperable objection to their being drawn from a single written source. See further W. Pesch, *Matthäus der Seelsorger*, Stuttgart, 1966.

138. G. D. Kilpatrick, op. cit., pp. 98, 79; cf. R. V. G. Tasker, *Matthew*, p. 172.

139. T. W. Manson, *The Sayings of Jesus*, p. 207, holds that Jesus was really referring to children in vs. 6f. Once it is remembered that Jesus used the metaphor of children to describe His disciples and that v. 6 should be punctuated as the start of a new section instead of being regarded as a parallel statement to v. 5 (cf. Huck's *Synopsis*) this view is seen to be unnecessary. Mark 9:42 indicates that the little ones are believers (which will include children but does not exclude older people

young in the faith), and in any case adult disciples certainly need pastoral care and attention. Cf. O. Michel in TDNT, IV, pp. 650–3.

140. T. W. Manson, op. cit., pp. 208f.

141. The possibility is admitted by T. W. Manson, ibid., although he does not regard the lost sheep (i.e. little ones) as disciples.

142. W. G. Kiimmel, *Promise and Fulfilment*, p. 56.

143. J. Schniewind, *Matthäus*, pp. 61f; cf. A. H. M'Neile, *Matthew*, p. 64. It would be wrong to follow E. Stauffer in finding a doctrine of purgatory concealed in 'the last farthing': 'The sinner can expiate his sin in Sheol and so escape Gehenna' (*New Testament Theology*, p. 212). That Jesus taught a doctrine of purgatory is vigorously denied by J. Jeremias, *The Parables of Jesus*, pp. 169–71, 185f.

144. J. Jeremias, op. cit., p. 97.

145. See above, and also T. W. Manson, *The Sayings of Jesus*, p. 139, 209ff.; B. H. Streeter, *The Four Gospels*, 1936[5], pp. 257f.

146. J. Jeremias, op. cit., p. 210.

147. Matthew 6:14 is usually regarded as dependent on Mark. R. Bultmann, *The History of the Synoptic Tradition*, p. 61, thinks that Mark 11:25 (like v. 26) was originally not a part of Mark, although on p. 148 he admits that Matthew 6:14f. is based on it. The arguments of H. F. D. Sparks ('The Doctrine of the Divine Fatherhood in the Gospels' in D. E. Nineham (ed.), *Studies in the Gospels*, Oxford, 1955, pp. 243–5) that Mark 11:25 is spurious and based on Matthew 6:14 are weak.

148. The variant reading εἰς σέ in Matthew 18:15 gives the sense correctly.

149. So G. Forkman, op. cit., p. 126. Thus in certain circumstances excommunication is possible, despite the teaching of the parable of the tares.

150. The procedure bears some analogy to the Jewish 'ban.' R. Bohren's attempt (*Das Problem der Kirchenzucht im Neuen Testament*, p. 27) to compare the two in detail probably goes too far in view of the difficulty of dating the rabbinic practice noted earlier. A better analogy may be found in the informal use of 'reproof' by the Rabbis and the Qumran sect and in the practice of excommunication by the Qumran sect; W. D. Davies, *The Setting of the Sermon on the Mount*, Cambridge, 1964, pp. 221–4; G. Forkman, op. cit., pp. 127f. Cf. Titus 3:10f.

151. K. L. Schmidt in TDNT, III, pp. 524–6.

152. J. B. Phillips, *The Gospels in Modern English*, 1957 edition, p. 254. See N. Turner, *Grammatical Insights into the New Testament*, Edinburgh, 1965, pp. 80–82. But the future perfect form may simply be equivalent to an emphatic future (cf. C. F. D. Moule, *An Idiom Book of New Testament Greek*, Cambridge, 1953, p. 18).

153. Cf. SB, I, pp. 738–41, 792f.; C. H. Dodd, *Historical Tradition in the Fourth Gospel*, Cambridge, 1963, pp. 347–9.

154. T. W. Manson, *The Sayings of Jesus*, pp. 210f. E. Schweizer, *Church Order in the New Testament*, 4f., p. 59, thinks that both possibilities must be combined.

155. R. Bohren, op. cit., pp. 102–6, thinks that the possibility of restoration is unlikely in Matthew 18. He argues that in the Old Testament the phrase about two or three witnesses is found where sins unto death are involved, and also that Matthew 18:6–9 indicates a complete severance of relations. But 2 Corinthians 13:1 and 1 Timothy 5:19 (as well as Deuteronomy 19:15, which is overlooked by Bohren) indicate that the Old Testament rule had a wider application; it is also doubtful whether Matthew 18:6–9 should be regarded as fixing the meaning at this point (*pace* Bohren). Matthew 18:10–14 is more important in this respect. G. Forkman, op. cit., pp. 130f., thinks that vs. 19f. refer to the certainty that the church's prayers for the restoration of a disciplined offender will be heard by God.

156. Predestination *may* be implied in Acts 1:16. The reference in Jesus' prophecy is of course to the culmination of the act of betrayal which was already in progress; Judas might have refused to continue what he had begun.

157. John 6:64 states that Judas was not a believer. See below, pp. 181f. Luke 22:3 and John 13:2 ascribe Judas' action to Satanic influence. The Lucan presentation is discussed in detail by S. Brown, op. cit., pp. 82–97, who argues that while Jesus' death was foreordained, the treason of Judas was not the inevitable result of scriptural prophecy.

158. The historicity is denied by G. Klein, 'Die Verleugnung des Petrus,' in ZTK, LVIII, 1961, pp. 285–328, and E. Linnemann, 'Die Verleugnung des Petrus' in ZTK, LXIII, 1966, pp. 1–32. In favour of the historicity see D. E. Nineham, *Saint Mark* (Pelican Gospel Commentaries), 1963, p. 399.

159. The verb and tense used imply that the desire was granted; A. Plummer, *Luke*, p. 503.

160. See S. Brown, op. cit., pp. 69–71.

161. J. Schniewind, *Matthäus*, p. 268.

NOTES TO CHAPTER 3

1. Since our aim in this work is to describe the beliefs of the early Church in general, it is not a matter of great moment whether Acts be held to give a faithful portrayal of the life and beliefs of the communities which it describes or an insight into the theology of Luke himself. Although the latter view is widely held today, the former view is to be preferred and is presupposed in our discussion. See the judicious survey in C. K. Barrett, *Luke the Historian in Recent Study*, 1961.

2. The word group 'to save' occurs 22 times in Acts, 25 in Luke, 14 in Mark, and 15 in Matthew. Many of the Gospel references are to physical healing.

3. Salvation is both a present experience and a future hope in Acts; W. Foerster, TNDT, VII, pp. 996f.

4. Cf. the knowledge of Christian prophets in Acts 11:27f.; 21:4, 11.

5. I. H. Marshall, *Luke: Historian and Theologian*, pp. 103–115.
6. See below, p. 142.
7. F. F. Bruce, *The Book of the Acts* (NLC), 1953, p. 283, n.; cf. the parallels in SB, II, pp. 726f. A number of scholars have argued that ἦσαν τεταγμένοι can be translated as a middle form with the meaning 'as many as had ranged themselves for eternal life' (R. J. Knowling, *Acts* (EGT), II, p. 300; E. M. Blaiklock, *Acts* (TNTC), 1959, p. 110). There are no parallels for this rendering. In the New Testament the middle voice of τάσσω has the same meaning as the active voice (Acts 28:23; Matthew 28:16), and the postulated sense would require the reflexive pronoun (1 Corinthians 16:15); cf. LS, *s.v.* II, 4.
8. The difficulty with this view is that the introduction of a fresh group of people in v. 44 may militate against an identification of the two groups in vs. 43 and 48. In any case, however, the group in v. 48 will include the proselytes in v. 43.
9. Cf. R. B. Rackham, *Acts* (WC), 1922[9], p. 327.
10. E. Haenchen, *Die Apostelgeschichte* (KEK), Göttingen, 1959[12], p. 612; cf. p. 70. Cf. F. F. Bruce, *The Acts of the Apostles*, 1951, pp. 27, 248.
11. S. Brown, op. cit., especially pp. 114–131, makes much of this point, and argues that Luke is concerned more with the perseverance of the church than of the individual. This is a valid insight, but it is taken too far.
12. F. F. Bruce, *The Book of the Acts*, p. 115.
13. S. Brown, op. cit., pp. 98–109, makes a good case that the basic element in the sin was a selfish attitude to wealth which issued in lying to the Spirit, and draws a parallel with the sin of Judas.
14. There is an obvious parallel with the incestuous man of 1 Corinthians 5, although this is denied by E. Haenchen, op. cit., p. 196.
15. J. D. G. Dunn, *Baptism in the Holy Spirit*, pp. 5–68, argues that since the disciples in Samaria had not received the Spirit they were in no sense Christians; hence Simon cannot be regarded as lapsing from a salvation which he had never received (cf. S. Brown, op. cit., pp. 110–114). But there is some uncertainty on this point, as E. Haenchen, op. cit., pp. 254f., points out. There is no indication that Simon was excluded from the laying on of hands and consequent gift of the Spirit (v. 17) that preceded his sinful request, even if that request seems incompatible with possession of the Spirit. What Simon sought (vs. 18f.) was not the gift of the Spirit but the (additional) power of conferring the Spirit on others.
16. E. Haenchen, op. cit., p. 255.
17. The fact that Simon appears in later legend, no doubt rightly, as an arch-heretic does not affect the theological point of the story here.
18. See the discussion in K. Lake and H. J. Cadbury, *The Beginnings of Christianity*, 1920–33, IV, p. 94. The possibility of forgiveness rests in the mercy of God. H. Windisch, *Taufe und Sünde*, pp. 92, 97, exaggerates the unlikelihood of acceptance, but Acts leaves the matter open.
19. E. Haenchen, op. cit., pp. 93–9.

20. Persecution plays no part in Acts as an inducement to apostasy. It is, however, taken for granted that entry to the kingdom is only 'through many temptations' (Acts 14:22).

S. Brown, op. cit., pp. 114–131, underestimates the importance of exhortation to Christians to persevere in Acts. A detailed discussion of his interpretation of Acts is not possible in the present context.

NOTES TO CHAPTER 4

1. In this chapter the Epistles from Romans to 2 Thessalonians will be examined. Since the Pastoral Epistles form a separate group, linked together by a common date, style, and subject-matter, they will be discussed in the next chapter, without prejudice to the question of authorship.

2. J. Weiss, *Der erste Korintherbrief* (KEK), Göttingen, 1910, pp. 25f. But reference to a present experience seems certain in Romans 8:24; 1 Corinthians 15:2; Ephesians 2:5, 8; 2 Thessalonians 2:10.

3. J. Weiss, *The History of Primitive Christianity*, 1937, II, pp. 543, 542, 561. The likelihood of perseverance is stressed by W. Neil, *1 and 2 Thessalonians* (MNTC), 1950, pp. 153, 160.

4. H. Lietzmann, *The Beginnings of the Christian Church*, 1953[3], p. 124. See also B. Rigaux, *Les Epîtres aux Thessaloniciens*, pp. 257, 372; E. B. Allo, *Première Epître aux Corinthiens* (EB), Paris, 1956[2], p. 283.

5. H. Lietzmann and W. G. Kümmel, *An die Korinther I, II* (HNT), Tübingen, 1949[4] , p. 168.

6. Romans 5:9 indicates that the decisive act of justification is in the past — at conversion; but the possibility of revoking one's justification is raised in Galatians 5:4.

7. The noun ἐκλογή can mean 'act of selecting, choosing' (Acts 9:15; Romans 9:11; 11:5, 28; 2 Peter 1:10) or 'that which is selected, chosen' (Romans 11:7). Here the former meaning is required. See G. Schrenk, in TDNT, IV, pp. 176–181.

8. It is not clear whether the ὅτι in v. 5 is causal or epexegetical; the meaning is scarcely affected.

9. Read by most MSS. and accepted by WH, RV, RSV, NEB.

10. Note that ἀρχή is found with the meaning of 'beginning' only in these two verses in Paul.

11. Although the divine plan of salvation was formulated in past eternity (Romans 16:25; 1 Corinthians 2:7; Ephesians 3:9; Colossians 1:26; 2 Timothy 1:9; Titus 1:2; 1 Peter 1:20; Revelation 13:8; 17:8), it is doubtful whether a pre-mundane election of particular individuals to salvation is taught in the New Testament.

12. The meaning is not greatly altered if the variant reading ἀπαρχήν is adopted (so B. M. Metzger, *A Textual Commentary on the Greek New Testament*, 1971, pp. 636f.; see, however, E. Best, *The First and Second Epistles to the Thessalonians*, 1972, pp. 312–314). In this case 'first fruits' may refer to the privileged position of the Thessalonians

either as early converts or with reference to their position at the last day in contrast with the doom of their persecutors.

13. The possibility of believers sinning is certainly present in Romans 6 and 8, and it is impossible to believe that Christian experience, whether normal or abnormal, is not mirrored in Romans 7:7ff. The opposite point of view is defended by H. Windisch, *Taufe und Sünde*, pp. 164–94.

14. In Romans 1:1f. (cf. Galatians 1:15f.) an individual 'separation' and call of Paul to apostleship is implied.

15. Genesis 18:19; Exodus 33:12; Numbers 16:5 LXX; Jeremiah 1:5; Hosea 13:5; Amos 3:2. See W. Schottroff in E. Jenni and C. Westermann (ed.) *Theologisches Handwörterbuch zum Alten Testament*, München, 1971, I, cols. 692–3; cf. R. T. Forster and V. P. Marston, *God's Strategy in Human History*, Bromley, 1973, pp. 144–169.

16. F. J. Leenhardt, *The Epistle to the Romans*, 1961, p. 233.

17. See the criticisms offered by W. Sanday and A. C. Headlam, *Romans* (ICC), Edinburgh, 1902[5], p. 217.

18. On the use of προορίζω see L. C. Allen, 'The Old Testament Background of (προ)ὁρίζειν in the New Testament,' in NTS, XVII, 1970–71, pp. 104–108.

19. The earlier references to glory in the chapter (8:17, 18, 21) may be thought to require a future sense here also. In that case Paul may be using the aorist here by analogy with the other aorists and to stress the certainty of the hope expressed (H. Lietzmann, *An die Römer* (HNT), Tübingen, 1933[4], p. 87). Cf. John 15:8: BD 333[2].

20. J. Wesley, *Explanatory Notes upon the New Testament*, 1754, adloc.

21. In Romans 11:1f. Paul raises the question whether God has rejected the people whom He foreknew (προέγνω). His answer is 'No.' Israel as a whole has been rejected, but this does not mean that every Israelite has been rejected. προγινώσκω is here used of a people rather than of individuals.

22. Note that Israel was cut off for failure to believe in Christ, but Gentiles are in danger of being cut off for falling from belief in Christ (Romans 11:20, 22).

23. F. J. Leenhardt, op. cit., p. 291, notes that a mechanical predestination is impossible at this stage in the argument.

24. What has been said above applies to the New Testament as a whole. In no case, except where divine 'hardening' is the penalty for sin, is human response to the Gospel due to divine predetermination. Faith is a response to the Gospel, not the result of a divine causation.

25. C. H. Dodd, *Romans* (MNTC), 1932, pp. 183–6.

26. Cf. Sanhedrin 10:1. See F. J. Leenhardt, op. cit., p. 293; W. Sanday and A. C. Headlam, op. cit., p. 336.

27. There is nothing to be said in favour of E. Stauffer's view (*New Testament Theology*, p. 224) that the condition 'by faith', falls away in Romans.

28. M. Dibelius and H. Greeven, *An die Kolosser, Epheser; an Philemon* (HNT), Tübingen, 1953 , pp. 62f.

29. καὶ τοῦτο in Ephesians 2:8 refers to the whole of the preceding clause. Faith is part of God's working in us, but it is regarded as *our* response elicited by His grace.

30. The image of the book of life in Philippians 4:3 'suggested no idea of absolute predestination' (J. B. Lightfoot, *Philippians* (Macmillan), 1881[6], p. 159).

31. 1 Corinthians 1:9; 10:13; 2 Corinthians 1:18; 1 Thessalonians 5:24; 2 Thessalonians 3:3; cf. Deuteronomy 7:9; 2 Timothy 2:13; Hebrews 10:23; 11:11; 1 Peter 4:19; Revelation 1:5; 19:11.

32. Cf. 1 Corinthians 1:8; Philippians 1:10f.; Colossians 1:22; 1 Thessalonians 3:13; Jude 24.

33. The καί may refer back to ἐβεβαιώθη in 1 Corinthians 1:6, or indicate that the process is not automatic (so J. Weiss, *Der erste Korintherbrief*, p. 10).

34. Romans 1:11; 16:25; 1 Corinthians 1:8; 2 Corinthians 1:21; Colossians 2:7; 1 Thessalonians 3:2, 13; 2 Thessalonians 2:17; 3:3; cf. Luke 22:32; Acts 18:23; Hebrews 13:9; 1 Peter 5:10; et al.

35. Jewish teaching looked forward to a large-scale outbreak of evil and apostasy in the last days (SB, III, p. 637; IV, pp. 977–86; Moore, II, pp. 354–63). According to P. Billerbeck this would be an apostasy by Jews, but an examination of the passages cited by him does not bear out his conclusion. Similarly, although the Qumran sect believed that Israel generally was apostate, they did not think of themselves as being involved in their apostasy. For Paul see B. Rigaux, *Les Epîtres aux Thessaloniciens*, p. 256; W. Neil, *1 and 2 Thessalonians*, p. 160. The view that Christians are involved in the apostasy is upheld by H. Schlier, TDNT, I, pp. 512–14, but his reasons are not convincing. See Further E. Best, op. cit., pp. 281–283.

36. E. Lohmeyer, *Die Briefe an die Philipper, Kolosser und an Philemon* (KEK), Göttingen, 1959[15], pp. 152f. The reference may well be to Christians who had turned against the cross, but this will have been due to Judaistic influences rather than to the fear of persecution and martyrdom associated with Lohmeyer's improbable understanding of Philippians as an Epistle of martyrdom. 1 Corinthians 16:21 is perhaps to be linked with this passage.

37. It is not clear whether 'those who are circumcised' here means the Judaisers, or the Gentiles who were being persuaded to adopt circumcision, or both. The first possibility is strongly defended by E. D. Burton, *The Epistle to the Galatians* (ICC), Edinburgh, 1921, pp. 353f., but his reasoning is not absolutely compelling.

38. There can be no doubt that in this verse Paul is speaking of the possibility of turning from faith in Christ to an attempt to be justified by the law, and that such an action leads to loss of salvation, since for Paul salvation is either by faith in Christ or by complete obedience to the law (which he regards as impossible in practice). What is not certain is whether the use of the aorist, κατηργήθητε, means that some Galatians had already taken the decisive step of submitting to the law.

The aorist may convey the sense, 'Your justification in law, which is but an attempt, has already resulted in separation from Christ as a fact' (E. D. Burton, op. cit., p. 276): it will then have the force of a strong warning to anybody who is tempted to go further along the road away from Christ.

39. In 2 Corinthians 11:1–4 Paul fears lest his converts may be led astray from Jesus to accept a different Gospel, but the thought is not developed further. Cf. Romans 16:17–19.

40. B. Rigaux, *Les Epîtres aux Thessaloniciens*, p. 511, is undecided between the two possibilities.

41. The connexion between idleness and expectation of the parousia is, however, not explicitly made; cf. B. Rigaux, op. cit., p. 74.

42. G. Forkman, op. cit., pp. 137–139, suggests that the names of offenders were to be written on a list (σημειόω), and they were to be excluded from the church's common meal, but not completely expelled from the church; cf. CD 20:4f.

43. E. Schweizer in TDNT, VI, p. 429.

44. Similar teaching to that in Galatians is given in Romans 6–8. Although the Christian is expected to live the life of the Spirit, Paul needs to insist that life according to the flesh will lead to death and to urge his readers not to live according to the flesh (Romans 8:12f.). O. Michel, *Der Brief an die Römer*, p. 135, n. 4, holds that Romans 6:16 allows the possibility of eternal death even for the baptized if they fall into sin.

45. The weaker brother was made 'still weaker till he fell from Christ and fell into eternal death' (J. A. Beet, *St. Paul's Epistles to the Corinthians*, 1885^3, p. 141); cf. Romans 14:20.

46. R. Bohren (*Das Problem der Kirchenzucht*, pp. 97–100, 102–107) found parallels to the Rabbinic light ban in 2 Corinthians 2:6–8; 2 Thessalonians 3:14; 1 Timothy 5:22 (cf. 1 Corinthians 16:22; Galatians 1:8) and to the heavy ban in Matthew 18:17; 2 Corinthians 13:2; Titus 3:10f.; 2 John 10; 3 John 9f. But it is doubtful whether the Rabbinic procedure in this form can be dated so early, and better analogies may be found at Qumran.

47. It is not clear whether the act of excommunication normally included the utterance of a curse. Denial that the act included excommunication (W. G. Kümmel in H. Lietzmann, *An die Korinther I, II*, p. 174) seems to be unnecessary.

48. Cited by E. B. Allo, *Première Epître aux Corinthiens*, p. 123.

49. For Satan as a murderer see Job 1–2; John 8:44; Hebrews 2:14; SB, III, p. 358.

50. The identity of the two offenders is usually denied, but has been recently defended by P. E. Hughes, *Paul's Second Epistle to the Corinthians* (NLC), 1962, pp. 59–63.

51. The suggestion of M. Goguel (*The Birth of Christianity*, 1953, p. 240) that the man was to suffer premature death instead of final loss of salvation is unlikely for the same reason; as Goguel himself admits, it would mean that Paul is here illogical and does not follow through his own soteriological principles. Nor is it likely that the man was to

atone for his sin by his suffering and death or by purgatorial suffering after death.

52. This was the view of some Greek fathers (J. Schneider in TDNT, V, p. 169 n. 8). Cf. B. Poschmann, *Paenitentia Secunda*, Bonn, 1940, p. 28. F. F. Bruce, *The Book of the Acts*, p. 114 n. 3, comments that some other form of physical affliction than death might follow the act of excommunication. E. B. Allo, op. cit., p. 124, also finds that the possibility of repentance and restoration to the fellowship of the Church is open to the offender.

53. A. C. Thiselton, 'The Meaning of Σάρξ in 1 Corinthians 5:5,' in SJT, XXVI, 1973, pp. 204–228. See also J. Cambier, 'La Chair et l'Esprit en 1 Cor. v. 5,' in NTS XV 1968–69, pp. 221–232.

54. E. Schweizer in TDNT, VI, pp. 435f.

55. W. G. Kümmel, op. cit., p. 186.

56. See R. F. Hettlinger, '2 Corinthians 5:1–10' in SJT, X, 1957, pp. 174–94; C. F. D. Moule, 'St. Paul and Dualism: The Pauline Conception of Resurrection,' in NTS, XII, 1965–6, pp. 106–23.

57. Cf. E. B. Allo, op. cit., p. 283.

58. Paul has Deuteronomy 32:15–22 in mind at this point.

59. It is not clear whether the man simply forfeits the reward due for good work or also in addition suffers some real loss.

60. A. Robertson and A. Plummer, *The First Epistle of Paul to the Corinthians* (ICC), Edinburgh, 1914[2], p. 67. C. K. Barrett, *The First Epistle to the Corinthians* (Black's New Testament Commentaries), 1968, p. 91, suggests that Judaizers are meant.

61. For this view of the construction (with inverted order of the clauses), see J. Weiss, op. cit., p. 346; A. Robertson and A. Plummer, op. cit., p. 332; E. B. Allo, *Première Epitre aux Corinthiens*, pp. 388f. Cf. NEB.

62. In 1 Corinthians 14:5; 1 Timothy 5:19 ἐκτὸς εἰ μή, means 'unless, except.' For the rendering 'otherwise' here, see H. Lietzmann, *An die Korinther I, II*, p. 76; NEB.

εἰκῇ may mean 'rashly' (J. Weiss, op. cit., p. 346; A. Robertson and A. Plummer, op. cit., p. 332) or 'to no purpose' (Romans 13:4; Galatians 3:4; 4:11; cf. Colossians 2:18).

63. J. Denney, 2 *Corinthians* (Exp. B), 1907, p. 225; E. B. Allo, *Seconde Epître aux Corinthiens* (EB), Paris, 1956[2], p. 173.

64. P. E. Hughes, op. cit., p. 217, categorically denies that the possibility of falling away is present. The possibility of grace being in vain is probably to be seen also in 1 Corinthians 15:10; C. K. Barrett, op. cit., p. 345. The need for perseverance in faith is also stressed in Colossians 1:23 (cf. Romans 11:20; 1 Corinthians 16:13f.; 2 Corinthians 1:24); here the construction, 'provided that . . .' (εἴ γε) allows, but by no means demands, the possibility that the condition may not be fulfilled. While the general tone is one of confidence that the Colossians will stand firm, it remains true that their standing on the day of judgement depends on their not shifting away from the hope contained in the Gospel.

65. The πῶς indicates uncertainty about the means to be employed

and so possibly about the end in view; cf. Acts 27:12; Romans 1:10; 11:14.

66. E. Lohmeyer, *Die Briefe an die Philipper, Kolosser und an Philemon*, p. 141.

67. The use of ἐξανάστασις may be due to a desire to draw a contrast with the other resurrection mentioned in 3:10 (M. Dibelius, *An die Thessalonicher I, II, an die Philipper* (HNT), Tübingen, 1937², p. 90). The parallel passages do not prove the required point.

68. E. Lohmeyer, ibid.

69. R. P. Martin, *The Epistle to the Philippians* (TNTC), 1959, pp. 150f.

70. Note how Paul goes on to assert that if any of his companions in the race are going astray God will reveal it to them and so give them the opportunity of amendment (Philippians 3:15; cf. 1 Thessalonians 4:9).

71. The verb δοκιμάζω simply means 'to test' or 'to discern' but often has the developed meaning 'to test something successfully,' i.e. 'to approve.' The adjective δόκιμος thus means 'approved by testing' and the negative adjective ἀδόκιμος means 'rejected after testing.' Men not only test themselves (1 Corinthians 11:28) but must also be tested by God (1 Thessalonians 2:4) and win His approval (James 1:3, 12; Romans 5:4).

72. 1 Thessalonians 2:19; Philippians 4:1; 1 Peter 5:4. The crown is salvation in 2 Timothy 4:8; James 1:12; Revelation 2:10; 3:11.

73. Cf. H. L. Goudge, *The First Epistle to the Corinthians* (WC), 1926⁵, p. 79: 'The text negatives the Calvinistic doctrine of "final perseverance"; even S. Paul was not sure of ultimate salvation. Nevertheless, his confidence seems to have deepened, as his life went on.' Cf. C. K. Barrett, op. cit., p. 218.

74. J. Weiss, op. cit., p. 249, held that there was a fusion of two letters in 1 Corinthians, with a suture at this point; but the unity of the Epistle is no doubt to be maintained. H. Lietzmann, op. cit., p. 44, stated that the use of γάρ here is stereotyped and that the word has no connective force. A closer connexion is seen by A. Robertson and A. Plummer, op. cit., p. 199.

75. Cf. 1 Corinthians 11:19; the genuine (i.e. approved) members of the church are those who test themselves before the Lord's Supper (1 Corinthians 11:28) or those who refuse to join in the various factions.

76. εἰ μήτι; the possibility is momentarily admitted. Cf. BD, 376.

77. P. E. Hughes, op. cit., p.481.

78. R. V. G. Tasker, *The Second Epistle of Paul to the Corinthians* (TNTC), 1958, p. 188.

79. On the important place of intercession in Paul's theology and practice see G. P. Wiles, *Paul's Intercessory Prayers*, Cambridge, 1974.

80. The nature of Church discipline in Paul is fully discussed by R. Bohren, *Das Problem der Kirchenzucht*, pp. 81–119. Most of the passages where matters of discipline occur have already been handled above.

81. No attempt has been made in this chapter to discuss the rich paraenetic teaching in Paul. A wealth of imperatives in his Epistles urge Christians to continued effort in their pursuit of love and holiness. There is a vocabulary of exhortation (see ἀντέχομαι, μαρτύρομαι, οἰκοδομέω, παραγγέλλω, παρακαλέω and παραμυθέομαι in the concordance) which bears witness to the constant need for believers to stand firm in the faith, to live lives worthy of God, to grow in the Christian graces and to love each other.

82. The view was popularized by J. H. Michael, *The Epistle to the Philippians* (MNTC), 1928, pp. 98–105, who cites P. Ewald in his favour. Cf. R. P. Martin, *The Epistle to the Philippians*, p. 111.

83. Philippians 1:19 certainly has a spiritual reference. 2 Corinthians 1:5 is surely spiritual also, but may refer to the Church as a whole.

84. R. P. Martin, op. cit., p. 111, takes κατεργάζομαι to mean 'to work at' rather than 'to work out.' But the verb often means 'to produce as an end result' (cf. 2 Corinthians 4:17; AG, s.v.). It refers either to the production of the fruits of salvation in Christian living (M. Dibelius, *An die Thessalonicher I, II; an die Philipper*, p. 83) or to the attainment of future salvation through perseverance in the faith (cf. 1 Timothy 6:12; F. W. Beare, *The Epistle to the Philippians*, 1968[2], p. 90).

85. The objection of R. P. Martin, ibid., that the traditional rendering introduces an individualistic, personal note which is out of place in a passage which urges the readers to think more of others than of themselves lacks force because even on the traditional rendering Paul is engaged in showing them that their salvation must be worked out in terms of a life which takes notice of other people.

86. It is better to take ἐν ὑμιν to mean 'within each of you' rather than 'in your midst.' Either translation is possible with ἐνεργέω, but the idea of God working to produce willingness and action 'in your midst' is strange.

87. R. P. Martin, op. cit., pp. 112f. Other possibilities are that the words express God's aim in working in us 'for his own chosen purpose' (NEB and most commentators), or that they express the purpose of pleasing God which is to be the Christian's aim (E. Lohmeyer, *Der Brief an die Philipper*, p. 105).

NOTES TO CHAPTER 5

1. Although many scholars favour non-Pauline authorship, there is a growing body of opinion in favour of the view that the Epistles either were written by Paul (whether directly or by an amanuensis) or were composed on the basis of Pauline material by a close disciple; see the surveys in D. Guthrie, *New Testament Introduction*, 1970; E. E. Ellis, 'The Authorship of the Pastorals,' in EQ XXXII, 1960, pp. 151–161. The precise relationship of Paul to the Epistles is hard to determine, and is in any case unimportant for the present study; since the Epistles

have been written in his name, it is simplest to refer to their author as 'Paul.'

2. Although the description is mainly in the future tense, the movement is regarded as being already under way; cf. 2 Timothy 3:1 and 6.

3. L. Boettner, *The Reformed Doctrine of Predestination*, p. 191.

4. J. Müller-Bardorff, 'Zur Exegese von 1 Timotheus 5:3–16,' in G. Delling (ed.) *Gott und die Götter* (Festschrift für E. Fascher), Berlin, 1958, pp. 113–133, finds only one group of 'real' widows, who practised sexual abstinence, gave themselves to prayer, and were supported by the Church.

5. It has been suggested that they had turned to immoral means of support (D. Guthrie, *The Pastoral Epistles* (TNTC), 1957, p. 101), but if this were so, surely they would have been sternly disciplined.

6. D. Guthrie, op. cit., p. 103.

7. μήποτε with the subjunctive implies some uncertainty as to fulfilment; cf. BD, 370.[3]

8. Cf. Wisdom 12:10, 19f.; Sibylline Oracles 4:168f.; Luke 24:47; Acts 5:31; 11:18; 17:30; 1 Clement 7:4f.; Barnabas 16:9; Hermas s. 8:6:1ff.; Epistle of Polycarp 11:4; H. Conzelmann, *The Theology of St. Luke*, 1960, p. 100n.

9. The verb παραιτέομαι is admittedly a strange one to use in this connexion; see AG, *s.v.* 2.

10. One of the men concerned reappears in 2 Timothy 2:17, alive and continuing his evil deeds! The counter-argument, that 2 Timothy was composed before 1 Timothy (B. S. Easton, *The Pastoral Epistles*, 1947), rests on very insecure foundations (M. Dibelius and H. Conzelmann, *Die Pastoralbriefe* (HNT), Tübingen, 1955[3], pp. 56f.).

11. E. F. Scott, *The Pastoral Epistles* (MNTC), 1936, p. 17.

12. Elsewhere in the Pastoral Epistles, laying on of hands is a rite of ordination, but at a later date laying on of hands was certainly part of the restoration of a penitent (Eusebius, HE 7:2). Since the whole passage deals with sin (in elders and others), the reference to restoration of sinners is not out of context. Cf. G. Bornkamm in TDNT, VI, p. 666, n. 93. For the other interpretation see N. Adler, 'Die Handauflegung im NT bereits ein Bussritus?' in J. Blinzler et al. (ed.) *Neutestamentliche Aufsätze*, Regensburg, 1963, pp. 1–6.

13. The meaning of 'elect' is a moot point. It may refer to those who have responded to the call of God; if so, the word salvation refers to that future possession of which they possess an earnest here and now (cf. B. S. Easton, op. cit., p. 229). Or it may express Paul's belief 'that among the mass of men there were those who had been chosen by God to receive salvation' (E. F. Scott, op. cit., p. 105; D. Guthrie, op. cit., p. 144). The reference to 'eternal glory' favours the eschatological meaning of 'salvation.' Further, the term 'elect' is not applied elsewhere to those who have not yet responded to the call of God. The words καὶ αὐτοί indicate Paul's desire that the rest of the elect may share his own certainty of perseverance.

14. ἀπιστέω here means 'to be faithless,' not 'to disbelieve.'

15. J. Jeremias, *Die Pastoralbriefe* (NTD), Göttingen, 1953[6], pp. 48f.; D. Guthrie, op. cit., p. 146. The view that God's 'faithfulness makes it impossible for Him to acknowledge those who deny Him' (R. F. Horton, quoted by D. Guthrie, ibid.) is unlikely.

16. It is uncertain whether we should identify the Church here with 'the group of genuine Christians who form the rock on which Christ will build His Church' (E. F. Scott, op. cit., p. 112) or give the term a more general reference. The meaning would not be essentially affected.

17. The Hebrew text and LXX differ from each other, but the difference is not important for us here, since Paul is using an Old Testament form of words rather than proving a point by means of a proof-text. Both this and the second text may have been modified in Christian usage; cf. M. Dibelius, op. cit., p. 84.

18. E. F. Scott, op. cit., p. 112.

19. E. F. Scott, ibid.

20. W. Lock, *The Pastoral Epistles* (ICC), Edinburgh, 1924, pp. 88, 90, 92.

21. M. Dibelius and H. Conzelmann, op. cit., p. 79; D. Guthrie, op. cit., p. 132. C. Maurer in TDNT, VIII, pp. 162–164. ἡ παραθήκη μου may mean not something entrusted to God by Paul, nor something entrusted to Paul by God, but the Gospel (cf. τὸ εὐαγγέλιόν μου, Romans 2:16; 16:25; 2 Timothy 2:8) entrusted by Paul to Timothy.

22. The interpretation of the passage in detail is obscure. The materials of which the utensils are made do not figure in the application of the metaphor. ἃ μέν. . .ἃ δέ. . . may mean 'the former . . . the latter . . .,' but the meaning 'some . . . others . . .' is preferable (cf. M. Dibelius and H. Conzelmann, op. cit., p. 84; AG, *s.v.* ὅς II, 2).

23. In the metaphor σκεύη εἰς ἀτιμίαν are vessels for menial purposes, such as containing refuse; in the application the idea seems to be uselessness and hence readiness for destruction; there may be an echo of Romans 9:21f.

24. τούτων (v. 21) probably refers to acts of ἀτιμία; it is unlikely that the reference is to the excommunication of evil-doers from the Church; see D. Guthrie, op. cit., p. 152.

25. Despite B. S. Easton, op. cit., p. 229.

NOTES TO CHAPTER 6

1. H. Windisch, *Der Hebräerbrief*, pp. 52–6; O. Michel, *Der Brief an die Hebräer* (KEK) Göttingen, 1960,[11] pp. 150–2; W. Telfer, *The Forgiveness of Sins*.

2. For this view in its various forms see B. F. Westcott, *The Epistle to the Hebrews* (Macmillan), 1903[3]; A. S. Peake, *Hebrews* (Century Bible), Edinburgh; W. Manson, *The Epistle to the Hebrews*, 1951; C. Spicq, *L'Épître aux Hebreux* (EB), Paris, 1952–3. The view that the Epistle was written to Gentile Christians is still widely held; see especially J. Moffatt, *The Epistle to the Hebrews*, Edinburgh, 1922; E. Käsemann, *Das wandernde Gottesvolk*, Göttingen, 1959[3]. The consensus of opinion at present appears to favour a Jewish Christian

destination, and the most recent studies have attempted to place the Epistle more precisely within a Jewish setting.

3. For these three points of view see A. Nairne, *The Epistle of Priesthood*, Edinburgh, 1913, W. Manson, op. cit., and E. Käsemann, op. cit., respectively.

4. B. F. Westcott, op. cit., p. xlviii. Cf. F. F. Bruce, *The Apostolic Defence of the Gospel*, 1959, pp. 78ff., and the same author's commentary, *The Epistle to the Hebrews* (NLC), 1964.

5. O. Michel, op. cit., p. 5.

6. O. Michel, ibid.

7. The conditional clause does not imply that the permission of God is necessarily doubtful.

8. Cf. A. S. Peake, op. cit., p. 143, who rejects this view.

9. This interpretation is accepted by C. Spicq, op. cit., II, pp. 153, 170f.

10. 'There is not the faintest suggestion that a second repentance might be produced by God when human effort failed,' J. Moffatt, op. cit., p. 79.

11. J. Calvin, *The Epistle of Paul the Apostle to the Hebrews and the First and Second Epistles of St. Peter*, Edinburgh, 1963, p. 76; J. Owen, *The Doctrine of the Saints' Perseverance*, pp. 638ff. Owen expressed the same opinions, often in the same words, in *The Nature of Apostasy* and in *An Exposition of the Epistle to the Hebrews* (*Works*, XVIII–XXIV — a wordy commentary of about 3,500 pages!).

12. The word 'enlightened' was later used of baptism.

13. J. Owen, *The Nature of Apostasy*, pp. 1ff.

14. Cf. J. Behm in TDNT, I, pp. 675–677; LS, *s.v.* γεύομαι.

15. A. S. Peake, op. cit., p. 143.

16. As suggested by E. Schweizer, TDNT, VI, p. 446.

17. J. Calvin, ibid.

18. J. Owen, *The Nature of Apostasy*, p. 24.

19. μέτοχος (cf. Hebrews 3:1, 14) is the equivalent of κοινωνός, used elsewhere in the New Testament for sharing in a common possession. For the thought, compare 2 Corinthians 13:13 and Philippians 2:1, where the phrase used probably means 'participation in the Spirit' (R. P. Martin, *The Epistle to the Philippians*, pp. 46–50).

20. J. Owen, op. cit., p. 26.

21. C. F. D. Moule, *An Idiom-Book of New Testament Greek*, p. 36.

22. J. Owen, ibid.

23. In the LXX παράπτωμα means 'transgression,' and παραπίπτω means 'to transgress' (Ezekiel 22:4 *'āsham*) and 'to act faithlessly, be treacherous' (Ezekiel 14:13; 15:8; 18:24; 20:27 *mā'al*). Cf. Wisdom 6:9; 12:2.

24. J. Moffatt, op. cit., p. 79.

25. B. F. Westcott, op. cit., pp. 153f. The view that ἀνα- here means 'sursum' rather than 'rursum' (F. F. Bruce, op. cit., p. 111, n. 7) is unlikely in view of the context; cf. E. Riggenbach, quoted by O. Michel, op. cit., p. 149, n.

26. A. S. Peake, op. cit., p. 145.
27. The phrase κατάρας ἐγγύς may reflect a certain mildness. Although J. Moffatt (op. cit., p. 82) holds that the phrase indicates an imminent doom which is only a matter of time, it may be that the words contain an indication that the fault must be total before such drastic action is taken; is there perhaps an echo of the teaching of Jesus in Luke 13:6–9?
28. T. Hewitt, *The Epistle to the Hebrews* (TNTC), 1960, pp. 109–11.
29. Hewitt quotes some half-dozen texts, and ignores the fuller evidence given by B. F. Westcott, op. cit., p. 167.
30. T. Hewitt, op. cit., p. 108.
31. This was the view of Tertullian; later writers held that it prohibited a second baptism for the *lapsi* but permitted *paenitentia secunda*; cf. B. F. Westcott, op. cit., pp. 167–9.
32. C. Spicq, op. cit., II, pp. 167–78.
33. Herveius, quoted by B. F. Westcott, op. cit., p. 169.
34. Compare and contrast 2 Timothy 2:25 where the possibility of God granting repentance is uncertain, although it is certainly envisaged as likely.
35. Cf. p. 12 above.
36. A distinction between sins of ignorance committed before baptism and deliberate sins committed after baptism is unlikely. Such a view would tend to place all post-baptismal sins on the same level, and the author obviously does not mean this.
37. T. Hewitt, op. cit., pp. 165f.
38. Cf. pp. 130f. above; O. Michel, op. cit., p. 234.
39. Cf. Matthew 5:13; 7:6.
40. Cf. O. Michel, op. cit., p. 236.
41. T. Hewitt, op. cit., p. 167.
42. O. Michel, op. cit., p. 234, n. 4.
43. O. Michel, op. cit., p. 308.
44. The verb ὑστερέω refers to falling away rather than to falling short; cf. R. V. G. Tasker, *The Gospel in the Epistle to the Hebrews*, 1950, p. 50. Cf. Hebrews 10:39 where falling back (ὑποστολή) results in destruction.
45. Jewish legends portrayed the sexual sin of Esau (SB, III, pp. 748f.), but there is no indication that these are in mind here, the allusion being simply to his contempt for the birthright.
46. Wisdom 12:10; 2 Esdras 9:11f.; 1 Enoch 65:11; 2 Baruch 85:12; 1 Clement 7:5; J. Moffatt, op. cit., p. 213.
47. But so C. Spicq, op. cit., II, pp. 401–3.
48. F. F. Bruce, op. cit., p. 368.
49. C. K. Barrett, 'The Eschatology of Hebrews,' in W. D. Davies and D. Daube, *The Background of the New Testament and its Eschatology*, Cambridge, 1956, pp. 363–93.
50. That angels are meant is argued by A. S. Peake, op. cit., p. 233, and E. Käsemann, op. cit., p. 28. But the parallels quoted for this use (Hermas, v. 3:4; Excerpta ex Theodoto 27:3ff.), which speak of the

angels as 'first-created,' are not sufficient to establish this meaning here. See B. F. Westcott, op. cit., p. 417, for the view adopted here. Cf. W. Michaelis in TDNT, VI, p. 881.

51. O. Michel, op. cit., p. 317, n. 2, holds that the reference is to election and nothing more.

52. Cf. Revelation 13:8; 17:8. But no more than an up-to-date list of those destined for the heavenly kingdom may be implied in Luke 10:20 and Philippians 4:3, and it is possible for names to be removed from the list (Revelation 3:5; cf. Exodus 32:32f.; Psalm 69:28). G. W. Buchanan, *To the Hebrews*, New York, 1972, p. 223, describes the book of life as 'a membership roll of the elect which God kept and brought up to date at the beginning of each new year.

53. It must be admitted that the Hebrew text (translated above) differs here considerably from the LXX which is normally used by the author.

54. E. Käsemann, op. cit., p. 22.

55. O. Michel, op. cit., pp. 98–100.

56. J. Moffatt, op. cit., p. 39, notes that the temptations facing Christ were those to avoid the suffering that led to the cross, while those of the readers are to slip into apostasy and give up their faith on account of the hardships which it involved.

57. B. F. Westcott, op. cit., p. 58.

58. See AG, *s.v.*; C. K. Barrett, op. cit., p. 383; O. Michel, op. cit., pp. 75–77; E. Käsemann, op. cit., pp. 79–82.

59. E. Käsemann, ibid.; also pp. 82–90.

60. Käsemann's view also requires taking ἀγαγόντα in Hebrews 2:10 as referring to Christ, whereas it must refer to God; cf. J. Moffatt, op. cit., p. 31.

61. O. Cullmann, *The Christology of the New Testament*, pp. 92f. Note that a cultic sense may also be present; cf. O. Michel, op. cit., pp. 76f.; G. Delling in TDNT, VIII, pp. 82f.

62. This means that the sacrifice of Christ is eternal in its validity, not that the perfecting of believers is a once-for-all act incapable of being undone. Perfection here is analogous to justification in Paul. It is not a change of nature which cannot (in theory at least) be reversed.

63. B. F. Westcott, op. cit., p. 397; J. Moffatt, op. cit., p. 196.

64. In Hebrews 9:14 it is Christ's blood which cleanses the consciences of men. Only in Hebrews 13:21 is the work of God through Christ in the believer mentioned.

NOTES TO CHAPTER 7

1. J. Jeremias, *The Sermon on the Mount*, p. 22; cf. M. Dibelius, *Der Brief des Jakobus* (KEK), Göttingen, 1957[9], p. 19.

2. M. Dibelius, ibid.

3. Reference to the new birth is, however, denied by L. Elliott-Binns, 'James 1:18: Creation or Redemption?' in NTS, III, 1956–7, pp. 148–61.

4. James 4:5 may refer to the dwelling of the Holy Spirit in the

believer (R. V. G. Tasker, *The Epistle of James* (TNTC), 1956, pp. 90f.), but a glance at the recent translations will show that its meaning is too uncertain to be the basis of a firm statement.

5. M. Dibelius, op. cit., p. 87.

6. J. H. Ropes, *The Epistle of St. James* (ICC), Edinburgh, 1915, p. 309.

7. M. Dibelius, op. cit., pp. 223, 235f.

8. J. B. Mayor, *The Epistle of St James* (Macmillan), 1892, pp. 162–4; R. V. G. Tasker, op. cit., pp. 134, 136f.

9. The brother is obviously a Christian believer; R. V. G. Tasker, op. cit., p. 142. Something more serious than the mistakes in James 3:2 is meant.

10. The view that premature death is meant is exposed to the same objections here as in 1 Corinthians.

11. It is not certain whose sins are covered, but a decision on this point does not affect the main point of the passage.

12. To raise the question whether a new life due to an incorruptible seed can possibly end in spiritual death is probably to press the metaphor of the new birth too far.

13. This is denied by H. Windisch, *Taufe und Sünde*, pp. 227–43, but his reasoning is not conclusive; he is correct in thinking that Peter urges Christians to be sinless, but wrong in imagining that he presupposes their sinlessness.

14. A. M. Stibbs, *The First Epistle General of Peter* (TNTC), 1959, p. 172; cf. J. Moffatt, *The General Epistles* (MNTC), 1928, pp. 62f. B. Lindars also notes that the use of Isaiah 8:14 in 1 Peter 2:7f. 'is a good way of warning his readers against apostasy' (*New Testament Apologetic*, 1961, p. 180).

15. J. W. C. Wand, *St. Peter and St. Jude* (WC), 1934, p. 37. Similarly K. H. Schelkle, *Die Petrusbriefe — Der Judasbrief* (HTK), Freiburg, 1961, writes: 'The forcible exhortations in 1 Peter (e.g. 4:15–19) attest that election is not yet final salvation.'

16. The situation and date of composition of the Epistle remain obscure. The heresy opposed was a species of libertinism, and shows some resemblances to the views held by some of the members of the church at Corinth in Paul's time; cf. E. M. B. Green, *2 Peter Reconsidered*, 1961, p. 26. The dates assigned to the Epistle by scholars vary considerably, but opinion seems to be settling in favour of a first century date. There is no convincing evidence against authorship by Jude, the brother of James; cf. J. W. C. Wand, op. cit., pp. 187–90; M. Green, *2 Peter and Jude* (TNTC), 1968, pp. 42–6.

17. The meaning is the same in 1 Peter 2:8 (D. H. Wheaton in NBC, p. 1241).

18. H. Schlier, in TDNT, I, pp. 469–71 holds that ἀρνέομαι implies a previous relationship of obedience and fidelity expressed in an act of confession and submission. If this were so, the false teachers would have to be regarded as having fallen from a faith which they once truly held. But this interpretation is doubtful. For the emphasis is not on contradicting an earlier confession but on disproving the reality of

one's profession by the character of one's life; cf. 1 Timothy 5:8; 2 Timothy 3:5; Titus 1:16.

19. J. Moffatt, op. cit., p. 231.

20. The order of words is strange, and it must be assumed that Jude's thoughts raced ahead of his words, so that he wrote 'twice dead' before explaining how the trees were twice dead.

21. Possibly also the metaphor is not to be pressed, and simply emphasizes that the false teachers were most certainly dead spiritually.

22. οὓς μὲν ἐλεᾶτε (ἐλέγχετε) διακρινομένους, οὓς δὲ σώζετε ἐκ πυρὸς ἁρπάζοντες, οὓς δὲ ἐλεᾶτε ἐν φόβῳ . . . This text is read, with variations, by Aleph, A, (B), 33, 424^{c}, vg, sy^{h}, bo, eth, and is translated in RV and RSV. B omits the first οὓς δέ to give a two clause structure. It is defended by B. M. Metzger, *A Textual Commentary on the Greek New Testament*, pp. 727–729.

23. Cf. J. B. Mayor, *The Epistle of Jude and the Second Epistle of Peter* (Macmillan), 1907, pp. lvi, cxc.

24. The reading ἐλεᾶτε is probably to be preferred in both clauses, and ἐλέγχετε will be an attempt to avoid tautology.

25. καὶ οὓς μὲν ἐκ πυρὸς ἁρπάσατε, διακρινομένους δὲ ἐλεεῖτε ἐν φόβῳ . . . This text is read, with variations, by P 72, the Liber Commicus, sy^{ph}, sa, Clement of Alexandria, and Jerome. See J. N. Birdsall, 'The Text of Jude in P 72', in JTS, n.s. XIV, 1963, pp. 394–9; C. D. Osburn, 'The Text of Jude 22–23,' in *Zeitschrift für die NT Wissenschaft*, LXIII, 1972, pp. 139–144.

26. J. B. Mayor, op. cit., p. cxci.

27. H. Windisch and H. Preisker, *Die katholischen Briefe* (HNT), Tübingen, 1951^{3}, p. 47.

28. Whatever text be adopted, the exclusion of the heretics from the fellowship of the Church is implied; cf. Matthew 18:17; Titus 3:10f. Cf. R. Bultmann, *Theology of theNew Testament*, II, p. 233.

29. A. G.*s.v.* ἐποικοδομέω.

30. For προσδέχομαι see Mark 15:32; Luke 2:25, 38; 23:51; Titus 2:13, all of which refer to awaiting the Messiah at His coming; cf. also Hebrews 11:35. For 'mercy' see 2 Timothy 1:16, 18; 2 Clement 16:2. Eternal life is also an eschatological concept.

31. It is noteworthy that in 2 Peter 1:10 those who do not stumble are those who are zealous to make their calling and election sure.

32. Among recent writers E. M. B. Green, *2 Peter Reconsidered*, pp. 10f., holds that a common source may have been used, rather than that one Epistle is dependent on the other.

33. J. Calvin, *Commentaries on the Catholic Epistles*, Edinburgh, 1855, pp. 433–434.

34. 8:15, in AP, II, p. 772. The words can scarcely be understood to refer to a superficial and unreal conversion. Cf. H. Windisch, *Taufe und Sünde*, p. 254.

35. J. W. C. Wand, op. cit., p. 171; cf. J. B. Mayor, op. cit., pp. 140–2. The opposite view is upheld by C. Bigg, *The Epistles of St Peter and St Jude* (ICC), Edinburgh, 1901, pp. 286f.

36. H. Windisch, ibid.; cf. *Die katholischen Briefe*, p. 87.

37. J. W. C. Wand (op. cit., pp. 165f.) draws attention to 2 Peter 2:5 in this connexion, but this is not a strong piece of evidence.

38. H. Windisch, *Die katholischen Briefe*, p. 87.

39. J. Moffatt, op. cit., p. 183.

40. H. Windisch, op. cit., p. 102, thinks that God's patience is for the sake of members of the Church who had been affected by the doubt of the false teachers (and not for the sake of the false teachers themselves).

NOTES TO CHAPTER 8

1. For the theology of Revelation see especially P. Feine, *Theologie des Neuen Testaments*, Berlin, 1953[9], pp. 373–9. Cf. G. B. Caird, *The Revelation of St John the Divine* (Black's New Testament Commentaries), 1966, pp. 289–301.

2. E. Lohmeyer, *Die Offenbarung des Johannes* (HNT), Tübingen, 1953[2], pp. 179f., 202, goes too far in describing the book as a *summons* to martyrdom.

3. H. Windisch, *Der Hebräerbrief*, p. 54; cf. *Taufe und Sünde*, pp. 316–20.

Two different understandings of the teaching of Revelation about victory have been offered by M. Kiddle and E. Lohmeyer.

According to M. Kiddle (*The Book of Revelation* (MNTC) 1940, pp. 61–5) a distinction must be made between ordinary believers and martyrs, and it is the latter alone who receive the title of conqueror. Various of the promises in Revelation 2–3 are regarded as being for martyrs only (Revelation 2:7, 11, 17, 26–8; 3:5, 12, 21); they alone are absolutely certain of eternal life, and it is only they who are promised a share in the first resurrection and the millennial reign of Christ over the nations.

This interpretation is to be rejected. It is probable that the second resurrection is purely of non-believers to judgement (E. Lohmeyer op. cit., pp. 162f.; E. Schweizer, *Church Order in the New Testament*, p. 134, n. 491), so that all believers participate in the first resurrection and the millennium. Further, the emphasis in the promises is on faithfulness to the end rather than on the one crisis of martyrdom. Endurance to the end need not imply martyrdom. (The view of R. H. Charles, *The Revelation of St John* (ICC), Edinburgh, 1920, II, pp. 183–5, that all Christians will have died before the parousia will not stand up to examination. Cf. G. B. Caird, op. cit., p. 209; I. H. Marshall, 'Martyrdom and the Parousia in the Revelation of John' in F. L. Cross (ed.) *Studia Evangelica*, IV, (TU, 102), Berlin, 1968, pp. 333–9). Finally, the rewards for conquerors in Revelation 2–3 are elsewhere assigned to all Christians (cf. Revelation 2:7 with 22:2; 2:11 with 20:6, 14f.; 2:17 with 22:4; 2:26 with 22:5; 3:5 with 22:14; 3:12 with 22:3f.; and 3:21 with 22:5); in particular, ruling is stated to be the privilege of all believers (Revelation 1:5, 5:10; 22:5). Cf. G. B. Baird, op. cit., pp. 32–4.

E. Lohmeyer holds that there is a distinction between martyrs and ordinary believers, analogous to the distinction between spiritual men and ordinary believers which he professes to find in 1 Corinthians 2 and in John, and that Revelation was written to persuade ordinary believers to become martyrs. The exegesis of Revelation 14:1ff.; 18:4; 21:6 and 22:7 on which this view is based is more than doubtful. That the way to victory and conquest is only by the path of literal martyrdom and that the 'thirsty' who are exhorted to take the water of life are believers who have not yet passed through martyrdom to heavenly bliss are assumptions which the text will not support.

5. On Revelation 22:19 see G. R. Beasley-Murray in NBC, p. 1309. For the book of life see G. Schrenk in TDNT, I, pp. 619f.

6. See M. Kiddle, op. cit., p. 251; G. Schrenk, ibid.

7. E. Lohmeyer, op. cit., p. 67.

8. G. B. Caird, op. cit., pp. 94–8, argues that the 144,000 (who are identical with the great multitude) are the prospective martyrs; they form, however, only a part of the whole people of God.

9. Cf. John 10:26. A dualism of this kind is accepted by the Calvinist theologian L. Boettner, *The Reformed Doctrine of Predestination*, pp. 282–296.

10. R. Bultmann, *Theology of the New Testament*, 1952–55, II, p. 23; cf. *Das Evangelium des Johannes*, pp. 171–4, especially p. 172.

11. Cf. C. K. Barrett, *The Gospel according to St John*, 1955, p. 68. Note that the language about the inscrutable operations of the Spirit (John 3:8) is to be understood in this context. Its purpose is to emphasize that salvation is due to the divine initiative and not to human achievement.

12. E. C. Hoskyns (and F. N. Davey), *The Fourth Gospel*, 1947[2], p. 429, comments on 'this glaring paradox.' 'R. Schnackenburg, *Das Johannesevangelium*, Freiburg, 1965 and 1971, II, p. 385, notes the fact that the thought of an unalterable exclusion from salvation (John 10:26) is excluded by the fact that the same Jews are exhorted to believe in verses 37f. See his detailed discussions in I, pp. 522–524; II, pp. 328–346.

13. W. C. van Unnik, 'The Purpose of St John's Gospel,' in TU, 73, 1959, pp. 382–411. This of course does not exclude its relevance for the thoughtful Gentile, as emphasized by C. H. Dodd, *The Interpretation of the Fourth Gospel*, 1954.

14. John 6:64. R. Bultmann, *Das Evangelium des Johannes*, p. 343, speaks of betrayal as the most extreme possibility in unbelief.

15. In view of John 6:70 it is probably that John 13:18 should be taken to include the choice of Judas among the twelve; see C. K. Barrett, op. cit., p. 370.

16. For this distinction see MH, I, pp. 67f.; AG, *s.v.*; R. Bultmann, op. cit., p. 189, n. 1; C. H. Dodd, op. cit., p. 183.

R. Bultmann, ibid., holds that the distinction is not carried through consistently and should not be made the basis of a theological argument. But the evidence is against his point of view. In John 5:24 the use of the dative refers to the necessity to give credence to God who speaks through Jesus as a prerequisite for attaining eternal life, and there is no need to suppose that the more profound element of trust is not also necessary (B. F. Westcott, *The Gospel according to St John*, 1882, p. 87). In John 6:29f., the two uses are brought into juxtaposition, but it is clear that intellectual credence is regarded as the necessary prerequisite to trust and committal. John 8:30f. is more controversial; here the second type of construction is followed by the first. Westcott's explanation (op. cit., pp. 132f.) in terms of two groups of people is not entirely satisfactory. It is better to follow RSV and NEB in beginning a new paragraph at verse 31, so that a new section commences in which Jesus addresses Jews who had not gone as far as the people described in verse 30 and who later showed that their belief was anything but adequate; in this case the linguistic distinction will stand. For 1 John 3:23; 5:10, see R. Schnackenburg, *Die Johannesbriefe* (HTK), Freiburg, 1953, pp. 185, 237, n. 3. 1 John 3:23 ('to believe in the name') is the only exception to the rule.

17. R. Bultmann, op. cit., p. 189, n. 1; cf. *Theology of the New Testament*, II, p. 71.

18. R. Bultmann, *Das Evangelium des Johannes*, p. 37, n.4.

19. R. Bultmann, op. cit., p. 231.

20. R. Bultmann, op. cit., p. 414.

21. C. K. Barrett, op. cit., p. 395, thinks that both Jews who failed to respond to Jesus and also apostate Christians (cf. ἐν ἐμοί) are meant.

22. This must be the meaning of σκανδαλίζω here (cf. John 6:61); C. K. Barrett, op. cit., p. 403.

23. It must be admitted that writers of the Calvinist school see no incompatibility between statements which assign the sin and unbelief of men to the fact that God has destined them to be reprobate and statements which declare that they themselves are culpable. But if this is the case, it would seem to follow that God Himself must also be regarded as the author of sin and as Himself culpable.

24. Cf. R. Bultmann, *Theology of the New Testament*, II, pp. 75–92.

25. On sinlessness in 1 John see especially R. Schnackenburg, op. cit., pp. 253–8; J. R. W. Stott, *The Epistles of John* (TNTC), 1964, pp. 125–7, 130–6.

26. It is not clear whether they had been formally excommunicated, although 2 John 10f. might be held to support this view.

27. E. Schweizer, *Church Order in the New Testament*, ch. 12b, p. 126.

28. R. Schnackenburg, op. cit., p. 279.

29. Cf. E. Schweizer, op. cit., p. 127, n. 474, for this possibility in 1 John 1:7, 10 (but not 2:1f.).

30. R. Schnackenburg, op. cit., p. 164.

31. The best discussion of this difficult passage (1 John 5:16f.) is to be found in R. Law, *The Tests of Life*, Edinburgh, 1914[3], pp. 135–42.

32. Cf. Numbers 18:22; Deuteronomy 22:26; Isaiah 22:14; Jubilees 21:22; 26:34; 33:13, 18; Testament of Issachar 7:1.

33. Most commentators think that apostasy is meant, but R. Schnack-

enburg, op. cit., pp. 247–50, counsels caution in making a decision on this point.

34. It is not forbidden. R. Law, ibid., suggests that it is *confident* prayer which is ruled out. For divine commands not to pray, see p. 32.

35. A E. Brooke, *The Johannine Epistles* (ICC), Edinburgh, 1912, p. 147; G. Forkman, op. cit., pp. 151–155. Cf. H. Windisch, *Taufe und Sünde*, p. 271: 'Perhaps he has the silent thought that God may still be able to intervene.'

NOTES TO CHAPTER 9

1. Cf. p. 241, n. 33 above.

2. K. Lake and H. J. Cadbury, *The Beginnings of Christianity*, IV, p. 95.

3. B. B. Warfield, 'Predestination,' in *Biblical Foundations*, 1958, pp. 303–5.

4. W. B. Pope, *A Compendium of Christian Theology*, III, p. 139. What the critic of the Augustinian and Calvinist position finds most distasteful is the arbitrariness which characterises the mercy of God in this system. We are asked to believe that God is just in showing mercy to this sinner and none to that sinner when it is agreed that there is no reason in the sinners themselves why God should treat one differently from the other. Any attempt to criticise this position is regarded as the application of human standards to God and as a contradiction of what God is actually said to have done in Scripture (D. B. Knox, 'Kept by the Power of God,' *The Churchman*, LXXXV, 1971, pp. 105–115). But the criticism must be made. Although this book has not been a specialised study of election and predestination as such, sufficient evidence has emerged to show that the Calvinist system often requires the reading into Scripture of ideas that are not there. Nor is the criticism based on applying human standards to God; a Christian would be justly censured on the grounds of scriptural teaching if he acted arbitrarily in the exercise of mercy. How much more is it necessary that God should be cleared of such a charge.

5. The strict Calvinist finds the explanation of human refusal to accept Christ in the inscrutable will of God; the alternative is to find the explanation in the irrationality and mystery of evil. Cf. J. K. S. Reid (ed.), *J. Calvin: Concerning the Eternal Predestination of God*, p. 44.

6. It should be clear from what has been written above that we have no desire to deny or quarrel with the biblical teaching on election and predestination, but rather to expound it correctly; and our contention is that the apparently rigorous teaching of certain passages is modified by other teaching in such a way that the biblical teaching as a whole will not fit into such a rigid, logical framework as that provided, for example, by the Five Points of Dort.

7. The cumulative force of such passages as Acts 8:22f.; 1 Corinthians 5:5; 2 Corinthians 2:7, 10; 7:10; Galatians 6:1; 2 Timothy 2:25f.; James 5:16, 19f.; 1 John 2:1; Jude 22f.; Revelation

2:5 (cf. Matthew 18:21f.) is decisively against any limitation of the scope of divine forgiveness.

8. The most important of these passages are: Matthew 24:10–12: Mark 13:22; Luke 8:13; 12:10; Acts 20:29f.; 1 Corinthians 5:3–5; 11:30–32; Galatians 5:4; 6:13; Philippians 3:18f.; 1 Timothy 1:19f.; 4:1; 6:10; 2 Timothy 2:26; 4:10; 2 Peter 2:18ff.; 1 John 5:16; Jude 22f.; Revelation 3:2. While there is naturally some uncertainty about the interpretation of some of these passages, at the very least they show that the possibility that the apostasy of genuine Christians is predicted and described cannot be ignored or dismissed.

9. This problem is not present to the same extent in the various background documents which we considered, for in them the two facts of reception of salvation in this life and of the divine keeping power are not emphasized as they are in the New Testament. See further note 26.

10. See in general R. Bultmann, *Theology of the New Testament*, especially the section on John, Vol. II, pp. 3–92.

11. R. Bultmann, op. cit., I, pp. 320–2.

12. Ibid, II, pp. 77f.

13. Bultmann has so little to say about this, that it can scarcely be a vital part of his theology.

14. R. Bultmann, *Essays, Philosophical and Theological*, 1955, pp. 6f.

15. Contrast Charles Wesley's 'Omnipotent Lord, my Saviour and King,' cited below, pp. 215f.

16. Cf. D. Cairns, *A Gospel without Myth?*, 1960, passim.

17. R. Bultmann, *Theology of the New Testament*, I, p. 336; cf. p. 333, where the gift of the Spirit is demythologized into 'freedom from the power of sin and death.'

18. Grand Rapids, 1958. See the summary by L. B. Smedes in P. E. Hughes (ed.) *Creative Minds in Contemporary Theology*, Grand Rapids, 1966, p. 91.

19. L. Berkhof, *Systematic Theology*, 1958, p. 548.

20. G. C. Berkouwer, op. cit., p. 90.

21. This is not to deny that faith is God's gift; cf. H. Hanse in TDNT, IV, p. 2.

22. K. Barth, *The Epistle to the Romans*, Oxford, 1933, p. 324; cf. p. 355.

23. Cf. E. M. B. Green, *The Meaning of Salvation*, pp. 231–6, for a discussion of the problem of perseverance and its solution very similar to our own.

24. Calvinism does recognize the possibility of attaining assurance of final perseverance (*The Westminster Confession*, 18). Popular evangelical religion holds together the more characteristically Methodist doctrine of the assurance of present salvation and the Calvinist doctrine of the irremissibility of that salvation.

25. Cf. A. M. Stibbs in NBC, pp. 1219–1221.

26. A study of the Apostolic Fathers lies outside our present scope, but examination would show that in these documents the characteristic New Testament teaching is given up in favour of a legalistic type of

religion in which the stress is placed on the need for continual repentance if the believer is to persevere, and very little is said about the gracious care of God for those who trust in Him.

27. C. F. D. Moule, 'The Judgement Theme in the Sacraments' in W. D. Davies and D. Daube, *The Background of the New Testament and its Eschatology*, pp. 464–81.

28. R. Bultmann, *Das Evangelium des Johannes*, p. 368, n. 5.

29. In view of such teaching as Luke 13:1–5 and John 9:1–3 modern Christians would be slow to attribute illness to the sin of the patient. Miraculous illness and death are probably to be regarded as belonging to the special conditions of the early Church in the same way and to the same extent as miraculous healing and other signs and wonders.

30. C. Wesley, MHB, No. 502.

EPILOGUE

The Problem of Apostasy in New Testament Theology

It may seem slightly odd that someone who knows Dale Moody only through the printed word and who has had no particular associations with the Southern Baptist Theological Seminary should take part in a symposium in Dr. Moody's honour, when there are doubtless many others who have a better claim than I. The basis for my invitation to contribute to the *Festschrift* is that Dr. Moody and I share a common interest in the subject of apostasy and have both written on it. Thus, I have been asked to write on the topic of apostasy and to do so in the light of Dr. Moody's work. I am well aware that the topic can easily raise theological hackles, and I trust that what follows will be taken as an attempt to understand the word of God in the Scriptures, since they alone can constitute our supreme authority in faith and in practice.

Perhaps an autobiographical word may be helpful as an introduction to the subject. In 1969 I published a book entitled *Kept by the Power of God* with the subtitle *A Study of Perseverance and Falling Away.*[1] The book was a shortened and somewhat simplified version of a thesis I had completed for the University of Aberdeen six years earlier. I did not find it easy to interest a publisher, a fact which may indicate that, quite apart from the shortcomings of the book in itself, the topic was not one of general concern to the theological public. The publisher for his part may have regretted his rashness in undertaking the assignment; he did not print a lot of copies and not many of them were sold, with the result that the book was withdrawn from circulation after a comparatively short time. Yet it found one 'convert'. My friend, Professor Clark H. Pinnock, confessed that my book had exercised a decisive influence on his thinking in this area, and, as a result of his enthusiasm for exposing the North American evangelical constituency to its arguments, the book was republished with some slight revisions in 1975.[2]

The line of thought I developed was not, of course, original. Dr. Moody had come to similar conclusions at an earlier date. He in turn was dependent on the great Baptist scholar, A. T. Robertson. He has developed his position in one of the chapters of his comprehensive study of Christian doctrine, *The Word of Truth.*[3] Another scholar who has also defended the same general position is Robert Shank, in his books *Life in the Son*[4] and *Elect in the Son.*[5] A similar position was taken earlier by scholars of the Arminian persuasion, including John Wesley.

The reaction of scholars in the strict Calvinist tradition is to reject the position of writers like Moody and myself. They find the position indefensible on three grounds. First, they regard the texts in the New Testament that appear to teach the final security of the believer as representing the clear and central teaching of Scripture. They say that other passages which may appear to teach differently, for example, by suggesting the possibility of apostasy, must be interpreted in line with the first texts on the grounds that scriptural teaching by definition is consistent.

Second, the systematic formulation of Christian dogmatics by Calvinist theologians leads to a set of basic and mutually related principles which include the final perseverance of the saints. If one grants that God determined from all eternity to save the elect, then the final perseverance of the elect follows logically. Similarly, if it is agreed that Christ offered an efficacious sacrifice and wrought a full salvation for the elect, then it is inconceivable that this salvation does not contain the element of perseverance.

There is a third reason that is also important, although it does not stand on the same level as the other two. This says that the thought is not congenial that I, a believer, may possibly fall away from my faith and my hope of ultimate salvation. Modern sociological study has shown us how much we need a sense of security if we are to cope with life and its problems, and the importance of a secure basis for early life in the caring love of parents has received the stress it deserves. If we need security on the human level, how much more do we need to be able to trust in God to keep us for time and eternity. How important it is that in our Christian life we have the security provided by God, and the knowledge that, whatever we do, nothing can separate us from his love or thwart his purpose for our lives.

Here, then, are three strong reasons for criticizing a position that acknowledges the danger of falling away from the faith, and for arguing that it rests on an unacceptable and false interpretation of Scripture. Some Calvinists will reject the position more or less out of hand. Others, however, recognize a genuine problem of biblical interpretation. Here, special mention must be made of two scholars. The one is Donald A. Carson, whose book, *Divine Sovereignty and Human Responsibility: Biblical Perspectives in Tension*, published in 1981, tackles the problem with particular reference to the Gospel of John and at a profound and scholarly level.[6] The other is Judy Gundry Volf, whose monograph on the problem of perseverance in the writings of Paul is certainly the most detailed and acute study of the topic thus far.[7]

What follows now is an attempt to look again at apostasy from an exegetical point of view using Moody's contribution as a starting-point. In the course of the discussion I shall, for sake of convenience, refer to theologians who believe in the final perseverance of the elect as 'Calvinists'. I shall refer to those who do not accept this doctrine in the way in which it was formulated at Dort[8] as 'non-Calvinists', since many of us who are unhappy with Dort are not happy to be lumped together as 'Arminians'.

While it is true that an important part of my own upbringing has been in the Methodist Church, I am by no means a 'dyed-in-the-wool' Methodist, and I owe a great deal to Christians in many other churches. My primary loyalty is to the word of God written in Scripture and not to any human denomination or theological group. My concern, therefore, is to establish what Scripture actually says, and I am grateful for the impulses from theologians of all camps who open my eyes to see things that otherwise any personal bias might prevent me from seeing. I hope that it is not inappropriate for me to regard it as part of my theological task to help other people to shed their blinkers.

1. SOME MORAL AND PHILOSOPHICAL PROBLEMS

First of all, however, let us mention briefly some of the theological and philosophical problems that the issue raises.

The upholders of the possibility of apostasy are not of course unaware of passages in Scripture that promise that God's people will persevere, but they make the point that these promises are for those who continue to abide in Christ and keep on following the Lord. But the Calvinist will ask whether that is an adequate form of assurance. It is some comfort to know that even if I turn away from the Lord, I can always turn back to him and find him willing to forgive. But knowing how fallible I am, I want the assurance that I can never turn away from the Lord to such an extent that I cannot turn back to him.

And here comes the problem. On the Calvinist view, the possibility of a return means that the Lord himself must so work in my life that I am preserved from the possibility of falling away by his overruling of my sinful will. Thus we find that perseverance depends on a divine determinism that overrules what I myself apparently do in freedom. And so, although the Lord may let me fall into sin, he never lets me sin to such a degree that I become totally deaf to his voice. He overrules my will so that I remain faithful. Indeed, he overruled my will in the first instance, so that I freely turned to him and became a believer.

To be sure, we all believe in the influence of the Holy Spirit in our hearts to transform our stubborn, sinful wills, and we insist that 'every thought of holiness, and every victory won are his alone', but this way of looking at things does raise some problems.

1. The Calvinist position cannot explain why it is that the converted sinner still sins sometimes and to some extent, and why God does not sanctify him entirely at conversion. In effect, God is left deciding to allow the convert to sin on some occasions (but never to the point of apostasy), and at other times to do good.

2. This means that in the end it is not the preaching or reading of God's word or any other external means of warning and persuasion that ultimately causes our salvation and holiness, but rather salvation all depends on the secret influence of the Spirit of God on our wills in accordance with a divine plan.

3. Consequently, the Calvinist view deprives the individual of real will power. When the person does wrong, it is because evil has control of him, rather than God. He is reduced to a mere automaton, apparently free to choose, but in reality at the mercy of the power of evil or the power of good. However, the believer does not know this, and perhaps it does not matter, because he acts as though he were free. The Calvinist can thus insist that divine determinism and human freedom are compatible. However, this view does seem to deny the reality of the personhood of God's creatures. Above all, it does not do justice to those passages in Scripture that clearly show that God treats people as free agents, able to decide for themselves.

4. The Calvinist position also has serious consequences for the doctrine of God, for it considers the individual's conversion

purely an arbitrary act of God. The convert had been a sinner because sin had taken control of him — he had been dead in trespasses and sins from the time of his conception. But God acted to take control of his life and to deliver him from sin. However, no reason can be assigned as to why God chooses some individuals and rejects others (or, if you prefer, passes them by). Thus the problem is that God appears to be capricious in granting his love. He may be steadfast in his love to the elect, but his choice of the elect is arbitrary. Of course, one may reply that God is free to show or to withhold mercy as he chooses, and so he is. But is it just to show mercy only to some? Shall not the judge of all the earth do right?

5. Finally, there is a philosophical problem in that this view presents God as the prisoner of his own predestining purpose. Were it merely a case of God's determining what other persons do, the problem would not be so great. In fact, however, predestination affects not only what God's creatures do but also what he himself does in relation to them. God decides whether or not he will act to save them. A solution to this problem may be to say that within God purposing and acting occur simultaneously since God is outside time, and therefore the idea that God first purposes and then acts is a mistaken one. But the determinist view does seem to me to make God the prisoner of his own will.[9]

The effect of these comments is to suggest that in the concept of predestination (whereby everything we do is predetermined) the basis of final perseverance contains moral and logical difficulties and leads to antinomies.

On the other hand, the non-determinist view also has problems. It does not explain how it is that God undoubtedly moves us at times by the working of his Spirit independently of our own wills. Also, it has to come to terms with those passages in Scripture that suggest that salvation from start to finish is the work of God who acts according to his own will. The nondeterminist position also shares with the determinist view the problem of explaining the relation of God to evil.

Thus there are problems for both Calvinists and for non-Calvinists. I believe that these difficulties are inherent in any attempt to explain both the actions of God, who is not bound by time and space, and the way in which his actions impinge upon the world he created. Even though we cannot understand in principle how the eternal God functions to cause events in this world, I have the impression that the Calvinist has the greater set of problems. However, I am not philosopher enough to take the matter any further, and therefore I would not want overly to emphasize the fact that I find the greater difficulties in the Calvinist position.

2. WARNINGS AGAINST FALLING AWAY

I therefore turn to the area where I feel more at home, namely asking what the New Testament says. A brief review of the textual material discussed by Moody affords a good starting-point for this investigation.

In regard to the Gospels, Moody is content to appeal to Luke 8.9–15. He is on strong ground in this passage. The interpretation of the parable of the sower indicates that there are people who receive the word but do not persevere or continue in faith. Commentators have seen two ways to apply the lesson of the parable. On the one hand, it may be seen as a warning to its hearers to beware of the temptations to give up believing and to stand firm against them. On the other hand, it may be seen as an explanation for the disciples of what will happen to different groups of people who respond to their mission. Either way, we have a clear warning against the danger, and therefore the possibility, of accepting the word and falling away.

There are various ways of avoiding this conclusion.

1. It can be argued that the presence of this and similar warnings in Scripture is part of the means by which God effectually keeps believers from falling away. The purpose of a warning such as this is not to describe actual cases of believers falling away but to describe the fate of hypothetical apostates in such terms that all believers who hear will be persuaded to remain in the faith. In other words, one of the means by which God enables his elect to persevere is through warning them in ways like this.

Now, if one holds that these warnings work in this way, one must also hold that God creates in the elect the correct response to these warnings and that his hidden action in the heart is what leads to perseverance at the end of the day.

But where is the evidence that this is the actual intent of Scriptures such as the present one? And is it not unreal to paint a picture of the fate of hypothetical apostates when such people do not and cannot exist?

2. It can be argued that the descriptions of people who fall away are in every case descriptions of people who had never in fact believed. They may have accepted the message with joy, but they did not believe. However, this explanation comes to grief on the wording in Luke. The presence of the word 'believe' in verse 13 and the contrast with verse 12 indicate that these are

people who believe for a time. It is necessary, therefore, to claim that a distinction may be drawn between real and temporary or half-hearted belief. Or the distinction is between those who merely believe on a human level and those in whose hearts the Spirit kindles true belief. However it be expressed, this interpretation would be that such passages as the present one do not describe the elect but rather those whose faith was never of the saving variety.

Of these alternatives the second would appear to be the easier to defend. But let us note clearly what is happening. What this exegesis amounts to is that Luke teaches that a person will not be saved unless his faith is marked, positively, by holding fast the word, bearing fruit and demonstrating endurance, and, negatively, by not ceasing to believe in times of temptation or by not yielding to temptations. In other words, the parable is about the attitudes that believers must show: they are commanded to persevere, and they are told that, if they do not, they will be lost, just like those people who never believed at all. Thus, at the end of the day it will be seen that they did not have saving faith, since their faith did not last and was not strong enough to overcome temptation. It would appear, however, that up to that point they did believe.

The parable says that saving faith is persevering faith. But this surely carries the implication that at any given moment it is impossible to say of a person that he has saving faith; the only proof of saving faith is that the person persevered in the faith and died believing. (We can ignore the problem of people who died at a point when it was not possible for them any longer to demonstrate conscious faith. No one is going to deny salvation to such people.)

If we put the point in this way, we have stated precisely what the defender of the possibility of apostasy is stating. For the parable does not teach that people will infallibly persevere in faith; it simply describes the fact that there are people who do. Certainly I cannot look at my faith at this moment and say, 'Yes, so far my faith has lasted, withstood temptation and brought forth fruit, and therefore I can be confident of my future salvation', for I do not know what tomorrow will bring — at least so far as this parable is concerned.

The Calvinist interpreter, then, is saying: people who do not bring forth fruit and persevere show that they were not of the elect and that they never had saving faith. A typical presentation of the position is: 'Men must hold themselves responsible to persevere; but if they do so, it is God's grace upholding them; while if they fall away, *they demonstrate that they were not true disciples in the first place*.'[10] The non-Calvinist says: if people wish to attain to final salvation, they must persevere in faith, and only at the end will it be seen whether they persevered. For the Calvinist there is a quality in the initial faith that guarantees perseverance (or, God who inspired the faith will enable it to persevere), so that we can say that such a person was and is 'a true disciple'. The non-Calvinist, while not disputing that one can distinguish broadly between nominal and true believers, insists that perseverance is not so much a quality inherent in true faith at the point of conversion, as it is simply the lastingness of faith that is shown from moment to moment throughout the Christian life.

Thus one can read the parable from a Calvinist perspective. But one must insist: (a) that this perspective is not necessary for understanding the parable in itself; (b) that the parable (and similar teaching) does not *prove* the Calvinist interpretation.

Hence such a parable as this does not *teach* final perseverance. To the Calvinist and the non-Calvinist believer alike it says: see that you persevere! Of itself it does not convey to the believer the assurance that he will persevere. We shall find that this is true for the 'warning' passages in general.

Moody briefly notes two passages in Acts that favour his position. One is the Ananias and Sapphira story (Acts 5.1–11). However, I do not think that any conclusions regarding the ultimate fate of the two sinners can be drawn from this passage. Acts 20.30 is a warning to the Church that fierce wolves will draw disciples away after them. Again, the Calvinist may claim that those who are drawn away were not 'true' disciples, but in order to do so it is necessary to demonstrate that Luke (or Paul) distinguishes between true and seeming disciples.

If the latter are meant, then (on Calvinist premises) the warning would appear to be futile because the seeming disciples do not belong to the elect. If it be argued that the purpose of the warning is to help any of these seeming disciples who are elect but not yet regenerate to come to true faith, then it must be remarked that this is a peculiar form of wording for the purpose. If the former group is meant, then the passage is being interpreted on the hypothesis that those who persevere to the end and do not become the prey of wolves are in fact the elect, and that they persevered because they were predestined to do so.

But does this really help? The fact is that no one can know for certain who are the true disciples and the false disciples. If a person is in the former group, he has still to heed the warning: only by so doing can he show that he is one of the elect. In other words, the Calvinist 'believer' cannot fall away from 'true' faith, but he can 'fall away' from what proves in the end to be only seeming faith. The possibility of falling away remains. But in neither case does the person know for certain whether he is a true or a seeming disciple. All that he knows is that Christ alone can save and that he must trust in Christ, and that he sees signs in his life which may give him some assurance that he is a true disciple. But these signs may be misleading.

It comes down to a question of assurance. Whoever said, 'The Calvinist knows that he cannot fall from salvation but does not know whether he has got it', had it summed up nicely. On this view, the ground of assurance is the evidence of a changed life. But this can be counterfeit and misleading. The non-Calvinist knows that he has salvation — because he trusts in the promises of God — but is aware that, left to himself, he could lose it. So he holds fast to Christ. It seems to me that the practical effect is the same.

Moody then turns to the epistles of Paul. Here he notes the encouragements and warnings to Christians and the fear that some would fall. The issues here are in principle the same as in the passages already discussed. And in a sense the exegetes are in agreement. For the Calvinist the warnings and the promises are the means by which God urges the elect to faithfulness on the empirical, human level, while he works in their hearts so that they respond positively. For the non-Calvinist the same passages are equally God's means of urging believers to persevere. In both cases it is recognized that the Spirit is the means of renewal without which believers would be unable to respond to God's word. The question is whether the Spirit always operates irresistibly and positively in the lives of some but not of others. Whether I am a Calvinist or not, I must heed the encouragements and warnings, in the former case to show that I am a real and not a seeming believer, and in the latter case for fear that I might fall away from the real faith that I have.

Most important are the passages in Hebrews to which Moody gives special attention. There are five of these: 2.1–4 (we must pay close attention to what we have heard, lest we drift from it); 3.7–4.13 (the danger of having an evil, unbelieving heart and thus falling away from the living God); 6.1–20 (the impossibility of restoring to repentance those who become partakers of the Holy Spirit and then commit apostasy); 10.19–39 (the punishment in store for those who sin wilfully after having been sanctified by the blood of the covenant); and 12.1–29 (the warning not to be like Esau who was given no opportunity to repent after he sold his birthright). The first and second passages can be understood by Calvinists like the cases of seeming believers above, but this is not the most natural interpretation of them. The third passage (Heb. 6.1–20) causes problems for the Calvinist because it is extremely implausible to interpret the passage as referring to people who were never genuine believers and then claim that the text describes a merely hypothetical danger. The same is true of the fourth passage, and (less clearly) of the fifth. That is to say, the view that the Hebrews passages speak of merely nominal believers is most unlikely. The Calvinist interpretation has to be that the dangers are purely hypothetical, since, it is claimed, God uses the passages effectively to warn all true believers against the danger of apostasy. But the passages in themselves do not require this interpretation, and it is safe to say that it would never have been offered except in the interests of a dogmatic theory that God will infallibly save a fixed group of the elect. However, even though the author of Hebrews emphasizes the faithfulness of God to his people, there is no suggestion in the text that the author shares this particular view of predestination.

3. ENCOURAGEMENTS TO PERSEVERE

We now have, on the one hand, a series of statements apparently addressed to believers, urging perseverance, warning against apostasy, and indicating the unpleasant consequences of apostasy. The believer must take these warnings seriously.

On the other hand, there are other strands of teaching that encourage the believer to persevere. These can be briefly summarized as follows:

1. The New Testament writers at least regard it as normal that believers will persevere and continue in their faith. Side by side with the warnings are statements that suggest that believers will travel safely to the end of their pilgrimage. The warnings are about behaviour that is regarded certainly as possible, but not as normal or inevitable.

2. The New Testament contains promises of heavenly glory to encourage believers to persevere in their faith. We have only to think of the promises to the overcomers in Revelation, and the fact that the author has visions of those who have overcome safely, reaching their final reward.

3. There are also promises that the powers arrayed against believers are not so strong that they must inevitably fall. In 1 Corinthians 10.13 Paul insists that there is no temptation so strong that believers must inevitably succumb to it, and insists that God will not let people be tempted beyond what they can

bear. He will provide a way out so that they can stand up under it. To be sure, they still need to be warned against the danger in which they stand (1 Cor. 10.12!), but they are assured that, if they want to overcome temptation, they can do so. If people resist the devil, he will flee from them (Jas. 4.7).

4. It is also quite clear that if a believer does fall and then returns to the Lord in repentance, he will be accepted. This is very clear from the Lord's Prayer with its petition for forgiveness, and also from 2 Corinthians where the problem of sin within the Church is discussed at length. Despite the strong words in Hebrews 6 and 10, it seems unlikely that any repentant believer would find the Lord refusing pardon for past sins. The sin in Hebrews 10 is that of rejecting the means of forgiveness, the death of Christ, and Hebrews 6 is probably to be explained in the same way; it is clear that the person who seeks forgiveness on the grounds of Christ's death will not be rejected.

5. Believers have the promise of spiritual power to overcome temptation. The presence of the Holy Spirit in their lives enables them to overcome temptation and guides them in the path of God's will.

6. All these points relate to means by which believers can overcome. They are like soldiers sent out to battle with full armour and the knowledge that the enemy, though strong, is not impregnable. They can go out with full confidence. But is that enough, and is it all? After all, the strongest armies have been defeated by the secret weapons of the enemy or by fifth-columnists within.

A vital element in perseverance is the assurance that God will certainly win in the end. This is an essential element in the faith of God's people; their faith is faith in the omnipotence of God, demonstrated in the death of Christ at which Satan and death were defeated (cf. Rom. 8.31–39).

Hence Christian faith is faith that one will persevere because God is almighty. Now if a person wonders whether he will persevere, he is doubting the content of his faith and is not believing. So the apostate is the person who has ceased to believe in the power and love of God. Hence by definition a believer is a person who believes that God will triumph — and that the triumph will include his share in it.

The person who falls away is thus one who prefers the pleasure of the moment — or the avoidance of the pain of the moment — to sharing the triumph of God, or who believes that God will not triumph. Falling away is giving up the faith that one will persevere by the power of God.

We must now consider whether the biblical teaching that speaks of God's election of his people and of his will to bring them to final salvation renders falling away impossible in principle.

In John we have some statements that indicate that believers will never perish. In his book, Moody draws attention to John 3.3–8 (those who have been born again cannot be 'unborn'); 5.24 (believers pass from death to life and do not come to judgement); 6.37 (all whom the Father gives to the Son will come to him); 6.39 (this is the will of God, that Christ should lose none of those given to him but raise them up at the last day); and especially 10.28 (my sheep shall never perish, and no one shall snatch them out of my hand).

Alongside these statements we have others that refer more specifically to believers as God's elect or chosen people. We find this thought in John 6.37, and also in such passages as Acts 13.48; 16.14 and 18.10. Above all, it surfaces in passages where God's people are specifically called 'the elect'. In one or two passages this phrase is conceivably used to refer to people who have not yet responded to the gospel, but who have been foreordained by God to do so (2 Tim. 2.10; Titus 1.1; Matt. 22.14; cf. Acts 9.15). We also read of God foreordaining people to be conformed to the image of Jesus and taking the necessary steps to bring them to that final goal (Rom. 8.28–30), and of his choosing people in Christ (Eph. 1.4f., 11). From these verses some would draw the conclusion that if God has a purpose for these people in electing them, then he will surely fulfil that purpose in their lives and bring them to final salvation.

Our problem is the relation between these statements and the former set. There can be only three solutions. The first is to give the election texts the primacy and to reinterpret the warnings to fit in with them by any of the means already discussed. This gives an unnatural rendering to the warnings. The second possibility is to recognize that there is a tension in the passages and not try to avoid it by twisting either set of statements. There is, of course, a third solution, which is to give primacy to the warnings and to twist the election statements to mean less than they apparently say. This is probably the least satisfactory solution. I am going to suggest that the election statements may be in danger of some misinterpretation, but I do want to take them seriously and to insist that they must stand alongside the warning statements.

So the question is what we make of the election and preservation sayings. I begin with a comment on the Johannine material. John 10.28 says that there is a group of people who are the sheep of the Good Shepherd. Whoever does not belong to this group does not believe. What leads to belief is not seeing signs that prove that Jesus is the Messiah, but hearing (that is, obeying) his voice and following him. Those who believe have eternal life and no one can take them out of the Shepherd's care — not even the evil one. The reason no one can do this is that the Father who gave the flock to Jesus is greater than any other power.

It is surely one thing for the devil to snatch the sheep away against the sheep's will — that cannot happen. It is another thing for the sheep to yield to temptation. How, then, is the activity of the devil seen? Does he merely tempt or does he cause people to fall? Is his appeal irresistible? It would be easy if we could say that he merely tempts and that it depends on us whether we fall.

Now on the level of exhortation and teaching, do we tell people that the devil is irresistible to Christians? Paradoxically, we do tell non-believers that they cannot avoid yielding to temptation, but since they are responsible they should not do so. The Christian schoolteacher does not tell his pupils that they cannot avoid doing what is wrong and that therefore he will not punish them if they commit wrong. Or do we tell people that the Spirit is irresistible, and that they can sit back and let the Spirit take control? Some may do so, but this attitude of 'quietism' would probably be rejected by serious theologians. What we actually do is to tell believers to resist the devil in the strength of God. They can win, but they will not win if they do not fight! Thus, whatever we believe about John 10.28, in practice we tell believers that they must resist the devil, or else they will fall. In other words, the force of a passage like John 10.28 is to encourage believers to resist the devil in the confidence that they can win because of the promises of God. Faith includes believing in the victory of God. Similarly, Jesus can look back in John 17.11f. and state that up to this point he has safely kept his disciples, and then confidently pray that they will continue to be protected. Yet even in this context we hear of the one who was not kept, the one destined for perdition. Thus the teaching in John is meant to be a source of encouragement to believers to persist in faith in the omnipotence of God.

Next, we can consider the concept of election. The words 'election' and 'elect', like the concept, are used in a number of theologically relevant ways: 1. to refer to Jesus as the Chosen One of God; 2. in the plural ('elect') to refer to the Church and its members collectively. The second is the most characteristic use. 3. 'Election' also refers to the calling of individuals to special tasks such as apostleship (Acts 1.24; 9.15). 4. in the singular, the term 'elect' refers to an individual Christian. There seems to be only one possible case of the last usage, namely, in reference to Rufus in Romans 16.13. The fact that Rufus is singled out in this way suggests that the word is used here in an unusual manner, perhaps to mean 'outstanding' or something similar.

It is important to note that 'elect' is always used of those who actually belong to the Church, not of prospective believers. The two possible exceptions are in 2 Timothy 2.10 and Titus 1.1, but there the expression means that Paul labours for the sake of believers so that they will attain to final salvation, and that he works in accordance with, or to further, the faith of God's people.

Next, we note that the term is ordinarily used to describe those who belong to the Church in terms of outward profession, rather than to distinguish between those who really belong and those who are merely professors. Thus the term is not used of a group within the Church secretly known to God. There is a possible exception in Matthew 22.14, but this verse simply refers to those who are invited to the wedding, some of whom are found unworthy; many are called, but only some of them respond and become part of the 'elect'. So the 'elect' are those who are called by God and who become members of his people by exercising faith. The word is not used of a group of 'real' believers in the Church, as opposed to seeming, nominal believers.

Where, then, is the source of the idea of a secret group of elect individuals previously chosen by God to be saved and to persevere in salvation? This idea does not come from the use of the term 'elect', but from other passages that may suggest that God has chosen some and passed by others. It is of course true that God chooses specific individuals for particular tasks — there is an element of particularity here that cannot be avoided. But are there any real grounds for extrapolating from the principle of the calling of some individuals to service the conclusion that there is a predestination of those who are called to salvation? And does it in any case follow that those called to service will necessarily obey?

Judas fell away from being one of the Twelve, and Paul gives the impression that he responded of his own choice (Acts 26.19). But it must be said that for a Calvinist the fact that somebody is said to respond to grace freely is no argument against effectual calling.

In John 6.64 Jesus states that there are some disciples who do not believe, for (says John) Jesus knew from the beginning who were the unbelievers and the betrayer. But there is nothing particularly problematic here: Jesus knows the hearts of people. Jesus goes on to say that people cannot come to him unless the Father enables them. He rejects the idea that people can 'control' him. Only if the Father calls can people come. But this does not necessarily mean that if a person is called he will respond with faith.

2 Timothy 2.19 has also been cited in this connection (the Lord knew those who were his people). But this text is only a recognition that the visible Church can contain plausible hypocrites who do not really belong to it, and no one denies that this can be the case.

More importance attaches to Romans 8.28–30. These verses say that the people who love God need not be afraid of tribulations (8.18), because the glory in store for them is greater than the tribulation; we can be confident that, no matter what painful experiences we have, all will be for the good of those whom God has called, because his final purpose for those whom he calls is their glorification. We know that because of two things. First, God's purpose for those whom he 'foreknew' was that they might share the image of Jesus, that is, share in his glory. Second, God has already started the process: God has called the people for whom he has this purpose. Calling was followed by justification, obviously of those who believed and thereby responded to the call. And justification is followed by a glorification that has already begun (2 Cor. 3.18). Thus this passage is meant to reassure God's people that his final purpose for them is glorification, a purpose that will be carried out despite their sufferings. The passage is not a statement about the effectual calling of those whom God foreknew. It is a guarantee that those who have responded to God's call with love (and faith) can be fully assured of his purpose of final glorification for them.

Finally, there is a group of texts in Acts that point to election. In Acts 13.48 we find that when Paul preached in Antioch of Pisidia the Gentiles who heard rejoiced, and all who were 'ordained' to eternal life believed. In 16.14 the Lord opened Lydia's heart to attend to what Paul said. And in 18.10 the Lord assured Paul that he had many people in Corinth, that is, many people who apparently were to be converted. These verses appear to suggest a divine plan to be carried out by Paul involving the salvation of individuals. With regard to Acts

16.14, however, no one would deny that people can hear and respond to the gospel only if the Lord takes the initiative. Acts 18.10 indicates the Lord's foreknowledge of the progress of the gospel in Corinth. But the text could also mean that, since there were now many Christians in Corinth, God's purpose for Paul was that he should continue there to teach them and ground them in the faith. Acts 13.48 could well mean that those Gentiles who had already begun to search for eternal life (like Cornelius in Acts 10) believed upon hearing the good news that salvation was now at last being offered to them through Jesus. Or it might mean that the Gentiles believed inasmuch as they had (collectively) been included in God's saving plan.

We have no desire to empty these verses of their meaning. It is beyond cavil that the Bible teaches that God takes the initiative in salvation, that he planned the creation of his people from eternity past, that it is he who calls to salvation, and that his Spirit leads people to faith in a way that we cannot understand. Calvinist and non-Calvinist alike believe that it makes sense to pray that the Spirit will lead unconverted people to respond. But whether we can conclude from this that a secret predestining will of God always operates when people are saved is doubtful.

Nor is there any question whatever that the Bible clearly teaches the loving purpose of God who keeps believers by his grace (1 Pet. 1.5). As Christians, we can and do rely completely on Christ, the Good Shepherd and we claim his promise that he will keep us and that he will not let us fall (Jude 24). We could not live the Christian life without these promises and their gracious realization in our lives.

What I am suggesting, then, is that the primary function of the election language in the Bible is to stress that God takes the initiative in salvation and that his purpose is to create a people who will attain to that salvation. But it is never said that this means either that there is a non-elect section of humanity who cannot attain to salvation or that there is a fixed group of previously chosen 'elect' who will be called, justified and glorified in some automatic fashion. We must not draw logical conclusions from the biblical material that go beyond its clear implications and which land us in logical contradiction with other biblical teaching.

It is this element of promise that needs to be emphasized to balance Moody's emphasis on the possibility of apostasy; Moody has deliberately offered a one-sided position in order to counterbalance a bias in the opposite direction that misinterprets important parts of Scripture.

4. CONCLUSION

What, then, are the theological and practical implications of our discussion? We have seen that:

1. The New Testament contains both encouragements to believers to persevere and warnings against the dangers of apostasy. These warnings are best understood as calls to believers to persevere in the faith in view of genuine dangers rather than (a) as calls that 'true' believers will inevitably heed because God has predetermined that they shall do so, and which are therefore empty threats because in fact nobody will ever apostatize, or (b) as warnings that are addressed to people who are not true believers, and thus are again unreal warnings in that such people need to be told to repent and believe rather than not to turn away from a faith which in fact they do not have.

2. The New Testament also teaches that God takes the initiative in salvation and leads people to faith by the work of the Spirit. Those who respond to the gospel become God's people, his 'elect'. He gives his grace and power to his people to enable them to persevere, and with divine help there is no reason why they should ever fall away from him. Yet the possibility of falling away cannot be excluded. We do not know whether any will in fact fall away and be lost eternally, although there are some possible cases in the New Testament.

3. It is better not to think of a group of people who at their conversion become 'true' believers (because of God's election and call) and whose faith therefore will inevitably persevere. What the Bible offers is promises that believers can persevere and, therefore, encouragements to them to persist in faith and not to fall away. The warnings are meant quite seriously.

4. Can, then, a person claim that he will never fall away and have an assurance that will carry him through every situation of temptation and worry? Can he, for example, say, 'I am elect, and therefore I am safe; no matter how far I fall into temptation and yield to it, in the end God will bring me safely through?'

According to L. Berkhof,[11] there is some difference of opinion among Calvinists on whether faith includes assurance. Berkhof himself allows that true faith 'carries with it a sense of security, which may vary in degree' and that believers can attain to a subjective assurance from contemplating their own experience of the work of the Spirit. But, while many believers in the Calvinist tradition undoubtedly do have assurance of salvation, both present and final (for mercifully God's gifts are not bound by what our theological systems allow him to grant), it is difficult to avoid the impression that a strict Calvinist can never be fully certain that he is one of the elect. So soon as he believes that he is one of the elect, he knows that he cannot fall from grace; may he not begin to trifle with sin, and thus prove that he never was elect? Consequently, even if a person says, 'I know that I am one of the elect', the possibility remains that he may commit grievous sin and thus show that he was not elect.

The same thing is true if we try to work in terms of 'true believers' as opposed to nominal ones or those with an unreal faith. For the reality of faith is shown only by its continuance. And who can say that he has such persevering faith?

What, then, can the believer say that is neither presumptuous nor self-deceiving? He can say that he knows the One in whom he has put his trust, and that he believes in a God who is able to keep that which he has committed to him (2 Tim. 1.12; whether this is the correct exegesis is totally immaterial!). He can listen to the apostle who tells him that he belongs to those who are 'kept by the power of God ready for a salvation ready to be revealed in the last time' (1 Pet. 1.5). That is to say, his assurance is rooted not in the fact that he has faith, but in the character and promises of God. And that is surely the point of the language of God's election and choice. It is an affirmation of the commitment of God to those who are his people; it is a declaration of faith that God, having brought us thus far, intends to bring us to final glory. It stands alongside those passages that declare that there is a condition to all this — 'provided that we also suffer with him' — and that warn us against unbelief.

And therefore the believer can and must affirm his faith and his assurance. If Paul can declare that he is sure that nothing in all the universe can separate him from the love of God, so too the believer can declare with full assurance in the words of Charles Wesley:

> No condemnation now I dread,
> Jesus and all in him is mine;
> alive in him my living Head,
> and clothed in righteousness divine,
> bold I approach the eternal throne,
> and claim the crown through Christ my own.

That note of solid assurance of final salvation comes from a so-called Arminian who believed what Paul said!

5. What, therefore, we have done is to insist that the warning

statements are to be taken with full seriousness, and that the promises, expressed in election language and other ways, are also to be taken with full seriousness as affirmations of belief in the saving power of God. And faced by these we walk by faith, not by sight, for the essence of our faith is that it is faith in the final victory of the God who has shown his almighty power on Good Friday and Easter Day.

What the New Testament says to the believer is: 'You belong to the elect, therefore constantly seek to make your calling and election sure.' The New Testament calls on all who believe in Jesus Christ to persevere in belief, that is, to keep on believing. Those who know that they are God's children, who have the assurance that their sins are forgiven, must go on believing and committing themselves to the saving and keeping love of Jesus. Their assurance of final salvation does not rest primarily upon the evidences of election but rather on their Saviour, and, if they are non-Calvinists, they know that the grace which has been openly revealed in Christ is not cancelled by a secret plan of God which may have excluded them from salvation even though they have experienced some taste of it.

It emerges that in practice the Calvinist believer is in no better position than the non-Calvinist. The non-Calvinist may believe that there is a danger of his apostasy, but he also believes in the revealed grace of God, and he knows that there is no secret plan of God which may conflict with his revealed loving purpose; on the contrary, he knows that he is included in the will of God to 'bring many sons to glory', and consequently he knows that he can trust in God with complete confidence.

On both views the possibility of apostasy exists at the experiential level. The Calvinist view allows that people may be seeming believers and of course in the end they will not be saved; they will not persevere in faith because they never had the 'real' faith which contains the virtue of perseverance. The non-Calvinist view also allows that people may believe and yet fall away because they did not persevere. But whereas the former view attributes 'apostasy' to the fact that God did not elect these people to salvation, the latter view attributes it to the mystery of evil.

It can be protested that neither solution is wholly satisfying. The former has to allow that God does not show mercy to all, which suggests that he acts immorally. The latter has to allow that, although God acts morally, for some mysterious reason he cannot always conquer the evil in human hearts; but the reason for this lies not in the reprobating will of God but in the mystery of evil. Perhaps, then, in the end it makes little practical difference whether we speak of the mystery of the divine will or of the mystery of evil.

But on the theological level there is a serious difference. In both cases we face the problem of evil and admit that we cannot solve it. The former solution is problematic because it questions the goodness of God and has to read into much of the New Testament a 'hidden agenda' in the divine plan for salvation. The latter solution is also problematic because it appears to question the absolute power of God,[12] but exegetically it perhaps has fewer difficulties.

Thus we find that both Calvinists and non-Calvinists affirm the reality of God's preserving grace and both allow for the possibility of apostasy in the Church. But an exegetical study of the New Testament makes it quite clear that in view of the complexity of the evidence and the impossibility of denying the reality of the danger of apostasy, we are best to admit that there is a tension in Scripture on this subject. In the last analysis this is due to the impossibility of explaining both the mystery of divine causation and the mystery of evil. Therefore we should recognize that the strict Calvinist approach offers an oversimplification and systematization of the biblical material. It is to the credit of Dr. Moody that he has expressed his unease with over-systematization of biblical theology and is content to live with mystery.[13]

NOTES

1. I. H. Marshall, *Kept By the Power of God: A Study of Perseverance and Falling Away* (London, 1969).
2. Ibid. (Minneapolis, 1975).
3. D. Moody, *The Word of Truth* (Grand Rapids, 1981), pp. 348–65.
4. R. Shank, *Life in the Son* (Springfield, 1961).
5. Ibid., *Elect in the Son* (Springfield, 1970).
6. D. A. Carson, *Divine Sovereignty and Human Responsibility: Biblical Perspectives in Tension* (London, 1981).
7. Judith M. Gundry Volf, *Paul and Perseverance: Staying in and Falling Away* (Tübingen, 1990).
8. At the 1618–19 Church synod held at Dort in the Netherlands the doctrines of the Remonstrants (the followers of Jacob Arminius) were condemned in a statement which outlined five key doctrines of Calvinism: the total depravity of mankind; God's unconditional election of those whom he chooses to save; the limitation of the saving efficacy of the atonement to the elect; the irresistibility of God's grace in saving the elect; and the infallible preservation of the elect to final salvation. It is the last of these points that is under discussion in this essay, but upholders of Dort would insist that all five points stand or fall together. For a brief account of the Synod, see (for example) W. Elwell (ed.), *Evangelical Dictionary of Theology* (Grand Rapids, 1984), pp. 331f.
9. For a fuller discussion of some of these points, see C. H. Pinnock (ed.), *Grace Unlimited* (Minneapolis, 1975).
10. Carson, *Divine Sovereignty and Human Responsibility*, p. 195; italics are mine.
11. *Systematic Theology* (London, 1969), pp. 507–9.
12. For a helpful discussion of the philosophical problem, see J. L. Walls, 'Can God save anyone he wills?', *SJT*, 38, 1985, pp. 155–72.
13. [1989] The issues treated in this and the preceding essay have now been carried further in C. H. Pinnock (ed.), *The Grace of God, The Will of Man* (Grand Rapids, 1989).

Select Bibliography

Note that where the place of publication of a book is not mentioned it can be assumed to be London.

Adam, D. S., 'Perseverance,' in ERE, IX, pp. 769–71.

Barrett, C. K., *The Holy Spirit and the Gospel Tradition*, 1947.

Berkouwer, G. C., *Faith and Perseverance*, Grand Rapids, 1958.

Boettner, L., *The Reformed Doctrine of Predestination*, Grand Rapids, 1932.

Bohren, R., *Das Problem der Kirchenzucht im Neuen Testament*, Zollikon-Zürich, 1952.

Bultmann, R., *Theology of the New Testament*, 1952, 1955.

Calvin, J., *Concerning the Eternal Predestination of God* (translated by J. K. S. Reid), 1961.

Institutes of the Christian Religion.

Carson, D. A., *Divine Sovereignty and Human Responsibility: Biblical Perspectives in Tension*, 1981.

Evans, O. E., 'The Unforgivable Sin,' in Exp.T, LXVIII, 1946–7, pp. 240–244.

Feine, P., *Theologie des Neuen Testaments*, Berlin, 1953.[9]

Forkman, G., *The Limits of the Religious Community*, Lund, 1972.

George, A. R., *Communion with God in the New Testament*, 1954.

Green, E. M. B., *The Meaning of Salvation*, 1965.

Harrison, A. W., *Arminianism*, 1937.

Noack, B., *Satanás und Soteriá*, Copenhagen, 1948.

Owen, J., *Works* (edited by W. H. Goold), 1850–55.

Pope, W. B.,*A Compendium of Christian Theology*, 1880.[2]

Poschmann, B., *Paenitentia Secunda*, Bonn, 1940.

Starbuck, E. D., 'Backsliding,' in ERE, II, pp. 319–21.

Telfer, W., *The Forgiveness of Sins*, 1959.

Volf, J. M. G., *Paul and Perseverance: Staying in and Falling Away*, Tübingen, 1990.

Wesley, J., *Works* (edited by T. Jackson), 1829–31.

Windisch, H., *Taufe und Sünde im ältesten Christentum bis auf Origens*, Tübingen, 1908.

Index of Passages

ACTS

ROMANS

Index of Authors